Dancing on the Canon

Also by Sherril Dodds

DANCE ON SCREEN: Genres and Media from Hollywood to Experimental Art

Dancing on the Canon

Embodiments of Value in Popular Dance

Sherril Dodds
Senior Lecturer in Dance Studies,
University of Surrey, UK

First published 2011 by
PALGRAVE MACMILLAN

Palgrave Macmillan in the UK is an imprint of Macmillan Publishers Limited, registered in England, company number 785998, of Houndmills, Basingstoke, Hampshire RG21 6XS.

Palgrave Macmillan in the US is a division of St Martin's Press LLC, 175 Fifth Avenue, New York, NY 10010.

Palgrave Macmillan is the global academic imprint of the above companies and has companies and representatives throughout the world.

Palgrave® and Macmillan® are registered trademarks in the United States, the United Kingdom, Europe and other countries.

ISBN: 978–0–230–57995–8 hardback

This book is printed on paper suitable for recycling and made from fully managed and sustained forest sources. Logging, pulping and manufacturing processes are expected to conform to the environmental regulations of the country of origin.

A catalogue record for this book is available from the British Library.

Library of Congress Cataloging-in-Publication Data

Dodds, Sherril, 1967–
    Dancing on the canon : embodiments of value in popular dance / Sherril Dodds.
       p. cm.
    Includes index.
    ISBN 978–0–230–57995–8 (hardback)
       1. Dance – Social aspects. 2. Popular culture. I. Title.

GV1588.6.D63 2011
793.3—dc22   2011011814

10 9 8 7 6 5 4 3 2 1
20 19 18 17 16 15 14 13 12 11

Printed and bound in Great Britain by
CPI Antony Rowe, Chippenham and Eastbourne

For James, Billy and Dylan

Contents

Illustrations

Acknowledgements

The ideas for this book began to emerge almost ten years ago and I would like to thank the following people for their support in the development of this work. First, I must extend my gratitude to the staff at Palgrave Macmillan. My editor Paula Kennedy has demonstrated a keen interest in dance publishing *per se*, as well as a commitment to this particular project. Within this current economic climate, I am grateful for her continued belief in the intellectual worth of dance studies. Thanks are also due to the good cheer of editorial assistant Benjamin Doyle, who patiently dealt with my constant stream of questions.

Second, thanks go to friends and colleagues who have been kind enough to share their intellectual expertise. Professor Janet Lansdale offered valuable guidance on material from Chapter 2 and Professor Marion Wynne-Davies kindly commented on my draft proposal.[1] Professor Theresa Buckland, who was instrumental in alerting me to the idea that popular dance could be a serious topic of scholarly enquiry, generously allowed me to discuss the content and structure of the book with her. Dr Melissa Blanco Borelli gave me much-welcomed feedback on Chapter 6, as did Professor Andrew Bennett on Chapter 7. Professor Susan Cook took precious vacation time to read the entire manuscript and I thank her for encouraging me to make stronger connections across its diverse intellectual threads. In all of these instances, I wish that time was a currency I could return. I am also acutely aware that I would have struggled to complete this project without the support and intellectual acumen of Professor Rachel Fensham. Not only did she allow me to squat in her MA Culture, Power and Difference module and offer generous and insightful commentary on various chapters in progress, but she also arranged for me to take a period of intensive research leave in the middle of a busy semester. Your support is much appreciated, Rachel. On a more formal note, I would like to acknowledge a Small Grant in the Creative and Performing Arts award from the former Arts and Humanities Research Board that allowed me to work on material for Chapter 3.

Finally, I would like to thank a range of people who have continued to spark my fascination with popular dance. I have been fortunate enough to teach some wonderful students who have enlightened me to a plethora of popular dance styles. I also appreciate the production and performance talents of those involved in the Korova Milk Bar and my current collaborator Baby Belle (aka Fiona Cameron) from La Bouche Burlesque who has shown how to be an exemplary friend while sewing on tassels. Over the past eighteen years, my partner James Powell has danced with me at gigs, festivals and celebrations. He talks to me about dance, reads my work and, along with my sons Billy and Dylan, tries not to complain too much when I disappear at night to observe and participate in popular dance events. Thank you, James. Special thanks also go to Billy and Dylan for continuing to fly the popular dance flag through the T21 hip hop crew. Lastly, my heartfelt appreciation goes to the participants who allowed me to interview them for the purposes of this book. I cannot thank enough the neo-burlesque striptease artists across London and New York, the punk, metal and ska fans who I approached on websites and at gigs, and the welcoming faces of Sunday Serenade for their willingness to share their thoughts on why they value popular dance. I will think of you always dancing.

Introduction: Let's Dance!

It's just thrilling the whole time and like a big cheer at the end is always great and usually people shut up a little bit if I do more than one kind of tassel twirling and they're more like kind of mesmerized a little bit and giggling and kind of quite excited about it and then at the end it's just great if you get a big cheer.

(Interview with Fancy Chance, 16 December 2008)

There's a Northern soul tune by Dobie Gray called *Out on the Floor*: 'that's where I get my kicks out on the floor', and it's a wonderful piece of Northern soul, but it beautifully articulates what it is about being on the dance floor that makes you burst with joy. I just love it; I think it's a fantastic thing to do and it's healthy, and it's good for you.

(Interview with Chris, 3 March 2007)

To me, dancing show(s) that you're a happy and sociable person. You like life, you like people. I mean, how can you hear music and stay still? Something must be wrong with you. I mean, even when I'm in pain and I hear music, I still can move.

(Interview with Francine, 2 June 2007)

The quotations above are taken from interviews with participants who are each engaged in a different area of popular dance practice: Fancy Chance performs as a neo-burlesque striptease artist and enjoys much acclaim for her tassel-twirling technique; Chris primarily works as a barrister, but also runs an evening ska club where he likes to dance; and Francine is a care worker who looks forward to every Sunday night when she attends Sunday Serenade, a British Caribbean dance hall. Their comments distinctively articulate what they value about dancing: for

Fancy Chance it offers the opportunity to demonstrate technical skill and enjoy the pleasure of audience response; for Chris it provides emotional wellbeing and good physical maintenance; and for Francine it is a means to convey herself to others and has the potential to transform how she feels. For these participants, dancing clearly engenders worth.

Following the Industrial Revolution of the nineteenth century, the mass production techniques of the early twentieth century brought about a clear separation between work and leisure time. Consequently, dance has occupied a significant proportion of recreational life and different social groups have created and disseminated a plethora of popular dance styles from the cakewalk to krumping. Currently, people participate in social dance events that range from formal classes to impromptu gatherings, and observe live dance entertainment from street performances to musical theatre. With the rapid development of mass communication systems, not only are popular dance forms expeditiously transmitted across the globe, but the media also act as an ideal platform for the representation of popular dance. Film and television screen a succession of dancing bodies set in Hollywood musicals, Bollywood cinema, pop music videos and light entertainment shows, and the internet offers numerous opportunities for the public to stage and view popular dance. Yet, while different dancing communities clearly express allegiance to specific dance styles through frequent and persistent engagement, there exists an absence of scholarly work that considers how participants create measures of value and what those embodied statements express.

Within the field of dance studies, value is implied but not addressed. For example, throughout my undergraduate degree studies in the late 1980s, the curriculum centred on theatre art dance. Even during my MA in the early 1990s, popular dance was tucked away in an anthropology module which only 2 of us attended out of a cohort of 15.[1] At both BA and MA level, dance analysis studies focused entirely on art dance practice and the question of evaluation was almost never entertained. While we were taught to develop complex interpretive strategies, we were equally trained to erase judgements of good and bad or likes and dislikes. Yet, ironically, dance studies pedagogy and scholarship constantly expressed matters of worth through favouring topics and making methodological choices. The disregard for questions of value, however, is apparent not just within dance studies. Traditionally, the logic of the hard sciences denies the messy issue of tastes and preferences, and the arts and humanities likewise seek to exemplify rigour by repressing any leakage of the personal (Connor, 1992).

Fortunately, frameworks of value are neither fixed nor inherent, so academic judgement and arts practice are subject to changing historical attitudes and social contexts of worth. Hence during the 1980s the dance studies curriculum gradually responded to broad cultural shifts that were increasingly pluralistic and less hierarchical regarding the division between high and low art. Consequently, it began to accommodate interest in popular forms of cultural expression. My interest in popular dance was partly shaped by 1980s British postmodern choreographers, such as Michael Clark and Lea Anderson, who readily integrated popular images and music into their stage dance and I jumped to take the MA anthropology module that allowed me to pursue an ethnographic project on female striptease performance. Thus, through my own intellectual development, I have witnessed a seepage of the popular into areas of study that were traditionally the preserve of high art practice.

I have titled this introduction 'Let's Dance!' partly in reference to my own investment in popular dance (as it is the name of a track by New York punk band The Ramones).[2] I recall jumping up and down in the midst of a tight sweaty throng as Joey Ramone, in his standard ripped jeans, biker jacket and baseball boots, spat at the microphone, 'we'll do the twist, the stomp, the mashed potato too, any old dance that you wanna do, well let's dance, well let's dance'. From a quick internet search, I note that 'Let's Dance' is also the title of a David Bowie hit, an NBC radio programme (1934–5), a 1950 film musical with Fred Astaire and Betty Hutton, a 2009 Bollywood film and the name of a Swedish, German and Slovak reality television show in which celebrities compete against each other with professional ballroom partners.[3] This breadth signals not only how the popular relies on transmission and dissemination through the global communications network, but also that it occurs across multiple performance contexts that span the recreational and professional. Furthermore, it highlights how the popular is open to a constant process of recycling and reinvention as the title 'Let's Dance' is adopted across different sites of dance and music production.

Within the context of this book, I conceive the term 'popular dance' as a historically contested label and employ it very broadly.[4] What interests me most about the category of the 'popular' is how it exists in a paradigm of value that dismisses it as mere entertainment or recreation, subject to easy commercial exploitation, intended for the lowest common denominator and conceptually light. Yet, as I hope to demonstrate, popular dance also constitutes a site of social and economic power that has the capacity to destabilize and transgress cultural norms. Its ability to unsettle beliefs and values renders it a potent cultural form, so

I intend to reclaim its worth as part of the project of this book. I have titled the book *Dancing on the Canon* in acknowledgement of the way that theatre art dance has dominated dance scholarship and cultural measures of worth. Yet, within the discipline of dance studies over the past decade or so, scholars have begun to work intensively in the area of popular dance, which has marked a clear re-evaluation of the popular's cultural and intellectual significance.[5] I imagine how the myriad participants of popular dance, from the solo hip hop dancer to the cancan chorus line, unite to dance upon and dismantle the hegemony of the Western art canon. In re-evaluating popular dance, I do not conceive this through an inverted binary in which the popular becomes 'good' and art dance 'bad'. Indeed, I would argue that the same kind of study of value formation could usefully be applied to art dance, which has traditionally occupied a position of greater cultural and intellectual worth.

Part of the motivation of this study is simply that I like popular dance, although I like some forms more than others. For instance, from a small number of classes I quickly decided that I preferred the Argentinian tango, which felt more contained and fluid, over salsa, which always seemed more jerky and flamboyant; I would rather pogo than head-bang, as the latter makes me dizzy and draws my attention away from watching the band; and I find the glossy celebrity of 'Strictly Come Dancing' lame in comparison to 'So You Think You Can Dance', in which members of the general public impressively master a range of choreographic styles in a bid to win a Hollywood contract. In making these claims, I imagine how readers might leap to defend their corner and this is precisely what excites me. I am not interested in absolute rights or wrongs, but rather in how people are committed to particular dance practices, how dancers express embodied worth and how they reflect upon those values.

With this book I therefore aim to show how and why popular dance exists within a system of values and how those engaged in popular dance practice are not only produced by a framework of value, but also have the capacity to negotiate and re-imagine the values they encounter through their dancing bodies. Thus value is both an external measure of worth constructed by 'outsiders' and an internal system of judgement created by the 'insiders' of a popular dance scene. Although the field of cultural studies has provided a rich theoretical apparatus for the study of popular practices, its attention both to the subject of value and to the dancing body is notably underdeveloped. I therefore situate this research as an interdisciplinary project that combines the discipline of dance studies, with its focus on corporeality, and the field of cultural studies, with its interest in popular forms and practices, as a framework within which to develop the concept of 'embodied value', that is the multiple enunciations of significance, judgement and worth that are expressed through the movement practices of different communities engaged in popular dance forms.

Part I of the book, 'Understanding Value', is more theoretical in scope and here I seek to question why popular dance has traditionally occupied a marginal position within the academy and attempt to develop a theoretical and methodological apparatus for the study of popular dance and its attendant value systems. I therefore set out the necessary intellectual framing that will allow me to investigate the values articulated by those who participate in popular dance practice. In Part II of the book, 'Dancing Values', I employ qualitative research methods to examine three case study examples of different dancing communities. Here I intend to explore how embodied value is produced and challenged through expressions of popular dance.

Given that Part I, 'Understanding Value', provides both an intellectual context and a theoretical apparatus for the study of popular dance, in each chapter I explore issues concerning the study of popular dance from different disciplinary perspectives. In Chapter 1, I commence with a broad overview of how value is conceived within the academy and how this impacts upon the relationship between the educational curriculum and the Western art canon. As research in cultural studies has centred on questions of the popular, I then move on to explore the relations between popular dance, cultural studies and value. In Chapter 2, I further unpack the institutional and intellectual values that underpin cultural studies scholarship to determine which theoretical approaches from this field can usefully be adopted in research on popular dance. I follow this with an examination of the treatment of popular dance within cultural studies research, which illuminates significant shortcomings in its neglect of movement analysis.

In preparation for examining approaches to popular dance within the field of dance studies, in Chapter 3 I consider popular dance as a historically contested term. I draw on the disciplines of cultural studies, popular music studies and dance studies to examine different conceptions of the popular and from this argue that popular dance is more usefully conceived as an approach to or way of understanding dance that takes place under a range of conditions, rather than as a fixed set of movement practices. In Chapter 4, I turn to dance studies to engage in a metacritical analysis of research on popular dance. From this I seek to illustrate the unfolding interests and concerns of the burgeoning area of popular dance studies to assert that popular dance demands an intellectual treatment that recognizes its distinct characteristics. In Chapter 5, I return to the concept of value to discuss a selection of theoretical models that offer potential strategies for understanding the production of value through popular dance practice. I initially look to the fields of philosophy, sociology and economics to consider paradigms of economic, class and artistic value and then detail three models of value that inform my analyses in the second part of the book.

In Part II: 'Dancing Values' I draw on three case study examples to explore localized articulations of value within particular dancing communities: neo-burlesque striptease, punk, metal and ska fans, and a British Caribbean dance club. My research methods are rooted in qualitative fieldwork, which encompasses participant observation techniques and formal semi-structured interviews, as a means to examine embodiments of value in popular dance. My choice of case studies was not initially motivated by a desire to interrogate value, but rather emerged from my personal interests, which I explain below.[6] Yet although I did not approach each case study with a systematic model of value against which I intended to 'test' each dancing community, my findings reveal some shared themes across the three sites: the idea of an 'imagined community'; the importance of 'play'; experiences of 'pleasure' in participation; and the possibility of an 'alternative existence' to quotidian life. I will return to these at the end of the book.

In the Introduction to Part II, I detail my methodological approach and reflect upon my own positioning in the field. In Chapter 6 I focus on female neo-burlesque striptease in the London and New York cabaret scene. My motivation for this area of research arose for several reasons. I had already conducted work on female striptease (Dodds, 1997) and had a continuing interest in the politics of 'dance and eroticism'. I was also keen to study at least one form of popular dance that was staged as a theatrical event. Furthermore, my intellectual interest in neo-burlesque striptease coincided with a personal investment as I had already attended events in London and New York for recreational purposes and, from this experience, decided to produce and choreograph a neo-burlesque show. Thus I approach this dancing community from the perspective both of observer and of performer.

In Chapter 7 I investigate pogoing, headbanging and skanking within the context of live music events. While the subject of 'youth subcultures' is well developed in popular music studies, sociology and cultural studies, it attracts little attention in dance scholarship. Given also that I spent many hours of my teenage years dancing in front of my favourite bands at popular music gigs, I wanted to foreground the importance of this corporeal expression in my own dancing history. I conducted this research through a series of interviews with participants who I contacted either through websites or through making introductions at live music gigs. Although I do not currently identify myself as a committed punk, metal or ska fan, I acknowledge my investment in this research as a popular music enthusiast.

In Chapter 8 my attention turns to a British Caribbean dancehall for the over-40s. Given how black expressive practices have distinctively shaped the field of popular culture, I was keen to privilege an area of black British dance culture. Yet as a white British researcher my relationship to this community was from the perspective of an outsider. The existence of this club was made known to me by one of my ska informants from Chapter 7, who occasionally attended this event. What I had not realized until my first visit was that this club catered for a more mature clientele. Consequently, this contributed to my decision to research this popular dance event as ageing dancers form a notable subject of neglect within dance studies (Thomas and Cooper, 2002).

Although each of the case study examples involves a relatively discrete dancing community, and my relationship to each one mobilizes different identity positions and degrees of knowledge, the commonality across all three events is that value is rendered at the site of the body. Yet these enunciations of worth are danced within material constraints as I locate the body within a dynamic set of aesthetic, social and economic relations. Therefore the popular dancing body is both shaped by and produces its own value framework and it is this tension I seek to explore.

Part I
Understanding Value

1
Dancing on the Canon

In *Ballroom, Boogie, Shimmy Sham, Shake: A Social and Popular Dance Reader*, dance scholar Julie Malnig (2009, p. 1) describes popular dance as 'a kind of poor relation within the scholarly hierarchy'. She calls upon the work of Brooks McNamara to argue that, while the grand visions of cultural production are revered within the academy, popular forms of entertainment traditionally remain 'hidden in the recesses of culture' (Malnig, 2009, p. 1).[1] Although the publication of Malnig's anthology indicates that popular dance no longer occupies such a marginalized position, it nevertheless raises the questions why we might privilege one artistic practice over another and how we make judgements of worth through our intellectual pursuits. In his essay 'The Good, the Bad and the Indifferent: Defending Popular Culture from the Populists' (1991), sociologist Simon Frith suggests not only that Charlotte Brontë's *Jane Eyre* is superior to a Mills and Boon romance novel, but that 'the Pet Shop Boys are a better group than U2 and that Aerosmith has no value at all' (1991, p. 105). In response, one might wonder whether it is his position as a university professor, being a self-proclaimed popular music fan or a precious universal quality located in these artists and their works that affords him the credentials to make such indisputable assessments of cultural worth.

I propose that the concept of value offers a key to understanding such frameworks of discrimination and in this chapter I seek to explore the tangled relationship between intellectual value and artistic worth. Throughout the 1980s and 1990s, the topic of value became of interest to scholars in the arts and humanities and I call upon this literature to inform this chapter (Connor, 1992; Fekete, 1987; Herrnstein Smith, 1983; Klamer, 1996; Squires, 1993). First I reflect on how the field of academic research produces its own set of values and then I consider how

11

the act of evaluation contributes to value formations. From this, I move on to explore debates concerning intrinsic versus relative values, how this duality underpins the construction and critique of the Western art canon and the position of popular dance in relation to it. In the final sections of this chapter, I consider the mutual relations between popular dance and cultural studies and, in view of these, how cultural studies deals with the vexed question of value.

Value and the academy

It is almost impossible to conceive a space in which human subjects operate outside the complex network of value systems that structure their existence. Values constitute the foundational principles of a culture or community as they are called upon to inform social structures, institutions, belief systems and policies (Weeks, 1993). From where we choose to buy our food through to which political parties we support, we habitually articulate our value preferences. As Fekete (1987) states, values inform all that social actors do, both at a micro (personal) level and at a macro (societal) level. In turn, human interactions in the social world produce, reproduce and modify values (Fekete, 1987). Consequently, values act both as a regulative medium, in that they provide guidance for how subjects should conduct themselves in life, and as a creative medium, in that they can be contested and reconfigured (Fekete, 1987). Yet in spite of the centrality of value in how we organize social, cultural, economic, intellectual and political life, in scholarly enquiry the concept of value forms a neglected topic (Ferguson and Golding, 1997; Herrnstein Smith, 1983; Morris, 1996).[2]

The failure to address the issue of value is due in part to the traditional division within the academy between positivist and scientific models of research, on one hand, and humanist and aesthetic approaches to intellectual enquiry on the other. Positivism is perceived as a 'value-neutral methodology' (Bernstein, 1987, p. 89) that relies on rigorous objectivism and empirical evidence as its epistemological strategy for conducting research (Fekete, 1987; Herrnstein Smith, 1983). Its scientific stance, which claims to deal with absolute facts and knowledge, conveniently leaves the issue of value out of the frame. In contrast, the type of humanist approach favoured in the arts and humanities takes on a more ethical perspective that requires an element of evaluation (Herrnstein Smith, 1983). In recognition of the humanist conception of the free-thinking individual, there is clearly more scope within this methodological tradition to allow subjectivities, ambiguities and personal values to enter the research field.

Thus, whereas the sciences are considered objective, neutral and value-free, the arts and humanities are perceived as subjective, biased and value-laden. Yet clearly these distinctions are questionable. Science is produced under particular social, historical and institutional conditions and the very concept of 'nature' is a social construct rather than an entity that is fixed and absolute (Herrnstein Smith, 1987). Equally, research in the arts and humanities often seeks to produce 'objective' readings through complex and logical argument or works with empirical data as a form of 'pure' evidence. Obviously neither the position of complete scientific neutrality nor humanist subjectivity stands when interrogated further, but these perspectives usefully expose the way that value is perceived to operate within the academy.

Although the division outlined above suggests that the arts and humanities subjects are predisposed to subjectivity and bias, the question of value remains largely ignored. The failure to examine how value operates within those disciplines primarily concerned with the processes and products of cultural existence is in part due to their preoccupation with interpretation. As Plotnitsky (1987) notes, the balance between evaluation and interpretation in aesthetic studies is skewed; while for interpretation many theories and approaches are at the scholar's disposal, this is not the case for evaluation, which is generally avoided. Indeed, several commentators identify a clear shift in the 1960s and 70s away from notions of discrimination and value towards issues of meaning and interpretation in the arts and humanities subjects (Connor, 1992; Squires, 1993).[3] Connor (1993, p. 32) rationalizes this transition towards interpretation as a consequence of the 'professionalization and institutionalization' of higher education from the 1960s onwards. This period was characterized by science-oriented approaches to the study of arts-based subjects, which favoured facts and knowledge over personal judgement (Connor, 1992). Hence the technical exercise of interpretation superseded the discretionary act of evaluation.

Yet as Agger (1992) argues, the descriptive and critical work demanded of interpretive analysis is perpetually informed by values even where adjectives of worth are not included. Plotnitsky (1987) reflects on how specific historical moments, that affect the kinds of theories available to the scholar, create constraints that delimit interpretative work. For example, the early Marxist scholars of the mid-nineteenth century would not have had at their disposal the Gramscian thinking of the early twentieth century that drew on 'hegemony' to explain how people 'consent' to the social structures that 'dominate' them; and the structuralist scholars of the 1960s would perceive that meaning resides in the 'text' rather than adopting the post-structuralist position that it is the 'reader' who constructs meaning (Barker, 2000; Strinati, 1995). In further reference to academic value judgements, Plotnitsky (1987, p. 126) suggests that, since interpretation has the potential to go on indefinitely, the scholar makes particular intellectual choices that bring closure to the analysis, hence demonstrating a 'structure of preference'. Connor (1993) states that this is particularly evident in the fields of cultural and critical theory, as scholars take an ethical stand through their personal interests regarding the politics of representation, social effects and the voices of marginalized groups for example.[4] Given that interpretation utilizes both frameworks of value and preferences of judgement, the following section considers evaluation as a social practice.

Acts of evaluation

Human subjects are constantly required to make evaluations in order to negotiate their everyday lives. Connor (1992) describes evaluation in terms of comparison, judgement, preference and estimation and states that these forms of assessment constitute the basic tools of transaction within social existence. He suggests that value arises through acts of evaluation and, as value is neither fixed nor absolute, it lies open to perpetual re-evaluation (Connor, 1992). Herrnstein Smith (1987) asserts that humans are continually exercising value judgements and interested in receiving them, not because this will guarantee an absolute truth, but since it potentially offers useful knowledge. She positions the process of evaluation in primarily economic terms:

> throughout our lives, we perform a continuous succession of rapid-fire cost–benefit analyses, estimating the probable 'worthwhileness' of alternate courses of action in relation to our always limited resources of time and energy, assessing, re-assessing, and classifying entities with respect to their probable capacity to satisfy our current needs and desires and to serve our emergent interests and long-range plans and purposes. (Herrnstein Smith, 1983, p. 19)

In making articulations of value in contemporary society, the human subject faces multiple and competing value systems. Consequently, evaluative practices can be complex, disordered and frequently the site of contradictions (Bernstein, 1987). Frow (1995) concurs, through his argument that cultural practices are produced through diverse groups that use criteria of judgement in often paradoxical ways. Yet in spite of this potential confusion and saturation of value practices, Herrnstein Smith (1987) insists that evaluations are always of interest to the individual, even if they are acknowledged as little more than subjective opinion. She notes that one is at least able to derive some sense of a product or practice's 'contingent value' in terms of how well it compares to other similar ones and the extent to which, for specific people within specific contexts, it fulfils certain desires (Herrnstein Smith, 1987, p. 5). Furthermore, she recognizes that the worth of an evaluation is dependent on the evaluative context, relations between those who produce and consume the evaluation, and the perspective of the evaluation itself (Herrnstein Smith, 1987). For instance, a scientific report may carry more *gravitas* than a tabloid editorial; a student may place more trust in the words of a professor than would a group of mutual friends in a pub; and a sensationalist headline might be taken less seriously than a balanced opinion piece. This attention to the social conditions in which evaluations take place would suggest that the act of evaluation is both contingent and constructed (Ruccio et al., 1996). It also implies an element of agency in that human subjects are responsible for producing structures of value through their acts of evaluation. Yet this notion that value is subject to contexts and practices of evaluation that are socially situated and contingent is at odds with Frith's (1991) insistence that certain cultural products, such as *Jane Eyre* and the Pet Shop Boys, possess great artistic value while others, such as Mills and Boon's romantic fiction and Aerosmith, do not. The following section therefore examines the debate concerning the intrinsic values of cultural worth.

Absolutism versus relativism

In this chapter, I have already made reference to the issue of whether value is fixed and inherent or contingent and socially constructed. This encapsulates one of the central tenets of thinking around value, which is expressed through the dialectic of absolute versus relative values. Absolutism supposes that cultural artefacts contain pure, intrinsic worth that is timeless and universal. Thus it privileges the 'object of value' rather than the process of evaluating (Connor, 1993) and within it values comprise fixed standards and judgements (McGuigan, 1997). In spite of Malnig's (2009) claim to the contrary, the absolutist position fully endorses the marginal standing of popular dance in relation to the revered spectacle of theatre practice and Frith (1991) would be perfectly correct in his claims concerning the worth of one piece of music or literature over another. Yet within the academy, at least, the authority of the absolutist belief is largely discredited. Van den Braembussche (1996) questions the existence of inherent value, since this measure of worth is informed by other systems of discrimination rooted in the social, historical, ideological and so on. Instead, he states that the value of art is always relative, sociohistorically constructed, biased and therefore contingent (Van den Braembussche, 1996). Similarly, Ruccio et al. (1996) position value as a discursive category that is neither universal nor intrinsic to any object. This would then explain how values shift in relation to certain cultural practices across time and place.

In response to the intractability of the absolutist stance comes relativism. The past few decades of critical thinking denounce the essentialist tenet of fixed and inherent truths and the consequence has been to expose that considered 'natural' as being 'constructed' (Weeks, 1993). Given that contemporary society is characterized by multiple and diverse beliefs, this raises the issue of how to separate and discriminate between them (Hirst, 1993). It is the relativist position that facilitates this. As Connor (1992) explains, relativism accepts rather than passes judgement on this pluralization of values; hence relativism celebrates difference and diversity. Yet, as with absolutism, the relativist perspective equally fails to offer any satisfactory answers as to how value is constructed and negotiated. Rather, absolutism and relativism are locked in a dialectic relationship that fixes value at two extremes. Indeed, it is almost conceptually impossible to assess the merits of both since each is epistemologically rooted in a rejection of the other. Although the relativist calls for an appreciation of all values as being equal for consideration, an irony lies in the insistence that relativity is valued over absolutism. In view of this, relativism is partly a product of absolutism since it privileges itself as a specified methodology (Hirst, 1993).

A further critique of the relativist position is that it exists as an apolitical intellectual strategy. As Connor (1993) propounds, to suggest that all values are equal negates the possibility for any meaningful value judgements and it devalues evaluation as a practice. Squires (1993, p. 1) suggests that, although postmodernism has brought an important critique to notions of hierarchy and truth, it is limiting in its rejection of 'principled positions'. She describes how the privileging of relativism has led to a domain of sameness in which no sense of aesthetic judgement, ethical duty or epistemological objectivity can exist (Squires, 1993). This is supported by Norris (1993) who also expresses concern that the liberalist rhetoric rejects a position of intellectual critique. Ironically Hirst (1993, p. 64) argues that 'a philosophically generalised and thoroughgoing relativism is incompatible with sustaining the conditions for a tolerant and pluralistic intellectual and political order'. Thus in the extreme, while relativism accepts all belief systems including those of radical fundamentalists, the values of those very groups may necessarily constrain or impact upon those unwilling to share their beliefs. It appears then that relativism is potentially hoist by its own petard. As Soper (1993) suggests, its inability to offer political challenge or critique leaves the scholar in a theoretical impasse.

In response, Hirst (1993) calls for a return to exercising value judgements. He argues that it is not enough to be an indifferent observer otherwise one's work becomes irrelevant, hence the need to determine what is valid or invalid. As he rightly indicates, it is necessary to challenge some social beliefs as invalid otherwise the consequences would have a serious social impact (Hirst, 1993). For instance, racial supremacy and religious fundamentalism are possible examples of how the values of one group may impact negatively on the civil rights of another. Hirst (1993) describes how liberal society endorses democratic relativism up to the point that a belief is potentially oppressive or dangerous. Yet in questioning how to determine the validity of some values over others, this argument gets locked in a relativist cycle. Hirst (1993) suggests that the plausibility of a value system is arrived at through logical reasoning, although consensus is not always achieved through methodological coherence and sophistication of argument. He also acknowledges that some values are time/place-specific and that some beliefs change over time or no longer appear valid; this proves unproblematic for social subjects in that they accept the contingent nature of value (Hirst, 1993). Yet where Hirst's (1993) position loses ground is in his suggestion that, within such a diverse society, some degree of relativism is necessary since a single methodology cannot hope to work neutrally across all of the belief systems in existence. Thus, while Hirst calls for the need to exercise value judgements as a means to assess the validity of social products and practices, his return to a relativist position fails to explain how one goes about making such judgements.

Unfortunately, the totalizing perspectives of the absolutist and relativist epistemologies fail to provide a coherent intellectual framework for interrogating how value is produced, adopted and re-envisioned. What they do offer, however, in returning to some of the initial concerns of this chapter, is an explanation for why popular dance and Mills and Boon novels are traditionally dismissed as devoid of cultural worth and consequently neglected within the academic arena. The tensions arising through absolute models of value confronting relativist equivalence usefully illustrate the construction and destabilization of the Western art canon.

Re-evaluating the canon

The privileging of particular artworks that are awarded high levels of artistic (and frequently economic) value has resulted in an elite aesthetic canon. Connor (1992) reflects that, until the mid-twentieth century, the humanities were informed by a Kantian logic in which cultural artefacts carried inherent value that could be validated only in its own terms, the consequence of which was that academic disciplines, such as literature and art history, simply sought to expose this intrinsic worth. This awarding of special value has produced the Western art canon as an absolute model of aesthetic quality.

Herrnstein Smith (1983, p. 28) identifies how the canon is a self-perpetuating phenomenon in that once a work enters this domain of high value, it acquires a level of security and its value becomes 'unquestionable'. Any negative attributes, such as sexist or racist content, are overlooked in favour of its formal properties and its historicity is repressed to make it appear timeless (Herrnstein Smith, 1983). Yet this sense of worth and endurance is not impartial and objective. As Herrnstein Smith (1983) notes, the institutions that preserve the canon are organized by power-holding subjects: accordingly, it is constructed to fit their needs. Significantly, those individuals who both create and preserve the canon possess considerable cultural, and associated economic, social and political, power and tend to reside in the dominant classes (Herrnstein Smith, 1983). Indeed, Frith (1991) suggests that it is the institutionalization of the canon, in the form of galleries, museums, universities and so forth, that separates it from other cultural activities. The institutionalization of the canon is then reproduced at the level of personal politics:

> cultural discrimination involves a constant negotiation of position with the aim of naturalizing one's own set of values, distinguishing them from the values of others, and attempting more or less forcefully to impose one's values on others. It is thus not just a matter of self-definition but also of struggle for social legitimation. (Frow, 1995, p. 85)

This very process of validation to which Frow refers can be seen in the evolution of dance studies and the legitimacy of its scholarship. In terms of dance practice, it is the serious endeavour of art dance that is awarded high levels of cultural value and, as several dance scholars reflect, the discipline of dance studies has perpetuated the hegemony of the canon. Malone (1996) and Thomas (2003) note how dance scholarship traditionally focuses on theatrical dance and Desmond (2000, p. 43) observes that 'work on the history or representational practices of concert dance, especially modern dance and ballet' predominates dance studies. Crease (2000, p. 110) suggests that, since the term 'dance' is typically understood to mean 'stage dance', other forms invariably remain marginal and problematic to define.[5] Buckland (1999a, p. 3) comments that the study of dance initially employed an Arnoldian approach, which sees an elite culture as 'the singular mark of civilisation'; consequently, choreographers, dancers and repertoire constituted the key subject of dance research.[6] Indeed, this privileging of art dance within the academy offers some explanation of why popular dance has occupied such a marginal or low position within dance scholarship: it lacked artistic legitimacy and concomitant cultural worth.

In spite of the social and intellectual frameworks that seek to ensure the continuity of the art canon, its stability has been called into question over the past few decades. McGuigan (1997) recounts how the need to rethink values in the 1960s and 70s prompted a challenge to the canon. With social frameworks changing around issues of gender and race, for example, this brought about conflicts of judgement in relation to value (Herrnstein Smith, 1983). Consequently, questions arose as to why more female artists or writers of colour, for instance, were not included in the art canon and the related educational curriculum. As Fekete (1987) proposes, the universal value systems of high art need to be reconceived to take into account popular practices and more pluralized audiences. This relativist influence has also impacted upon dance studies in which there has been a notable shift towards popular forms of expression. Buckland (1999a) identifies in recent decades a more pluralist perspective in which cultural production is treated relatively rather than hierarchically. Likewise, Malnig (2009, p. 1) reflects on how 'the widespread efforts in the 1980s to expand the traditional literary, artistic, and historical canons carried over onto dance studies'. This is certainly evident in the last decade and a half in which there has been a proliferation of key texts that address popular dance practices.[7]

To return to the question of value, the existence of the canon and the various challenges to it raise important issues of cultural worth. In spite of the relativist discourses that have brought it under critique, as an organizational system it continues to impact upon the discourse of value. Herrnstein Smith (1983) insists that to ignore the judgement frameworks that inform cultural criticism allows inherent values, such as 'great works' and 'good taste', to exist unquestioned. Frow (1995) also identifies the difficulty of theorizing value in relation to the problematic dichotomy of a high/low culture, which has historically shaped the value systems of aesthetic practice. Indeed, Herrnstein Smith (1987) identifies how the language around evaluation creates a simplistic binary of 'personal preference' versus 'genuine judgement'. Whereas the former is subjective, biased and individualized, the latter is objective, fixed and absolute. Furthermore, this discursive strategy facilitates the hegemonic position of the canon in that one may dislike its contents at the 'personal' level, while 'genuine judgement' insists that its contents are 'good art'.

In reference to judgements of 'good' and 'bad', it is worth exploring how several scholars have attempted to deal with these slippery assessments of worth. In recognition of the contingent nature of evaluation, Weeks (1993) characterizes good (and for that matter bad) as a collectively produced construction that emerges through social practice and experience, and of which there are multiple configurations. This argument avoids both the limitations of individualized personal preference and the fixity of absolute values, but it does not offer any insight into how such consensus occurs. Ruccio et al. (1996) propose that notions of good and bad are articulated through reference to one another. Whereas pronouncements of good are tied to discourses of presence, assessments of bad are based on an absence or lack (Ruccio et al., 1996). They suggest that what is good needs to be defined in order to reference that which is bad (Ruccio et al., 1996). Indeed, this can be seen on a scale in which the bad is described in terms of how much good it does not possess (Ruccio et al., 1996). Yet they conclude that these are indeterminate judgements and that uncertainty exists about whether something is truly good or bad (Ruccio et al., 1996). In an attempt to challenge the dominance of the Western art canon, they call for a privileging of bad art:

> if bad art defines a separate realm of existence which it only weakly shares with good art, then its 'goodness' for different purposes and for different reasons may be easier to establish. (Ruccio et al., 1996, p. 65)

Through this methodology, they claim that this positive assessment of bad art has allowed popular forms, such as B movies and comic books, to move away from their subordinate position in relation to art (Ruccio et al., 1996). Yet I would argue that this entire intellectual strategy relies on an inverted binary whereby the bad is celebrated, and that it assumes stable assessments of value in that to reclaim bad art as good, there must be *a priori* good art. Even if good art is seen as a social construction of value, then these labels have little sense of worth as everything can conceivably be seen through relativist notions of good. This is not to suggest, however, that the labels 'good' and 'bad' or 'high' and 'low' should be left in exile. As Frow (1995) argues, the critique of the high/low binary is not a rejection of the activities that it covers, nor a desire to side with either high or low art. Rather it is an opportunity to acknowledge the existence and operation of this regulative structure and its concomitant values and contents (Frow, 1995). Indeed, in Chapter 5 I make explicit a strategy for how I propose to conceive and interpret value, in preparation for Part II where I aim to explore how dancing participants construct their own discourses of value that are neither the result of an absolutist claim to inherent value nor the product of an apolitical relativism. I now seek to focus on the field of cultural studies (and its relationship to dance studies) as I employ this disciplinary frame as part of my methodological approach precisely because cultural studies has invested in a radical intellectual critique of the canon.

Popular dance and cultural studies

Since its inception, cultural studies has sought to eschew canonical and hierarchical paradigms of culture: hence, much of its focus is directed towards the study of popular forms (Agger, 1992; Inglis, 1993; Nelson et al., 1992). A well developed body of literature exists within cultural studies that offers specific theoretical apparatus for the study of definitions, meanings and functions of popular culture (During, 1993; Grossberg, 1992; Storey, 1998; Strinati, 1995). Yet in spite of this, the subject of popular dance forms a notable area of neglect within this field. Paradoxically, given that dance studies has begun to focus on popular forms of expression, in response it has adopted new research paradigms.[8] Sklar (2000, p. 70) identifies a nascent direction in dance studies, which she describes as 'sociopolitical: it draws on the rapidly developing ideas and language of cultural studies'. Desmond (2000, p. 43) relates a similar account: 'many scholars in dance studies have produced exciting new work by bringing to bear on their research those questions and methodologies that are loosely part of "cultural studies"'. This raises the question why cultural studies has devoted so little attention to the study of popular dance.

Desmond (1997, p. 29) states that dance is 'undervalued and under-theorized' within academia in general and that cultural studies could benefit from a greater engagement with the subject of dance. She continues that the cultural analysis of dance can offer a wealth of information on how social identities are formed and negotiated within specific historical frameworks (Desmond, 1997). Likewise, Thomas (2003, p. 1) notes that 'few social or cultural theorists of the body have been drawn to address dance systematically as a discursive or situated aesthetic practice'. McRobbie concurs that cultural studies is 'negligent' of dance (1990, p. 39) and berates this serious oversight. She comments that the study of dance can produce significant scholarly findings in that the social contexts in which dance occurs reveal key information about the lives and values of those involved (McRobbie, 1990). Thomas and Cooper similarly note that dance has only a 'shadowy presence' (2002, p. 54) in cultural studies and 'despite the recent overwhelming interest in the study of the body in the humanities and social sciences, the human body as a moving agent in space and time remains somewhat ignored' (2002, p. 57).

Desmond (1997) asserts that dance's neglect within cultural studies is indicative of the latter's bias towards verbal and visual texts and that any research which does address the body tends to examine its representations and discursive formations rather than its movement and action. She goes on to note that dance is either dismissed as a trivial leisure pursuit (in its social and popular performance contexts) or else considered unworthy of study because of its preconceived association with marginal groups, particularly women and people of colour (Desmond, 1997). Here, Desmond's critique clearly calls attention to the social and cultural values that inform how certain subjects are privileged within the academy and others are subsequently marginalized. Ward (1993) also identifies the scant attention paid to dance in 'sociological literature' and offers a number of reasons for this absence.[9] He proposes that the lack of an available score or text and a universally accepted mode of recording dance creates problems for academics wishing to research this area. Yet he counterpoints this argument in his suggestion that this has not prevented scholars without knowledge of music notation from pursuing the study of music. Ward (1993) traces another line of argument which claims that since dance, as a non-verbal practice, is situated outside the formal bounds of language, it cannot be approached discursively. Again, he is critical of this intellectual trajectory:

this conception holds that, as a non-verbal form of communication, dance is non-rational and thus more important within pre-literate than other social structures. From which it follows that within rational and industrial/post-industrial societies dance will be peripheral to the main forms of activity and social relations. (Ward, 1993, p. 18)

Here Ward speaks to a continued marginalization of the body (and its expressive movement practices) that has left scholars outside the domain of dance studies ill equipped to deal with questions concerning corporeality and its multiple articulations (Shilling, 1993; Thomas, 2003). Indeed in the latter part of Chapter 2 I examine how a small body of scholars within cultural studies has tackled the subject of popular dance within wider cultural events to demonstrate the limited and problematic ways in which the dancing body is read.

Yet although cultural studies has generally overlooked practices of popular dance, I nevertheless recognize that cultural theory offers a rich lens through which to examine popular forms of expression. In Chapter 2 I discuss at length the value of cultural studies as an intellectual field but, in advance of this, I seek to explore how cultural studies deals with the concept of value.

Cultural studies and value

The issue of value has prompted recent debate within cultural studies, largely because of its neglect (Ferguson and Golding, 1997; Morris, 1996; Murdock, 1997), and much of this discussion is rooted in the absolutist/relativist tensions examined above. In response to the elitist canon of high culture, one of the key tenets of cultural studies is a privileging of all cultural activities as worthy of academic investigation (Agger, 1992). Yet several commentators note that such a perspective is problematized by the influence of postmodernism and its relativist position. The rejection of the totalizing discourses of grand narratives in favour of local forms of knowledge has created a situation of pure equivalence and critical indifference (Agger, 1992; Frow, 1995). Morley (1997, p. 122) notes that cultural relativism means that it is difficult to express judgement without being accused of 'ontological imperialism', which places cultural studies in an apolitical stance. Although McGuigan (1997) asserts that absolute values of judgement have rightly been dismantled, value is a fundamental constituent of social experience; humans are 'valuing subjects'. I therefore turn to three scholars, John Fekete (1987), Simon Frith (1991) and John Frow (1995), who offer more considered examinations of value within the framework of cultural studies and I reflect on how I propose to use these ideas within the context of popular dance research.

Fekete (1987) observes that a watershed of new thinking around the concept of value came about in cultural studies informed by postmodern and post-structuralist theory. Within postmodernism a single unified theory of value cannot exist; instead the discipline offers a more pluralized understanding of value that recognizes greater 'narratives of action' and the 'play of value' (Fekete, 1987, p. x). This position clearly speaks to the relative and socially situated nature of value. He goes on to suggest that post-structuralism conceives value neither as fixed to an object, nor deriving from personal needs or desires; instead, he positions it as a 'regulative medium of preference' (Fekete, 1987, p. 65). For Fekete (1987) value produces effects rather than static representations. This conceives value as a dynamic entity within the field of social relations that avoids becoming objectified in the form of treasured cultural artefacts. Thus, while value is not an entirely determining social force, nor is it arbitrarily constructed: social subjects both shape and are shaped by value systems. This position neither awards value itself nor affords the social subject complete agency over the production of worth. I therefore use this understanding of value, which is produced, negotiated and reconceived through a dynamic exchange between human subjects and their social conditions, as a means to examine the embodied articulation of value within my case study examples.

Yet another perspective that Fekete offers assumes a less balanced conception of value. Drawing on the work of Jean Baudrillard he proffers that postmodern society is characterized by a hyperreality in which sign values only ever refer to other sign values in an endless simulacrum (Fekete, 1987). These simulations or empty sign values are oversaturated and it is only the consumer that gives them meaning (Fekete, 1987). Fekete conceives this as a kind of 'vampire value' in which fixed meaning or worth is drained from these value signs. Yet, like relativism, this arguably dystopian representation of postmodern life is an ultimately unhelpful position. The notion of multiple and vacuous free-floating values, which leaves the subject without any means to discern between them, is an overly pessimistic reading of cultural engagement. As I demonstrate in Part II, the dancing communities under investigation are incontrovertibly able to articulate judgements of worth and preference. Although such assessments are not necessarily fixed or consensual, neither are the dancing subjects overwhelmed and unable to occupy rationalized and discriminatory positions.

To offer his ideas further context, I now to return to Frith's (1991) essay which opened out some of the debates at the beginning of this chapter concerning absolute and relative values.[10] Frith is another who suggests that value is a neglected topic within cultural studies, and he argues that value judgements are as relevant to popular forms as they are to high culture (Frith, 1991). He historicizes the disregard for value through suggesting that mass culture theory, in particular the work of the Frankfurt School, positioned popular forms as constituting negligible cultural worth (Frith, 1991).[11] Yet in more recent cultural studies scholarship attention has turned to cultural values associated with acts of consumption (Frith, 1991). He describes how 'cultural populism' has resulted in an uncritical valuing of popular culture (Frith, 1991).[12] For him, the problem is a methodological one in that the academic locates the process of analysis in readings of worth, rather than in field-based research that focuses on the values of those communities directly involved in the consumption of cultural practices (Frith, 1991). Thus the relativist position of academic populism within cultural studies creates a 'flattening' of value in which all cultural activities are privileged and celebrated at a purely theoretical level. Yet Frith contends that 'to deny the significance of value judgements in popular culture (to ignore popular taste hierarchies) is, if nothing else, hypocritical' (Frith, 1991, p. 105).

In order to consider how one negotiates issues of 'worth' Frith (1991) proposes that it is necessary to examine the arguments employed to exalt certain practices over others. Indeed, he suggests that the same debates of worth in high culture can be applied to popular culture (Frith, 1991). Yet I would question whether there is a danger that he perpetuates the potential for an absolutist and canonical privileging of popular forms. It is at this point that he asserts the superiority of *Jane Eyre* over a Mills and Boon novel and the Pet Shop Boys over U2. While his assessment of *Jane Eyre* simply offers consensus with the literary canon, it would appear (given that U2 have received both critical and commercial acclaim) that his assessment of their musical worth is based on personal preference.[13] Although his absolute conviction is perhaps a playful provocation to invite the reader to think about value, it is still frustrating that he exercises aesthetic judgement without explaining the criteria against which he constructs these measures of value.

Where Frith's work is perhaps more useful is in his call to examine the social construction of value within its frameworks of production:

> to understand popular cultural values we need to look at the social contexts in which value judgements are deployed, to look at the

social reasons why some aspects of a sound or spectacle are valued over others. (Frith, 1991, pp. 105–6)

In relation to popular music, he suggests that the value judgements that circulate around it are constructed in three key domains: the creators (i.e. the musicians), the producers (those personnel involved in the production and dissemination of the music) and the consumers (Frith, 1991). Indeed, the circuit of production, transmission and consumption may well be a useful way to track the range of values that surround popular dance forms. I therefore take from Frith (1991) the importance of qualitative methods that engage directly with the creators, disseminators and participants of popular dance to establish how they constitute frameworks of value within the socially situated contexts of their dancing communities.

Frow (1995) provides the final consideration of the question of value and its theoretical neglect within cultural studies. He commences by challenging received ideas concerning value in his assertion that the elitism and authority of the high art canon over a domain of culture denigrated as low, mass or popular is a dichotomy that is no longer justifiable (Frow, 1995). First, high art is also part of the free market economy and can be equally subject to mass production techniques or popular commercialization. Second, in place of a singular, dominant belief system, a range of hierarchies is at play and, although high art still holds a specialist position, mass culture also participates in the formation of our cultural values. Third, the high/low cultural divide traditionally suggests a class correlation, which is outmoded given that mass audiences are characterized by inclusion rather than exclusivity. Finally, rather than a disdain for all things mass, there is an increasing play between high and popular forms. In Chapter 3, I explore further the fragility of the high/low paradigm that informs the art canon.

In reference to cultural studies, Frow suggests that rather than address the issue of value, it has simply adopted an inverted value hierarchy so that popular forms are privileged over elite culture (Frow, 1995). Although Frow (1995) critiques the high/low binary as an untenable paradigm, he recognizes the difficulty of moving away from a model that is entrenched in the social fabric. He acknowledges that it performs convenient ideological work in unifying and differentiating cultural practice into an oppositional hierarchy that would otherwise break down into heterogeneous forms and practices. Thus he suggests that it is necessary to recognize the high/low binary as a descriptive category, but that it does not need to be accepted as a given. For Frow (1995), value as a universal model does not exist; however, the concept of value informs all areas of life. In Chapter 5, I explore Frow's ideas further and employ his notion of 'regimes of value' to demonstrate in Part II how popular dance communities create localized and sometimes contested structures of value.

Frow's (1995) other area of critique identifies a key problem within cultural analysis. Methodologically, researchers traditionally seek to suppress value judgements; yet this then skews how they would ordinarily engage with cultural texts, and the object of study potentially loses its meaning. As Frow notes,

> cultural studies has been prolific of attempts to reconcile the division of knowledge, to overcome the split between reflexive knowledge and its others. The characteristic masks in which it performs have been those of the organic intellectual, the fan, the participant observer; or more deceptively, it has worn the invisible mask of a humanism which supposes the common identity and the common interests of the knower and the known. (Frow, 1995, p. 2)

Thus the conduct of research as a valuing researcher throws open a range of epistemological and ontological questions around the extent to which perceived objectivities and subjectivities are balanced. In light of this, Weeks (1993) argues for the need to be explicit about the epistemological and ontological rationale underlying the frameworks of value employed by scholars, although he recognizes that even this approach is a value position in itself. This conundrum clearly affects the field research data that informs Part II of this book and there I tackle questions regarding the tensions between my multiple subjectivities as researcher, performer, participant and fan.

The return to value in popular dance

In this chapter I explore the shifting measures of value attached to popular dance in relation both to the academy and to arts practice. Given that evaluation is a socially situated act, individualized, collective and institutionalized assertions of worth are the means by which value is constructed, negotiated, revisited and modified. I conclude that neither the absolutist notion of inherent worth nor the relativist assertion of cultural equality offers a satisfactory lens to explore how value operates in relation to popular dance. The field of cultural studies potentially offers a useful entry to the question of value with its focus on popular forms of expression: Fekete (1987) argues for a dynamic conceptualization of value in which subjects both shape and are shaped by frameworks of value; Frith (1991) suggests that value is constituted among different communities of people and that field-based methods offer an appropriate research tool through which to access the systems of worth articulated by these producers and users; and Frow (1995) raises important methodological issues regarding the ontology of the researcher. As this book examines popular dance through intellectual perspectives drawn from cultural studies, I now seek to explore the institutional and intellectual legacy of cultural studies as a discipline.

2
The Value(s) of Cultural Studies

In this chapter I seek to reflect upon the social, institutional and theoretical values that inform cultural studies to demonstrate how this field of enquiry can inform popular dance research. First I provide an historical overview of the social and institutional conditions under which cultural studies arose. This historicization of the discipline reveals shifting attitudes towards the popular and I draw on this material in Chapter 3 to illustrate differing approaches to defining popular dance. Second, I consider how cultural studies scholarship conceives the notion of culture. This not only illuminates its interest in the popular idiom, but also the way in which cultural studies understands popular culture as a site of contestation shapes how I then conceive and analyse popular dance practice. The assertion in cultural studies that popular culture constitutes a terrain of competing power relations allows me to demonstrate in Part II how the popular dancing body negotiates values of difference, inequality and contradiction. In view of this, my third area of exploration centres on the key intellectual strategies that cultural studies research brings to its subject of enquiry. I consider the main theoretical and methodological approaches employed in cultural studies and reflect upon how I can employ these paradigms in popular dance research. The literature that I call upon to investigate these three areas emerged from the 1990s, which marked a period of reflection and re-evaluation in cultural studies as scholars working in the field set out to define and critique this broad subject domain (Ferguson and Golding, 1997; Storey, 1996; Turner, 1990).

Although I suggested in Chapter 1 that the subject of dance forms a notable absence in cultural studies, several key studies focus on aspects of popular culture in which dance plays a significant role: youth (sub) cultures and club cultures. In the fourth section of Chapter 2, I therefore provide a critique of cultural studies texts that focus on popular dance events. While I argued earlier that cultural studies offers robust intellectual frameworks for the study of popular culture, I demonstrate in this literature review how the discipline is less equipped to analyse the corporeality of the dancing body and its capacity to articulate values in motion. For this reason, as a conclusion to this chapter I argue that popular dance research can benefit from an interdisciplinary investigation that combines theories and methods located in cultural studies with the attention to the expressive and responsive capacities of the moving body as developed within dance studies. Accordingly, this chapter both traces the intellectual values of cultural studies and presents an exposition of the value of cultural studies for popular dance research.

The social and institutional context

The foundation of cultural studies is located in post-war Britain and its intellectual preoccupations emerge from these specific conditions. The late 1940s marked a period of capitalist prosperity and by the 1950s differences between the working and middle classes were diminishing as workers became more affluent and had increasing access to the cheap commodity goods made available through mass production techniques (During, 1993; Green, 1996). Furthermore, the gradual acquisition of washing machines, refrigerators, record players and television sets, for example, redirected social existence from one of labour to one of consumption (During, 1993). This combination of increased spending power, labour-saving domestic appliances and access to mass communications placed greater emphasis on leisure time. The influence of American mass-mediated culture brought about feelings of insecurity in relation to the stability of British cultural life (Barker and Beezer, 1992), and I suggest below that some of the early work in cultural studies reacted against this rapid cultural change. Yet Agger (1992) asserts that the post-war baby boom generation acquired its cultural knowledge and identity through the mass media and it is this media-literate audience which now engages in the activity of cultural studies.

Another post-war development fundamental to the advent of cultural studies arose from greater opportunities for education through the welfare state (Green, 1996). Whereas higher education had previously been the preserve of the middle classes, its elitist outlook was inevitably dismantled by the inclusion of young people with alternative world views. Likewise, the adult education movement of the 1930s and

40s offered opportunities for the working classes to engage with subject matter relevant to their own experience (Barker and Beezer, 1992). This democratization of education brought about changes to the curriculum and this is evident from the opening of the Centre for Contemporary Cultural Studies (CCCS) at Birmingham University in 1964 (Barker, 2000; Turner, 1990).[1] Two scholars closely linked to the early work of the Centre are Richard Hoggart and Raymond Williams (Barker and Beezer, 1992; Inglis, 1993).[2] Significantly, both came from working class backgrounds and both taught in adult education (During, 1993, Nelson et al., 1992).

English literature studies formed the intellectual lineage of Hoggart's and Williams's work (Green, 1996; Turner, 1990) and, in order to understand their distinctive scholarly contributions to cultural studies, it is necessary to turn to the literary criticism of F. R. Leavis. Leavis was an exponent of the 'culture and civilization' tradition, which feared the rapid proliferation of mass culture and the resulting decline of folk cultures (Johnson, 1996; Turner, 1990). Leavis sought to use the education system to distribute knowledge and, within that, promoted a restricted canon as a means to improve moral standards (During, 1993). It is in relation to this paradigmatic framework that the work of Hoggart and Williams can be situated.

Hoggart's seminal work, *The Uses of Literacy* (1957) draws on the disciplines of literary studies, sociology and anthropology to illuminate his personal experience of working class life (Grossberg, 1993; Turner, 1990). On one hand, by privileging the values and meanings of working class culture he challenges the Leavisite canonization of literature and its implicit hierarchy of high and low culture (Hall, 1996a). Yet, on the other, *The Uses of Literacy* is an extension of Leavisism in its attempts to legitimate working class culture through a critique of mass culture (Grossberg, 1993). Williams is considered equally influential and in *Culture and Society* (1958) he focuses on literary history but within the context of changes in social, political and economic life (Hall, 1996a; Turner, 1990). As did Hoggart, Williams also measures different cultural formations against Leavisite value judgements (Turner, 1990). His interest in definitional concepts of culture (which I take up in the following section) and the need to address contextual issues continues with *The Long Revolution* (1961). This book examines the impact of the media on British cultural life and deals not only with aesthetic questions, but also with institutional and ideological frameworks. Yet *The Long Revolution* also stands accused of promoting 'idealist and civilizing' definitions of culture (Hall, 1996a, p. 34).

Although these foundational texts reproduce Leavisite perspectives, their impact on the field of cultural studies should not be underestimated. First, they took the subject of culture seriously in their interrogations of how it reflected key historical changes in industry, democracy and class (Hall, 1996a). Second, they defined culture 'as ordinary', a sentiment which stood in opposition to the conservative post-war rhetoric of heritage and tradition (Green, 1996). This understanding of culture as part of the practice of everyday life has been highly influential in the field of cultural studies and in the following section I examine more closely the development of this thinking.

Culture as a site of contestation

One of Williams's major contributions to cultural studies is his attempt to offer a more clarified and considered explanation of the term 'culture' than had previously existed. Earlier definitions of culture were underpinned by a humanist or aesthetic understanding; the former conceives culture as a process of spiritual and intellectual development and the latter refers to elite aesthetic objects as the constituents of culture (Johnson, 1996; Storey, 1998). Williams, however, is responsible for expanding the definition of culture and employing it in an anthropological sense to include a 'whole way of life' (Bennett, 1993; Hall, 1996a). Although there have been a number of critiques of this particular definition of culture, a consensus does prevail over the desire to postulate an inclusive notion of culture.[3] This approach assumes an anti-canonical perspective, which has led to legitimization of the previously neglected area of popular culture as an object of academic enquiry (Agger, 1992; Inglis, 1993; Nelson et al., 1992).[4]

Yet not only do cultural theorists value popular forms of cultural expression, but they also conceive culture in a particular way: as a terrain marked by difference and contest. Consequently it is conceived as a site of political critique (Nelson et al., 1992), out of which emerges an interest in relations of power, ideology and resistance (Barker and Beezer, 1992). The interconnections between culture and power hinge on a dialectic of whether culture is imposed on people 'from above' or whether people participate in the construction of cultural meanings themselves (Agger, 1992; Barker and Beezer, 1992). The notion that people are passive recipients of a culture produced from an omnipotent source is located in theories of dominant ideology and hegemony. Within this theoretical framework, culture is no longer seen as an expression of everyday life, as in the work of Williams and Hoggart, but as a 'system of domination' (During, 1993, p. 5).

The dominant ideology thesis refers to historically situated discourses that appear universal and transparent, but which secure and maintain dominant power structures (Barker, 2000; During, 1993). Hence culture is said to reflect the dominant political perspective. Much of this work is located in the thinking of Louis Althusser, who sees individuals as ideologically constructed subjects, a condition which allows the state and capitalism to reproduce themselves without the threat of revolution (During, 1993). Bennett (1993), however, critiques this unidirectional model in which power emanates from a single source and can only be challenged or opposed from the outside. Another model of power is developed in the influential work of Antonio Gramsci, in particular his concept of hegemony in which domination is secured through consent rather than coercion (Barker, 2000; During, 1993).[5] Yet culture can also be read as a ground of empowerment as well as constraint. Recalling the work of Stuart Hall, Storey (1996) argues that, although culture is where hegemony is produced and secured, it is also a place in which socialism could be constituted. The notion of resistance, which occurs in the act of consumption, is pertinent to this opposing perspective. In Chapter 3, I explore how these dialectical conceptions of power, as a form of domination or resistance, have informed frameworks for defining popular culture and how this can be read back into popular dance.

Since culture is conceptualized as a field of conflict and struggle, cultural studies is associated with a political agenda. In its pursuit of theoretical knowledge cultural studies seeks to expose and challenge power structures and to institute change (Blundell et al., 1993; Johnson, 1996; Storey, 1998). In this regard the humanist legacy of the arts and humanities is evident in the constitution of cultural studies scholars as politically engaged subjects, so it is not surprising that social, political and intellectual values are inextricably linked. Yet there is a danger that political engagement in cultural studies stays at the level of the theoretical and I take up aspects of this debate in the following section and in Chapter 3.[6] At this stage, I conclude that cultural studies has legitimized the study of popular forms and conceives the popular as a framework of power politics. First, this informs my argument in Chapter 3 that 'the popular' is more appropriately understood as an approach through which to examine a range of dance practices that exist under particular conditions, than as comprising a discrete set of movement forms. Second, the idea that popular culture constitutes a site of dynamic power relations shapes the way that I approach the multiple and conflicting values that I encounter in the case study examples under investigation in Part II. I now move on to consider the intellectual strategies developed in cultural studies to make sense of popular culture as a site of contestation.

Theories, methods and their positions of value

Historically, the work that emerged from the CCCS was divided between 'culturalism' and 'structuralism'. Although this bifurcation is now somewhat outdated, these different approaches and the debates surrounding them mark an important division of intellectual values within the field. Culturalism initially dominated the Centre through the work of Williams and Hoggart and is rooted in a 'social humanist perspective' (Grossberg, 1993, p. 27). Through this intellectual lens culture is viewed as ordinary and its emphasis is on human agency and lived experience; consequently, the research is empirical in character and explores how people actively create cultural meanings (Barker, 2000).[7] By the 1970s, culturalism had largely been superseded by structuralism, which applies a linguistic model to the study of culture and is distinctly anti-humanist in perspective (Grossberg, 1993; Hall, 1996a).[8] These competing interests undoubtedly underpin the intellectual legacy of cultural studies and I now seek to examine three key modes of enquiry that have come to characterize cultural studies research: textual analysis, political economy and consumption studies. Each approach carries with it specific intellectual values that have the capacity to deny as well as privilege ideas.

The method of textual analysis, which has been highly influential in cultural studies research, arises from the structuralist tradition outlined above and seeks to conduct a formal interpretation of cultural artefacts (Barker, 2000). While this method facilitates a systematic reading of a text (Johnson, 1996), it has also prompted a number of concerns. Billig (1997, p. 205) notes that cultural studies research tends to focus on manufactured artefacts rather than on people's lives and thus conceives the field as a 'depopulated discipline'. His contention is that attention has turned to the media texts and commodities of mass culture, thus neglecting lived practices and the ways in which people make use of these material and symbolic goods. Agger (1992) asserts that cultural studies is in danger of becoming a technical method that lacks any grounding in a social, historical or political context. Although textual analysis may demonstrate intertextual flexibility and interpretive versatility, as Agger (1992) states, a close analysis fails to address the reception process or prompt social transformation. Ferguson and Golding (1997) also support this dissatisfaction with textual approaches that divert attention from the material context of cultural analysis. They note that, within the textual paradigm, power struggle occurs at the level of theory rather than within real historical and material circumstances. Jensen and Pauly (1997) suggest that a methodological consequence of the swing towards textual analysis is that audiences also become 'textual constructions' and therefore people's understandings of their own experiences are overlooked.[9] In light of this, several scholars (Frith, 1991; McRobbie, 1997) have called for a return to experiential research that engages with the users of popular culture. I also support the need to give voice to participant experience and for this reason employ qualitative research methods in examining the popular dance case studies in Part II.

The second key area of focus is rooted in a political economy approach. Barker (2000) suggests that this has developed as research in cultural studies has primarily centred on industrialized cultures organized through capitalist frameworks of production. The underpinnings of a political economy approach derive from the work of Karl Marx, which privileges the conditions of production as determining social organization and cultural formations (Johnson, 1996). Hence questions regarding ownership of cultural production and modes of distribution are primary concerns (Barker, 2000). While much of the early work of the CCCS employed Marxist frameworks of thinking (Storey, 1996), the shift towards textual analysis has directed cultural studies away from issues of production (Garnham, 1997).

Garnham (1997) suggests that scholars within the field of cultural studies are wary of a political economy approach because of its perceived determinism: the classic Marxist paradigm centres on the belief that the economic 'base' determines the social 'superstructure'. Although Garnham (1997) acknowledges that the mode of production sets the terms for the superstructure, he queries the essentialist critique applied to the political economy model. He asserts that the base/superstructure relationship is historically variable and can be subject to crisis and contradiction.[10] Garnham (1997) goes on to insist that a political economy approach does not privilege production over consumption, but instead sees the two as interlinked in a supply-and-demand dialectic. On one hand people's needs and desires are formed through what producers make available; but on the other producers act in response to people's needs and desires.

In light of such critiques, several scholars call for a move to recognize the relations between production and consumption through a return to questions of the political economy in cultural studies research (Kellner, 1997; Murdock, 1997). Its strength lies in the acknowledgement that material conditions can affect and be affected by cultural expression. I would concur that questions of economic value are germane to the study of popular dance, which is often located in commercial production contexts. In Chapter 5 I therefore explore in further detail the specifics of Marxist thinking, which then allows me to consider questions of how popular dance is shaped by and responsive to economic values in my analysis of the three case studies in Part II.

The third area of focus lies on the notion of consumption. This strand emerges from literary reception studies, which assert that understanding is always from the position of the reader: hence audiences are actively involved in the creation of meaning through their engagement with cultural formations (Barker, 2000). Yet, although this approach potentially offers a fruitful examination of how people actively make sense of the cultural products with which they engage, it draws less on the culturalist (and therefore experiential) mode of enquiry advocated by Hoggart and Williams than on the structuralist preoccupation with the, meanings and values that 'readers' invest in cultural texts. The development of consumption-oriented research in the 1980s has come under serious attack within the field of cultural studies for the populist perspective through which consumption came to be conceived (Agger, 1992; During, 1993; Gitlin, 1997; McGuigan, 1992, Webster, 1996).[11] 'Cultural populism' posits that the consumers of popular culture are active readers who are always situated in a position of resistance through the pleasures, meanings, values and uses located in their engagement with popular forms (Morris, 1996).[12]

Agger (1992, p. 171) refers to populism as an 'affirmative postmodernism' that simply celebrates consumerism rather than critiquing it, and Gitlin (1997) sees it as an inversion of the traditional high/low hierarchy in which popular culture is uncritically extolled. Yet it is the populist disregard for the potentially manipulative or pernicious operation of popular culture that appears to cause most concern.[13] There is clearly a danger that this uncritical populism fails to acknowledge the ideological operation of cultural products (Agger, 1992; Garnham, 1997) and to articulate the precise form that this resistance takes (Kellner, 1997). Although Morley (1997, p. 125) is at pains to dismiss the idea of 'textual determinacy', he is equally keen to dispute the notion that cultural texts are completely open-ended. A further charge against cultural populism is its lack of engagement with material and political circumstances, in that textual resistance does not prompt actual social change. McGuigan

(1997, p. 141) contends that the populist focus on the 'micro narratives' of consumption leaves little space for 'transformative struggle'. The implication is that the field of cultural studies is trapped in an undiscriminating vacuum and returns to arguments (discussed in Chapter 1) that populism has left researchers in the value-free domain of an apolitical relativism.

Excavating these key theoretical and methodological approaches within cultural studies reveals how analytical frameworks reflect their own value systems, which offer both uses and limitations in the conduct of scholarly research. Throughout Chapter 3, in which I explore definitions of popular dance, and Chapter 4, in which I critique how the field of dance studies engages with popular dance practice, I continue to make reference to these distinct intellectual approaches. They inform specific conceptions of the popular idiom and offer a robust apparatus for the study of popular dance. In particular, I seek to privilege an understanding of popular dance that focuses on the experiences of its participants, so adopt a qualitative approach; yet, in recognition that popular dance takes place under specific social, economic and aesthetic parameters, I take into account the conditions of production. While the field of cultural studies offers appropriate research paradigms for the analysis of popular culture (more broadly defined), thus far I have drawn little attention to its treatment of the dancing body in particular. In the following section I therefore explore how scholars in cultural studies have attended to the subject of dance.

Dancing in youth (sub)cultures and club cultures

Since the early work of the CCCS, a number of projects have emerged that examine cultural events in which dance plays a significant role. A cluster of work has developed around the theme of 'youth (sub)cultures' and 'club cultures' and in this section I seek to examine how a selection of these texts tackles the subject of popular dance.[14] The work under examination spans a period of 20 years and I have focused on six monographs and one book chapter in which the authors make reference to the dance practice that takes place within different cultural groups. In so doing, I hope to reveal precisely how the dancing body is valued within this intellectual tradition.[15]

In 1979 Dick Hebdige published *Subculture: The Meaning of Style* (1979) which comprises a semiotic analysis of youth subcultures, such as mods, teds, rockers and skinheads, to demonstrate how 'spectacular subcultural styles' undergo a cycle of resistance to and incorporation into hegemonic culture. For Hebdige, style refers to 'the plane of aesthetics: in dress, dance, music' (1979, pp. 44–5) but, in spite of this claim, he pays scant attention to subcultural dance. In total, there are two pages devoted to the subject of punk dancing:

> punk did more than upset the wardrobe. It undermined every relevant discourse. Thus dancing, usually an involving and expressive medium in British rock and mainstream pop cultures, was turned into a dumbshow of blank robotics. (Hebdige, 1979, p. 108)

Yet he fails to expound on how dancing in mainstream rock and pop was 'involving and expressive', and why punk transgressed these values. In reference to the pogo, he describes it as 'a caricature – a *reductio ad absurdum* of all the social dance styles associated with rock music' (Hebdige, 1979, p. 108). Although he offers a brief description of the movement, as 'masculine jostling at the front of the stage' (Hebdige, 1979, p. 108) and 'leaping into the air, hands clenched to the side, to head an imaginary ball' (Hebdige, 1979, p. 108–9), his interpretation of it is limited. First, although he implies that the pogo lacks sociality, the spatial limitations dictated by the venues in which punk bands played, meant that audience members inevitably came into immediate physical contact with each other, so that the dance almost resembled a form of combat.[16] Second, he fails to comment on how the aggressive physicality of the pogo might be meaningful to the dancers. Thirdly, I also question Hebdige's description of the dance in terms of 'masculinity'. This gendering of the dance is less a description of movement quality, than an omission of the place of females within early subcultural research (Thornton, 1997), even though key female figures in music are emblematically associated with the punk movement.[17]

In contrast to Hebdige, Michael Brake's *Comparative Youth Culture* (1985) offers a wider examination of youth cultures across America, Britain and Canada. Yet his attention to dance and the role it plays in the identity formation of subcultures is also minimal. In Chapter 3, Brake discusses a range of British youth subcultures, and although he closely examines the dress, music, idols and commodities of each subculture in some detail, the subject of dance is completely overlooked. In Chapter 5, attention turns to African American subcultures. Brake briefly mentions 'dancing' in a generic sense, but offers little detail in the way of movement content. Furthermore, he draws problematic links between dance and sexuality:

> there is a belief in the superiority of their dancing and rhythm, which is a metaphor for the superiority of their sexuality, a fear in

white people that explains some of the irrational features of racism. (Brake, 1985, p. 124)

Although he attempts to argue that the dance and music act as an empowering identity-marker for African Americans, his suggestion that dance signifies sexuality speaks to an essentialist understanding of the black body.[18] While Brake refers to an 'irrationality' within this discourse, it is unclear whether his critique is aimed at an irrational fear of the superiority of the black body or at the contested relationship between the black body and a virile sexuality. The absence of movement analysis and the reduction of the dance to a functionalist expression continue in a brief reference to breakdancing as a form of 'resistance' (Brake, 1985, p. 126) and dance as a type of 'courtship ritual' (Brake, 1985, p. 170). Ultimately Brake (1985) gives no consideration to how this embodied practice facilitates the social functions to which he refers.

Iain Chambers's *Urban Rhythms* (1985) focuses specifically on a range of popular music associated with youth subcultures and there are numerous references to dance within this volume. Indeed, Chambers places the body, and specifically dancing, at the interface between popular music and leisure: 'it is above all the body, enveloped in sound, in dance, that stands at the cross-roads of pop music and leisure time' (Chambers, 1985, p. 17). Yet although he frequently refers to 'dance music' and 'dance venues', his discussion of specific dances is negligible. For instance, while he mentions the twist, the pogo, the block and the ska in passing, these references do little to evoke a well formed picture of the dance. Chambers (1985) also reads dance through a problematic duality. On one hand, he links dance to marginalized and disempowered groups: for example, disco and homosexuality (1985, p. 149), jiving and 'girls' (1985, pp. 41–4) and the generic label of 'stylised dancing' as the 'inseparable partner' of 'black musics' (1985, p. 118). Yet when he discusses 'progressive rock', a form associated with white male youth, attention shifts from the physicality of the body to the rationality of the mind:[19]

> dance rhythms became less imperative – the body had discovered other ways to be 'transported' – and musical effect was increasingly concentrated in the 'head'. (Chambers, 1985, p. 91)

Thus the dance is located in a Cartesian dualism that privileges the mind, along with masculinity, heterosexuality, whiteness and rationality, in opposition to the body, which is linked to femininity, homosexuality, blackness, and eroticism. Although these stereotypes pervade popular thinking, Chambers makes little attempt to problematize them, either through a deconstructive critique of these hierarchies or through offering alternative readings of the dancing and the dance event.

Research into youth culture continues with Paul Willis's *Common Culture* (1990), an ethnographic study of popular youth culture. Although Willis (1990, pp. 65–8) devotes attention to the dance, he reduces it to an embodied expression of music rather than an end in itself: 'dancing is the principal way in which musical pleasures become realized in physical movement and bodily grounded aesthetics' (Willis, 1990, p. 65). This is followed by a reductionist reading of dance as a sexual function: 'the sensual appeal of popular music is at its greatest in dance music, where its direct courting of sexuality generates a heightened sense of self and body' (Willis, 1990, pp. 65–6). Yet he also raises some pertinent issues regarding how young people experiment with dance as a form of symbolic cultural work and how dance forms are transmitted across different social groups, in particular from black British to white youth.

In general, the strength of this writing is that he privileges the cultural practices of young people and acknowledges the sophisticated level of work and understanding that goes into their dance activities. For instance, in reference to breakdance he notes, 'with their often elaborate and sophisticated moves, these more worked-up forms of popular dance have their own grounded aesthetic criteria for those that practise them, criteria of originality, wit and flexibility' (Willis, 1990, p. 67). It is also notable that Willis allows the participants' voices to emerge, thus enabling them to articulate understanding of their dance practice. Yet in spite of his references to a number of dance styles, such as skanking, Bhangra and breakdance, he gives no information about the character of these dances and the contexts in which they occur. In a final statement about the role of dancing, Willis dismisses it as a kind of compensatory activity for the unemployed: 'besides being an alternative way of filling in time, "working" and controlling the body might be some kind of consolation for the shrinking sense of power and control experienced elsewhere' (Willis, 1990, p. 68). Thus the value of dance is reduced to a work-function displacement instead of being a legitimate activity in its own right (Ward, 1993).

One piece of writing that stands out against the texts discussed so far, in the attention it devotes to dancing *per se* and its legitimization of dance as a significant cultural activity, is Angela McRobbie's book chapter 'Dance and Social Fantasy' (1984).[20] As Ward (1993) identifies, the analysis is largely directed at examples taken from popular fiction, film and television rather than from participatory practice. The importance of McRobbie's essay, however, is the cultural value she places on dance as a key activity of identity formation. In reference to the dance examples she selects from popular fiction and visual texts, she describes dance as a vocation that offers satisfaction and reward for young women and, although she highlights conventionalized links between the female body and sexuality, she problematizes this reductive position and offers alternative (feminist) views of dance. Yet what limits her reading is the link she draws between dance and fantasy:

> the dancehall or disco offers a darkened space where the dancer can retain some degree of anonymity or absorption. This in turn creates a temporary blotting-out of the self, a suspension of real, daylight consciousness, and an aura of dream-like self-reflection. (McRobbie, 1984, p. 144)

By situating dance is the realm of fantasy, she dislocates it from the real world in which it can act as an agent for social change. Thus any kind of personal transformation or political contestation occurs within this world of fantasy, not at a concrete or material level.

More recent scholarship has focused on club dance and Sarah Thornton's influential study *Club Cultures* (1997) clearly recognizes the centrality of the body in clubbing practice: 'dance styles...need to be *embodied* rather than just bought' (original emphasis, 1997, p.3). The research, which employs an ethnographic methodology, uses Bourdieu's notion of 'cultural capital' to explore hierarchies of taste within club subcultures.[21] Thornton (1997) argues that 'subcultural capital' can be both objectified and embodied and, in relation to the latter, she offers examples of how clubbers can display distinctions of taste through clothes, language and dance. As part of a historical overview, Thornton acknowledges the symbiotic relationship between popular dance and music. This diachronic perspective is useful as it calls attention to how the production and reception of music is inextricably linked to popular dance.

Thornton recognizes, not only that the act of dancing is key to 'club dance music', but that genres such as pogoing, slam dancing, moshing and 'air guitar' solos form an important component in the consumption of live music gigs. Yet, irrespective of Thornton's assertion that dance forms a significant indicator of the way that clubbers classify dance music cultures within hierarchies of taste, she neglects to make any comment about the character of the dance practice itself or, as Thomas (2003) identifies, of the clubbers' 'experience' of clubbing. Consequently she fails to explicate how dance constitutes a marker of subcultural style.

In a vein similar to Thornton's monograph, Ben Malbon's book *Clubbing: Dancing, Ecstasy and Vitality* (1999) employs ethnographic research as the methodology through which to examine clubbing practices. Where the two texts differ is that Malbon (1999) devotes considerable attention to the clubbing event through explicit references to his field data, and so a much more coherent picture begins to emerge. Malbon's research examines how clubbing affects experiences of particular territories, through which he argues that clubbing is a form of play that can shape and transform clubbers' identities and identifications. In the preface to the book, Malbon provides a diary of a night out in which he places great emphasis on the interaction of music and physical expression. This early reference to the centrality of the active body in the clubbing experience is echoed later in the volume in which an entire chapter, titled 'The Dancer From the Dance: The Musical and Dancing Crowds of Clubbing', focuses on the role of dance within club culture.

In comparison to the literature thus far, Malbon (1999) offers a more rigorous and sustained consideration of dance. For instance, he argues that dance acts as a marker of individuality and that the clubbers' experience of music is expressed through dancing to the extent that it is a form of 'creative listening' (Malbon, 1999, p. 82). Thus his discussion directly addresses how the dance itself is a *locus* of identity formation and creative expression, rather than simply suggesting that these social functions occur at an event where dance takes place. Malbon describes dancing as 'a mode of behaviour in which the relationship between movement and thought (or motion and emotion) is central' (Malbon, 1999, p. 86). Therefore he conceives dance not just as a physical response to a given stimulus, but also as a reflective, critical and intellectual investment in the body. In general, the strength of this research is that it interrogates how dance reflects significant social meanings and values. Through his study, Malbon (1999) argues that dance is a basis for social interaction; it is tied to issues of belonging and identity through which it has the potential to influence other areas of clubbers' lives.

What is also important with regard to the rigour of this research is that Malbon employs the voices of the participants to substantiate his ideas and engages with scholarly literature from the field of dance studies through which to debate them (Thomas and Cooper, 2002). Yet what is lacking is a delineation of the dance practice itself. Although there is a detailed examination of where, when and why clubbers dance, there is no consideration of how they dance: movement content is absent. The failure to analyse movement vocabulary in any depth is characteristic of all of the literature under investigation here. Although Malbon (1999) and McRobbie (1984) are commendable in their sustained consideration of how the dancing body itself plays a vital role in the construction of social identities and interactions, a detailed analysis of how the body moves and how this corporeal expression articulates cultural meanings marks a serious oversight.

Investing in popular dance

Given that cultural studies has sought to legitimate and interrogate the topic of popular culture, this raises the question of what this field can offer popular dance research. The shifting social circumstances of post-war Britain, which brought about rapid cultural change, sparked the intellectual focus of the discipline as commentators sought both to critique and to reflect upon the new 'mass culture'. The post-war democratization of education also impacted on the institutional evolution of cultural studies as some of its early scholars sought to research the 'ordinary culture' that had come to characterize their working class lives. This engagement with 'everyday practices' therefore had an indelible impact on conceptual definitions of culture. It no longer pertained to an elitist canon of aesthetic excellence, but an expanded understanding of culture that embraced the practices, institutions, representations, customs, values and traditions that constituted all 'ways of life'. As I go on to demonstrate in Chapter 3, these broad social changes have informed intellectual approaches to definitions of the popular idiom.

Yet what is most distinctive is the way in which cultural studies conceptualizes the operations of culture. Culture is conceived as a site of struggle and instability through which complex power relations are played out. It is this asymmetrical characterization of culture that has prompted the political dimension of the field, which seeks to expose and critique power imbalances in cultural formations. This perspective (understanding culture as a domain of conflict) offers a useful apparatus through which to approach the multiple and often paradoxical values that characterize popular dance practice. Furthermore, it highlights the tensions that exist between the producers and institutions that might seek to regulate cultural norms and the participants who choose to negotiate and question dominant value systems. In Part II I therefore seek to examine these dynamic power relations through the three case study examples.

This broad interest in culture as a contested terrain, and the desire to explore its interactions with power, open up the potential to employ diverse theoretical and methodological frameworks that offer important conceptual apparatus though which to analyze the production, circulation and consumption of popular forms. For the purposes of this book, I specifically value the experiential voices of those involved in popular dance; accordingly, I take from cultural studies theories and methods that pay attention to the creation of and participation in popular dance. It is important to note, however, that this not only is from the perspective of the participants, but also takes into account the existing network of social, economic and aesthetic values that shape and inform popular dance practice.

While a body of work within cultural studies centres on sub- and club cultures, the dance is frequently reduced to a functionalist role and the authors make assumptions of class, gender, sexuality and race that convey essentialist perspectives. Although some of the later research begins to consider how dance can articulate social identities and interactions, there is never sufficient investment in how the dancing body articulates these complex social values and exchanges as movement description is very rarely addressed. For this reason I propose an interdisciplinary model of popular dance research that takes from cultural studies its broader interests in production and consumption, but which also provides a detailed interrogation of the movement and a consideration of how this corporeal expression gives rise to the social formations under discussion. I therefore call for an investment in the popular dancing body that traces both how it is shaped by its contexts of production, transmission and reception and how it negotiates and re-articulates itself in response. As a dance studies scholar, I am interested in how the contested values of the popular are articulated by bodies in motion. Therefore in Chapter 4 I consider how dance studies 'writes' the popular dancing body and what this literature can offer my study of value.

Before I look to existing dance studies research on popular dance, I come to the troubled question of what constitutes 'popular dance'. I have suggested already that, rather than defining popular dance as a collection of movement forms, a more fruitful strategy may be to conceive it as an approach to a range of practices that occur under particular conditions. It is with this in mind that I now tackle the question 'what is popular dance'?

3
What Is Popular Dance?

Positioning the popular historically

A burgeoning interest in popular dance came to the fore in the 2001 winter edition of *Dance Research Journal*, which was devoted to 'social and popular dance'. That an entire issue centred on dance practices situated outside the hallowed ground of the theatre dance canon indicated a nascent shift in dance studies towards an increasingly relativist position. In the introduction, editor Julie Malnig (2001) comments that the dances which fall within this category reveal a wide range of forms, skill levels, degrees of professionalism and performance contexts. Yet this potentially rich diversity also encounters vexing questions of classification. As Malnig asserts, 'one of the fascinating aspects about the category of social dance itself is... the continually fluid interchange among what we call social, vernacular, and popular dances' (2001, p. 7). Yet she only remarks on the leakiness of these terms rather than providing any delineation of their distinct characteristics. While Storey (2003) suggests that definitions of the popular are both constructed and reconceptualized by intellectuals, I would argue that the meanings and values attached to categories of popular culture carry currency within the social world. It is for this reason that I focus on the question 'what is popular dance'?

In recent studies of early modern England (1500–1800), historians challenge the notion of a fixed divide between an elite culture that belonged to the dominant classes and a popular culture constituted by the masses (Burke, 1999; Harris, 1995; Reay, 1998). They argue that the concept of a singular, monolithic popular culture is limiting and instead propose that the 'popular cultures' of this period were fragmented, multiple and fluid (Burke, 1999; Harris, 1995; Reay, 1998). This pluralization of the term moves beyond a class-based definition to include variations of region, religion, gender, age and occupation (Reay, 1998). Reay (1998, p. 199) proposes that the elite–popular polarity also neglects the 'cultural exchange' that occurred between the two groups and comments that, although 'the people' did not participate in elite culture, the gentry certainly took part in popular forms. Harris (1995, p. 16) further disputes the elite/popular division to draw attention to the cultural activities of a 'middling society'.[1] Indeed, many of these points regarding the myriad ways in which cultural practice operates recur throughout this chapter. It is the period of industrialization and urbanization from the mid-nineteenth to the early-twentieth century, however, that cultural studies scholars mark as key to the development of contemporary popular culture (Baroni and Callegari, 1983; Chambers, 1986; Collins, 2002; Storey, 2003). This epoch brought with it vast social and cultural change and mobilized a series of responses regarding its impact on life across Europe and America. Within this chapter, I therefore call on some of those historically constituted debates to interrogate the classification of 'popular dance'.

I initially turn to dance studies to examine how the field deals with definitions of the 'popular' but, given their interest in the popular idiom, I also look to popular music studies and cultural studies to assess how scholars within those disciplines conceive the popular. In music scholarship the attention to popular forms arose as a reaction against the long-held tradition of valuing 'art music' as epitomized by the classical canon (Frith, 1997) and in Chapter 2 I highlighted the preoccupation in cultural studies with popular processes and products. Yet the desire to formulate a definition of the popular has proved troubling and elusive within those disciplines. Since 'popular music' encompasses a diversity of styles, genres, traditions and functions (Fiori, 1983; Shuker, 1998), scholars argue that its content and parameters are unclear (Cutler, 1983; Stratton, 1983). Equally, outside the arena of academic study, this nebulous category is rarely tackled in standard music dictionaries and in 1991 the Broadcasting Act in Britain struggled to create a definition that satisfied both artists and representatives from the music industry (Shuker, 1997). Similarly, as 'popular culture' also embraces a multitude of objects and practices (Frith, 1997; Sedgwick and Edgar, 1999), it is problematic to unify such diversity within a single theoretical model. Consequently, 'popular' is frequently applied to cultural phenomena independently of a definitional framework (Frith, 1997); accordingly, the term is reliant on common-sense or intuitive understandings.

The concept of the 'popular' is clearly a slippery classification, but one that continues to be used to delineate specific products and pastimes. In this chapter, I therefore seek to examine constructions of the popular as a historically contested label specifically in relation to processes of industrialization and urbanization. I employ an interdisciplinary methodology to consider how the term is conceived across the fields of dance, popular music and cultural studies and I draw on three dance examples – tap dance, the pogo and ragtime – to illustrate how robust those definitions are in practice. As I demonstrate, different intellectual understandings produce distinct definitions of what constitutes a popular culture. I therefore suggest that the popular is more usefully conceived as an approach than as a fixed set of objects and practices. To commence I focus on dance studies to consider how it deals with definitions of 'popular', 'social' and 'vernacular dance'. I then begin to integrate ideas from popular music studies and cultural studies to explore different definitions of the popular: a paradigm that marks it as distinct from folk and art cultures; classifications that conceive it through theories of mass culture as a force of manipulation; and conceptions that articulate it through positions of power. Within this discussion, I show how different approaches reveal specific value judgements in their construction of the popular. In conclusion, I argue that popular dance cannot be understood as an absolute definition, but encompasses a way of understanding a range of dances that take place under particular conditions. From this, I offer a working definition of popular dance that foregrounds how I choose to address the popular idiom within the context of this book.

Popular, social and vernacular dance

To return to Malnig's (2001) observation that a wide collection of dances are variously described as 'popular', 'social' and 'vernacular' it is worth examining how those terms have been employed within dance scholarship with a view to qualifying why I have selected to use the label 'popular' over other possible definitions. In an early piece of work that sought to tackle the thorny issue of classification, Buckland (1983) set out to consider definitions of 'folk dance' and in so doing also looked at concepts of 'classical' and 'popular'. In this article, she offers a cursory definition of popular dance as a:

> fashionable dance form: can be associated with popular music recordings. Tends to be transmitted through fashionable centres for

dancing, including schools of dance, or nowadays through television. Tendency to innovation. (Buckland, 1983, p. 326)

This brief description is part of a triadic paradigm in which the popular is set in contrast to an extended consideration of a 'classical' and 'folk' dance binary; hence 'the popular' is both marginalized and defined through what it is not.[2] Almost 20 years later, in the special social and popular dance issue of *Dance Research Journal*, Cohen-Stratyner (2001) is no further forward in resolving the issue of what characterizes 'popular dance'. Although her concern is with 'social' dance, there is a tendency in her writing to conflate 'social' with 'vernacular' and 'popular', either by using the three terms interchangeably or by dividing them with forward slashes to suggest an 'either/or' rhetoric.

Crease (2000, p. 110) is consistent in his use of the term 'vernacular dance', which he describes as 'the kind in which people dance amongst themselves, spontaneously, without professional training, in ordinary spaces without sharp borders between participants and spectators'. Yet he does not provide a satisfactory rationale for the label he has selected to describe these dances. He questions the term 'vernacular', which he states is 'awkward and academic-sounding' and, although he refers to the possible alternatives 'social' and 'popular', he dismisses them as 'misleading' without expounding on why he does not favour them (Crease, 2000, p. 110). Furthermore Crease (2000, p. 110) excludes 'standardized practices of ballroom dancing' from his definition, which is questionable in that, although ballroom can be highly theatricalized in its exhibition form, it can also take place in precisely the sort of contexts he describes as vernacular. While I acknowledge that vernacular dance is a term commonly used within dance scholarship to describe live participatory dancing (Jackson, 2001; Malone, 1996; Stearns and Stearns, 1994; Valis Hill, 1992), I would be keen to include this within a broader set of 'popular dance' practices that I will come to shortly.

One of the most recent conceptions of 'popular dance' is articulated by Malnig in her anthology *Ballroom, Boogie, Shimmy Sham, Shake: A Social and Popular Dance Reader* (2009). Malnig (2009, p. 4) also makes reference to 'vernacular' dances as those that 'spring from the lifeblood of communities and subcultures and are generally learned informally, through cultural and social networks'. Yet her preference is to employ the term 'social' to encompass these dances, as 'vernacular' is also used to include folk genres which are rooted in the 'preservations of heritage and group traditions' (Malnig, 2009, p. 4). For Malnig (2009, p. 4), 'social dance' better conveys the way in which its participants become 'a community *as a result* of the dancing [original emphasis]' rather than through a shared social or cultural heritage. Although she acknowledges that social and popular dance can be employed interchangeably, in that both are participated in by many and both are generally situated as distinct from 'art dance', she specifically describes popular dance 'according to a specific *process* by which local, vernacular, and social dance traditions become popularized in the public sphere [original emphasis]' (Malnig, 2009, p. 105).[3] Here she refers to the mediation of social dance through apparatus such as dance manuals, instruction songs and music video. While I would concur that many popular forms are subject to theatricalization and mediation, her notion of 'popularization' implies a quantitative understanding of popular dance as existing initially within a 'private' or 'pre-mediated' context, but then circulated to a wider 'public sphere' (i.e. more people). Later in the chapter I will problematize quantitative definitions of the popular, but I would also argue that there is a continual exchange between so-called 'private' and 'public' cultures and that neither remains discrete. That said, I therefore question whether an uncontaminated 'social' dance can exist prior to the process of mediation, which then makes it 'popular' in character.

Although Nahachewsky (1995) does not focus on 'popular dance' as such, he contributes an important debate to the issue of classification within the field of dance anthropology. Nahachewsky (1995) advocates defining all dance practices on a continuum or spectrum that spans 'participatory' and 'presentational' contexts. To illustrate this in practice, he traces how the *kolmyika*, a Ukranian dance, changes as it is performed in two different situations. Yet Williams and Farnell (1995) identify some flaws in his supposition. They suggest that the notion of a 'context' for classifying dance is a useful, although not exclusive, approach. They argue that Nahachewsky conflates 'context' with 'types of dance' and that the key difference in his participatory/presentational axis is rooted in the 'recipient' rather than the context or the dance. They also assert that to characterize differences across the 'same dance' performed in different contexts must be to suggest that they are somehow different and must be recognized as such (Williams and Farnell, 1995). Williams and Farnell (1995) conclude that it may be more fruitful simply to conceive dance as a 'cultural tradition' rather than tackling elusive definitions. I would suggest, however, that since both the scholarly community and the general public use the classifications 'popular', 'social', 'art', 'folk' and so on both to frame and to value dance practice, these typologies require serious consideration.

For the purposes of this book I have chosen to employ the term 'popular' rather than 'social' or 'vernacular' dance as it offers a more inclusive definition. As the two latter terms emphasize 'liveness' and 'participation', they exclude forms of dance that are performed, staged or screened but which do not fall easily within categories of art dance. In line with cultural studies, I prefer to use the term 'popular' to include both participatory and representational cultural practices. Although I am sympathetic to Malnig's (2009) attentiveness to processes of mediation and theatricalization, it is almost impossible to see the 'social' and 'popular' as discrete practices. In light of this, I employ 'popular dance' to include live participatory forms that exist in mutual exchange with mediated and staged productions of dance. My aim now is to consider how the development of industrialization and urbanization brought with it new understandings of the popular idiom and how I can read these definitional frameworks back into the concept of popular dance.

Classifying culture as folk, art and pop

Storey (2003) traces how, from the mid-nineteenth through to the early-twentieth centuries, processes of industrialization and urbanization altered British cultural life and brought with them new conceptions of culture. Fears concerning the disappearance of traditional cultures prompted an interest in 'folk cultures' and, as a means to preserve the past, folk collectors set about studying traditional song, story and dance (Storey, 2003). This project spoke to a romantic mythology of an unchanging rural community absorbed in the collective production of cultural practices (Burke, 1981; Shepherd, 1983). It also served the purpose of creating a discrete national identity and indigenous culture, particularly for those European countries under foreign domination (Burke, 1981; Storey, 2003). While on one hand anxieties regarding industrialization sparked a return to pastoral ideals, urbanization produced middle class concerns regarding the industrial working classes (Storey, 2003). Collins (2002, p. 3) identifies how, in the first half of the nineteenth century, cultural practices existed side-by-side in the same contexts: 'concerts included arias as well as popular songs of the day...museums included both European masterpieces and stuffed exotic animals'. Yet from the mid-nineteenth century, middle class audiences began to carve out and institutionalize an area of culture designated as elite (Storey, 2003). This caused a divide between the nobility of high culture (which was privately funded and a marker of good taste) and popular entertainments that were profit-seeking and deemed vulgar in character (Storey, 2003).

It is possible to see how these distinctions between 'folk', 'art' and 'popular' (or discourses of 'high' and 'low') have fed into intellectual definitions of culture. Conceived as a paradigm of opposition, Buckland's (1983) interrogation of 'folk', 'classical' and 'popular' dance provides a useful example of this.[4] She commences with a clear delineation of classical and folk within a binary framework. On one hand, classical dance possesses a written body of criticism; it demands formal institutions of training and performance; there is a clear demarcation between creator and performer and between performer and observer; it is supported by a wealthy elite; and its transmission is reliant on national and international acclaim. In contrast, folk dance possesses no written body of criticism; it does not require formal contexts of training and performance; it is participatory in style as there is no division between performer and audience; it is not dependent on subsidized patronage; and its continuity does not rely upon national or international validation. Certainly her model of classical dance falls into the institutionalized practices of elite culture as outlined above, whereas her understanding of folk dance is very much in line with vernacular definitions of dance. Where this model becomes clouded, however, is in relation to popular dance, which Buckland (1983) positions on a continuum between classical and folk. Since she does not conceive popular dance in relation to the key attributes that define and contrast classical and folk, the popular is left out on a conceptual limb.[5]

A similar oppositional model to the one Buckland (1983) proposes is evident within popular music studies and cultural studies, although in these instances the popular is clearly dichotomized rather than existing on a continuum. In popular music studies, popular is set against 'classical' and 'folk' (Fiori, 1983; Kassabian, 1999) and in cultural studies it is polarized with 'high culture' (Chambers, 1986; Miller and McHoul, 1998). Birrer (1983) describes this as a 'negative definition' in that each classification is defined through what it is not. Whereas classical music is primarily an object of consumption that is individual in its creation, non-participatory and independent of commercial pressures (Cutler, 1983; Shepherd, 1983), folk music is fundamentally participatory and refers to the traditional practices of agrarian communities (Cutler, 1983; Kassabian, 1999).[6] Many of these characteristics overlap with definitions of 'high' and 'low' within cultural studies. Whereas high art is profound and individualized, low culture is serialized and exists for commercial gain (Frow, 1995; Storey, 1997); and while entertainment is the key feature of the popular, high art is concerned with transcending body, time and place (Miller and McHoul, 1998).

Although some sense of the character of each classification begins to emerge through the defining principles outlined above, this structural model is fraught with contentions and exceptions. As addressed in Chapter 1, it reveals a value system in which classical or high art is privileged and folk and popular practices are marginalized. Storey (2003) usefully situates the construction and destabilization of the high–low division in relation to modernist and postmodernist conceptions of popular culture. Whereas the early-twentieth century tenets of modernism excluded the masses through the production of art that was esoteric and obscure, postmodernism sought to critique this elitism through effacing the boundaries between high and low art (Storey, 2003). Yet it is not only the relativism of postmodern thinking that has called into question the stability of the high–low paradigm. Historically situated studies of cultural practice reveal how different forms have moved across the boundaries of high and low culture.[7]

An examination of tap dance can demonstrate the fluid and unstable character of the high/low dichotomy. Throughout its history, tap has shifted across a range of contexts from participatory, vernacular settings through to the theatricalized presentations of film and stage (De Frantz, 2002b). Sommer (1998) suggests that tap developed between the mid-1600s and early 1800s as a hybrid of West African and British traditional dances. It initially evolved as a vernacular dance form, which was then appropriated for the minstrel stage throughout the 1800s, and during the twentieth century it was further exposed and commercially exploited at travelling black road shows, on the vaudeville and Broadway stage and in Hollywood film musicals (Sommer, 1998; Stearns and Stearns, 1994). In the twenty-first century, this diversity of performance contexts is still apparent. While, on one hand, tap dance is taught to children and adults in the vernacular settings of school halls and community leisure centres, it also forms a vocational syllabus for young people training for careers in musical theatre and the commercial media. Contemporary 'performance' tap dancers, such as Savion Glover and Tobias Tak, appear at venues associated with high-art practice and are treated as 'serious artists' in terms of their virtuosity and choreographic innovation (De Frantz, 2002b; Levene, 1997b; Ostlere, 2003).

In contrast, commercial shows such as *Tap Dogs* (1995) seek consciously to make tap accessible to contemporary audiences through its heavily amplified tap dancing, hard-bodied performers and rock music score. Although some critics are scornful of the skill and artistry of *Tap Dogs* (Christiansen, 2001; Crisp, 2003; Levene, 2001), Prentice (1998, p.

17) notes that Dein Perry, the creator of *Tap Dogs*, received two Olivier Awards for his choreography and comments that '[the dancers'] true mastery of the art has earned them surprising credibility in the notoriously snobbish dance world'. In current dance scholarship, tap is recognized for its complexity and sophistication in both improvised and choreographed work and key practitioners are heralded as significant exponents of the form, not unlike the canon of art dance choreographers and performers (Malone, 1996; Stearns and Stearns, 1994; Valis Hill, 2000). Thus, although the origins of tap are located in a vernacular context, its transmission to a presentational stage context and the critical celebration of the technical and choreographic prowess of star performers place tap within a set of discourses traditionally applied to high art.

A reciprocity also exists between high and low that further problematizes their defining boundaries. Prato (1983) identifies how classical and popular music often draw upon characteristics of the other and Mukerji and Schudson (1991) state that high and popular culture share commonalities as social practice. This mutual exchange between high and low culture can be seen in an examination of punk rock and its related dance activities. Seminal punk band, The Sex Pistols' debut performance was at St Martin's School of Art (Wicke, 1993).[8] Frith and Horne (1987, p. 2) comment on how art schools straddle the high–low binary and portray art students as 'petit-bourgeois professionals who, as pop musicians, apply "high art" skills and identities to a mass cultural form'. Wicke (1993) asserts that Malcolm McLaren, manager of The Sex Pistols, was influenced by the art movement the International Situationists, and Frith and Horne (1987) describe punk performance in terms of a 'shock value' typical of the avant garde. They suggest that art school provided 'the only audience that would appreciate the aesthetics of incompetence, would dance or jeer with glee at the inversion of style' (Frith and Horne, 1987, p. 58). Indeed it could be argued that the pogo embodies these sentiments in that its aggressive, minimalist and repetitive 'anti-dance' style played to the 'shock value' of the avant garde. Conversely, high art has appropriated images and ideas from punk. Sabin (1999) traces punk's interface with, and influence on, literature and visual art and, in the field of dance, the choreography of Michael Clark and Karole Armitage is characterized by a punk sensibility (Duerden, 1999; Greskovic, 1999). On one hand, the mutual appropriation of ideas and images across punk and art demonstrates the fluidity of the high–low binary; on the other, the appropriation of the popular into the realm of high art might be a way to legitimate this cultural form.

Although the folk/art/popular triad or the high/low binary undoubt-edly informs how cultural practice is categorized, such practice is hierar-chical and partial. Shepherd (1983, p. 87) views this as a form of cultural imperialism: 'in shaping a phenomenon to suit a label, analysts become selective in their understanding of the phenomenon, admitting and emphasising some characteristics at the expense of others'. Yet Frow (1995, p. 22) notes that, although these defining frameworks lack theo-retical rigour, they are 'historically real'. This 'negative definition' of the popular, which is constituted as 'not folk' or 'not art', comments more on its structural relationship to other categories of culture, and the val-ues that underpin them, than it does on its content and context.

Mass culture and the manipulationist debate

As the forces of industrialization continued across Europe and America, in the early-twentieth century existence came to be characterized in terms of a mass culture, both through its assembly-line production tech-niques and the mass-media forms of radio, film and television (Strinati, 1995). This developing mass culture prompted the late-nineteenth cen-tury reformer Matthew Arnold (followed by F. R. Leavis in the early-twentieth century) to denounce mass culture as a threat to moral value and social stability (Storey, 2003). Thus 'popular culture' came to be read as a 'mass culture' and this informs intellectual definitions of the popular that are concerned with mediation and quantity. One of the ways in which Buckland (1983) distinguishes popular dance from clas-sical and folk is in its relationship to the mass media as a key mode of circulation. Similarly, Middleton (1997) identifies a techno-economic definition of popular music, which associates it with systems of mass communication, while Strinati (1995) asserts that popular culture is tied to the development of the mass media of the 1920s and 30s.

The emerging technologies of the analogue media and the develop-ing urban centres of the early-twentieth century offered the perfect conditions for dance to flourish and this can be seen in the case of ragtime. Industrialization produced new structures of time regulated by factory hours, thus creating a clear divide between labour and leisure (Chambers, 1986), and as industry moved to cities, urban life became a site for activities such as cinema, theatre and dance halls (Malnig, 1998). It is in this sociohistorical context that ragtime dance was dis-seminated. Although ragtime music and dance originated from African Americans, agents of the leisure industry were quick to exploit its com-mercial potential (Cook, 2000; Malnig, 1998; Robinson, 2009). One avenue for entrepreneurial scope was teaching and public performance. Vernon and Irene Castle adapted a collection of ragtime dances to suit white North American tastes and exploited these new forms through exhibition dancing and private lessons (McDonagh, 1979). In a study of the impact of the phonogram on ragtime dance, Cook (2000) examines how the recording industry sought to market music through dance. Initially this was presented as music to accompany African American dances, which white North Americans would have only observed; yet, by 1912, a number of recordings were released for the purposes of participation by white consumers. Cook (2000, p. 77) notes, 'in August [1913] *Talking Machine World* reported on the presence of a new profession, popular dance instruction, an unexpected and profitable development for the industry as it increased both sales of machines as well as recordings'.

This attention to the relationship between cultural production and mass markets speaks of another understanding of popular culture that is rooted in a quantitative classification. Buckland (1983) refers to a definition of popular dance that conceives it as practised by a large proportion of the population and this approach, which is rooted in a positivist methodology, can also be identified within the fields of popular music studies and cultural studies. The thinking behind such a strategy is that the term 'popular' refers to an object or practice that is widely consumed (Shuker, 1997; Storey, 1997). As consumers determine what is popular with their economic capital (Burnett, 1999), popular forms are then quantifiable through indicators such as sales figures, audience capacity, ratings, chart position and frequency of airtime (Shuker, 1997; Storey, 1997). In this case, the popular is constituted through numerical value.

Yet this quantitative approach is clearly problematic. To commence, there are no parameters to delimit the point at which a commodity becomes popular (Fiori, 1983; Storey, 1997; Wicke, 1983). In the area of musicology, Middleton (1983) highlights a range of methodological problems, which are both ideologically and empirically situated, in employing a positivist model. First, he questions the reliability of sales data, which can be subject to manipulation. Second, he identifies a tendency for this mode of research to privilege the youth market, which traditionally apportions a considerable amount of disposable income to music purchases, thus neglecting the consumption of music by older age groups. Thirdly, the focus on sales exclusively addresses the 'moment of exchange' and so the 'moment of use' is a glaring omission (Middleton, 1983, p. 6). Finally, he states that this approach only acknowledges commodity forms of music, which completely bypasses popular music that exists in vernacular contexts, for instance.

The bias towards the activities of the market in defining popular forms is a critique voiced by other scholars. By placing emphasis solely on those commodities that succeed in the market place, a vast range of cultural products that are potentially popular but commercially unsuccessful is consequently neglected (Cutler, 1983; Fiori, 1983; Frith, 1997). As Wicke (1983) notes, only a small proportion of popular music actually reaches 'the masses'. Another factor that skews a quantitative analysis is the manipulative character of the market in that it does not directly reflect consumer choice. Cutler (1983, p. 4) argues that buying practices are complex and partial in that they are limited by 'taste-formation' and 'demand-creation'. The reliance on market success to define popularity is further problematized if the high–low dualism is brought into play. Whereas some high culture achieves vast sales figures, certain popular forms appeal only to niche audiences (Shuker, 1998; Storey, 1997).

It is somewhat problematic to look at popular dance in purely market terms as it is a movement practice rather than a commodity *per se*. To some extent, dance can be presented in commodity form and audience size/sales figures can reflect 'relative popularity'. For instance, in the case of *Tap Dogs* statistics based on ticket sales or consumption of the show through video or DVD purchases could reveal its popularity. Yet this cannot always be applied to dance practices that take place in a vernacular setting. There are no definitive figures for how many people participated in ragtime at dance halls or what percentage of the audience pogoed at punk gigs or even in the privacy of the home.[9] Additionally, numerical popularity does not automatically tally with a dance form's classification as popular dance. Whereas some forms have been notably characterized by the extent of participation, such as during the 'dance craze' years of ragtime (Cook, 2000), others are exclusive and only involve comparatively small numbers, such as the pogo which was part of a minority youth subculture. Clearly, to focus exclusively on the market place and extent of consumption is to neglect other significant features of the popular, such as its history, meanings and context of production (Cutler, 1983; Middleton, 1983). As Miller and McHoul (1998) note, although market figures indicate what people buy, they do not reveal what people will tolerate, how they make sense of it and why markets fail.

Clearly popular dance has a close alliance with the mass media in terms of its circulation and dissemination. Yet one of the difficulties of linking the popular idiom to the mass media is that in theoretical terms this relationship has traditionally been rooted in an underlying manipulationist model. Building on the legacy of Arnold and Leavis, theorists of the Frankfurt School perceived the new mass culture as deeply detrimental to social existence (Storey, 2003; Strinati, 1995).[10] Storey (2003, p. 27) recounts how Theodor Adorno and Max Horkheimer developed the notion of 'the culture industry' to 'describe the products and the processes of "mass culture"'. For the exponents of the Frankfurt School, the commodities of mass culture are homogeneous, formulaic and serve to maintain the capitalist order (Burnett, 1999; Strinati, 1995). This is said to have an ideological function in that it produces a passive consumer who unquestionably accepts these standardized forms. Closely related to this is the mass culture theory of Dwight McDonald, which sees culture as 'imposed from above' (McDonald cited in Storey, 2003, p. 29) and its recipients as a manipulated mass. Although Burnett (1999) critiques this simplistic determinist perspective, which reduces the complex process of consumption to a simple psychological effect, it raises important issues of power regarding how mass culture is conceived. The following section therefore examines the classification of popular culture as a site of power relations.

The culture industry versus the people

In Chapter 2 I suggested that, within the field of cultural studies, culture is understood as a site of contestation. In view of this, another strategy for defining popular practice is to locate it within a power model that relates to its modes of production and consumption, and this hinges on the dialectic of whether culture is created 'from above' or 'below'. On one hand there is the supposition that cultural commodities are imposed by the dominant 'ruling classes' for the purposes of mass consumption; on the other is the argument that cultural practices are created and participated in by 'subordinate groups' and are therefore authentic and countercultural in character (Hanna, 1979; Middleton, 1983; Sedgwick and Edgar, 1999). Thus, within the realm of popular production, there is a conceptual tension between 'the culture industry' and 'the people'. Whereas the former perspective is rooted in mass culture theory, the latter is evident in a branch of cultural studies that focuses on the agency of the consumer (McGuigan, 1992; Strinati, 1995). As I suggested in the previous section, mass culture theory is generally discredited as the notion of a homogeneous culture that is passively received by the people has been critiqued for its manipulationist and essentialist understanding of culture. The shift towards regarding the consumer as an active participant able to resist the ideological forces of popular culture is a more recent concept in cultural studies and hinges on some of the 'cultural populism' debates that I addressed in Chapter 2.

Before examining these tensions in relation to dance practice, it is necessary to tease out how 'the culture industry' and 'the people' are conceptualized across dance, popular music and cultural studies. The intrinsic relationship between popular dance and the market place is noted by Buckland (1983). She describes how popular dance is employed to delineate commercial products that seek to be continually innovative, but allow minimal opportunity for creative participation. This is clearly rooted in a mass-market understanding of popular culture in which the continuous novelty of new commodities (whether they are songs, dances or clothes) perpetually seeks to maintain consumer interest, but the formulaic nature of such products ensures a short lifespan in terms of personal gratification. Baroni and Callegari (1983) assert that popular music is a reaction to, and expression of, the conditions and values of complex industrial societies and, as several writers state, since popular culture exists in a capitalist, free-market economy, its motivation is to maximize profit (Burnett, 1999; Frith, 2001; Shepherd, 1983; Storey, 1997). Consequently, popular culture is perceived as a commercial project produced through the 'culture industry' of a dominant capitalist system. Tied to this is the idea that popular forms are therefore steeped in the ideologies of capitalism and I will return to this issue shortly. First, however, I want to consider the opposing argument that popular culture is produced by 'the people'.

Bennett (1986) argues that 'the people' is a fixed and ahistorical category as a critique of the way that scholars have conceptualized this grouping as an abstract homogeneous mass. Significantly, different schools of thought offer different definitions of who the people are. Cohen-Stratyner (2001, p. 121) asserts that within European dance scholarship 'popular' is conceived as traditional dance forms that are 'of the people' or 'the folk'; in American academia it is associated with the new and linked to youth; but she also describes popular dance as 'the performance vocabulary of class structure'. These shifting definitions are also mirrored in popular music studies and cultural studies. Whereas high culture is linked to the ruling elite (Cutler, 1983), popular forms are said to reflect the tastes of 'ordinary' (Frith, 1997; Gammond, 1991) or 'working class' people (Bennett, 1986). The supposition that it is 'the people' who create popular culture, and that they are variously conceived as the 'folk', the 'youth', the 'ordinary' or the 'working class', further clouds the question of the parameters of the popular. The links between the popular and different social groups also evoke an essentialist discourse in that cultural preference is determined by social position.

The question whether popular culture is produced through the subjugating ideologies of a capitalist culture industry or through the spontaneous and countercultural practices of the people raises important questions of domination and resistance. Storey (2003, p. 51) suggests that the work of Antonio Gramsci is instrumental in conceiving popular culture as 'an arena of struggle and negotiation between the interests of dominant groups and the interests of subordinate groups'. As identified in Chapter 2, Gramsci's notion of 'hegemony' ensures the continuity of the dominant social framework, but operates through consent rather than coercion in a process of negotiation between those who hold power and those who do not (Miller and McHoul, 1998). Drawing upon some of the earlier case study examples, it is possible to see how issues of domination and resistance are articulated through interaction between the commercial industries and individual agents responsible for creating and disseminating a dance.

To take the example of ragtime dance, it operated both as a medium of social regulation and as a discourse of resistance. Cook (2000) suggests that the dance's illicit associations with 'black bodies' constituted a source of anxiety and this sense of social unease is supported by Robinson who describes how

> there was vociferous public criticism from many members of the middle classes, religious leaders, and social dance teachers, who could not or would not accept ragtime's new bodily aesthetics of play, angularity, casualness, inventiveness, and abruptness. Such people associated this new style of dancing with wanton sexuality, social vice, and delinquency among youth. (Robinson, 2009, p. 92)

In response, teaching associations sought to modify the movement to be acceptable to all sectors of society. In 1914, dancing master Oscar Duryea taught the Foxtrot to the Imperial Society of Teachers in Dancing in Britain: the dance was codified and set as a 'disciplined technique' that could be staged as 'competition dancing' (Franks, 1963, p. 186). Likewise, Vernon and Irene Castle 'refined' a collection of ragtime dances to suit white North American tastes and exploited these new forms through exhibition dancing and private lessons (McDonagh, 1979). Clearly the cultural anxiety that surrounded ragtime exposed the racist discourses that underpinned the dance practice and the desire to modify the dance served as a regulatory social framework. George-Graves offers an eloquent Gramscian reading of ragtime in her assertion that, while the primitivist discourses, which constituted the dance as uncivilized and vulgar, served to reinforce dominant racial codes, 'they also served blacks by giving them a sense of ownership over important cultural forms' (George-Graves, 2009, p. 66).

Yet an area in which ragtime dance was associated with shifting social attitudes was in its promotion of the 'new woman' in dance periodicals. Malnig (1998) observes the links between the press, ragtime dance and the ideologies of the Progressive era. Dance periodicals available in the nineteen-teens, such as *The Modern Dance Magazine* and *Dance Lovers Magazine*, promoted the latest dance practices as well as current social issues, for instance women's health, the suffragette movement and the 'new leisure culture'. Malnig (1998) argues that the dancing images evident in these periodicals embraced a spectrum of female role models and taught women about the cultural values and beliefs of the Progressive era. Although these were often idealized images, many emerged from the suffragette movement, which had sought to give women greater social, political, economic and sexual freedom; thus ragtime became intertextually associated with these transformative discourses and represented women's progressive entrance into previously male-dominated activities (Malnig, 1998).

With punk, there is a notable tension across the narratives that document its evolution and ideological positioning. Wicke (1993) states that it is seen either as an expression of a disaffected, unemployed youth or as a capitalist strategy to stimulate the record industry during a period of recession. To some extent, there are arguments to validate the role of 'music fans', rather than agents of the recording industry, in the creation and dissemination of punk music. As punk developed through art schools and the pub rock scene, this provided space for fans and musicians to create and perform music independently of the major labels (Laing, 1985). There was also an emphasis in punk on 'self-reliance', with those involved in the scene creating independent record labels and publishing fanzines (Laing, 1985). Although this 'do-it-yourself' mentality places agency at 'grass-roots' level, the punk scene did not remain isolated from the record industry. As bands sought greater recognition, independent labels hooked up with major record companies that would manufacture and distribute records in return for a share of the profit (Laing, 1985).

With regards to the pogo itself, Sid Vicious is credited as its originator. Laing (1985) writes that, prior to Vicious joining the band, he started jumping up and down and knocking into those around him at a Sex Pistols gig at the 100 Club. Irrespective of whether this 'myth of origin' is true, it would appear that the pogo had little commercial potential and remained an embodied response to the music by the participants in the scene.[11] What is important to note here is the dialectic between the participants and the industry. It would seem that punk music, with its concomitant fanzines, dance form and styles of behaviour and dress, neither came directly from the musicians and fans, nor was a complete commercial fabrication. Instead there is a crucial play between both parties in the creation and circulation of the music and its visual and embodied style.

There is much debate as to the extent to which punk rock disrupted the social order. Wicke (1993) suggests that punk challenged traditional values and, although some commentators doubt the extent to which it caused wider social change, it nevertheless brought about alternative modes of music production and consumption that eroded the divide between producers and consumers of music (Laing, 1985; Wicke, 1993).[12] Laing (1985) proposes that, whereas the stadium rock music that preceded punk was characterized by passive, stationary audiences, consumers of punk took an active role both in the production of music and how they responded to it: 'dancing had been one way of being active for an audience, and punk fans surging to the front of an auditorium to pogo responded in the same way as teds jiving in the aisles in the 1950s' (Laing, 1985, p. 82). Although the pogo can be read as a corporeal response to the apathy of progressive rock fans and musicians, Shaar Murrray (1991) argues that the recording industry remains extremely powerful overall. Wicke (1993) even suggests that those involved in the scene did not set out to overturn the commercial remit of the music industry. Indeed, as Laing (1985) notes, punk rock was inextricably linked to capitalist concerns as both the record labels and the punk musicians were reliant on music sales for their economic survival.

In terms of tap dance, I want to focus specifically on *Tap Dogs* which, in direct contrast to the countercultural readings of punk, is located in a set of discourses that speaks to the commercializing and manipulationist operation of a dominant mass culture. Jays (1996, p73) comments that shows such as *Tap Dogs* 'are like pioneer enterprises, built on ever-tapping feet, as if pounding stakes into the ground to mark their merchandising passage'. Indeed, the Executive Producer of *Tap Dogs* was explicit in his economic design as he stated 'our criterion is commercial viability' (Brown, 1996, p. 7). The fruits of this aspiration are evident as the show has become a global franchise with multiple productions touring simultaneously (Hutera, 2001; Levene, 2001), and the performers have featured at promotional events for BMW, Toyota, Audi and Mercedes Benz (Conrad, 2001). In terms of reception, *Tap Dogs* is dismissed by some critics as a formulaic and one-dimensional product that contributes to the construction of a passive spectator since it lacks intellectual challenge and fails to be innovative. Levene (1997a, p. 10) describes 'crowd-pleasing mega-hits' like *Tap Dogs* as 'undemanding spectacles that bypass the brain'. Other writers meanwhile comment upon its promotion and celebration of male stereotypes. Jays (1996, p. 75) describes it as 'all dick', Ross (1995/1996, p. 48) states that it is 'testosterone out of control' and Van Ulzen (1997/1998, p. 24) asserts that 'masculinity is mostly what the show is about'. Furthermore, it raises awkward matters of race given that the contribution of African American dancers to the history of tap is notably erased, since the show is performed by an all-white cast.

In line with the Gramscian model of power, the examples above illustrate how the dominant capitalist framework remains firmly in place, although there are clearly different degrees to which the popular can be interpreted as a slick entertainment product that does little to challenge the prevailing order or as a politically motivated entity that negotiates and destabilizes existing social norms. It is also evident that the 'culture industry' and 'the people' are not abstract and omnipotent entities, but instead are specific agents and institutions that operate within particular sets of social, historical, economic and political parameters. Within the previous three sections I have reflected on how different definitions of the popular arise from historically constituted debates: in opposition to folk or art culture; as a mass-produced and therefore quantifiable form that is ideologically manipulative in character; or as a power structure that serves the interests of the dominant classes but which facilitates opportunities for negotiation and resistance. In the final section of this chapter, I seek to construct a working definition of popular dance.

Towards a working definition of popular dance

It is evident from the above discussion that definitions of the popular within dance studies closely parallel those tendered in popular music studies and cultural studies. Yet in practice many of these conceptual models prove to be theoretically fragile, from which it is clear that an absolute definition of popular dance does not exist. Furthermore, the notion that the popular resists characterization as a fixed and knowable entity explains its capacity for resistance and reinvention. While I would not wish to propose a rigid definition, I draw on some of the material above to delineate the conditions under which popular dance occurs, rooted in matters of historical context, economic structure, physical location and sociopolitical framework.

In terms of its historical evolution, processes of industrialization and urbanization across Europe and America offered the necessary technological advances and shifts in social organization to create a cultural environment in which popular dance practice could be produced and disseminated. Although popular dance is not necessarily subject to 'mass participation', it is frequently transmitted through, or closely allied to, the mass media. In economic terms, popular dance is rarely subsidized through public funds or private donors: it is either created at low cost by individual agents/communities or else constructed for the purposes of commercial means by institutions such as the record industry, private dance schools, and film and television companies. Notably, the relationship of these communities and institutions to popular dance is often close, through mutual cultural exchange. Although popular dance frequently develops within particular communities, it rarely stays at grass-roots level as private corporations perpetually seek out new commercial enterprises. In turn, dancers within vernacular contexts draw on media representations of dance to inform their practice or endeavour to exploit their dance commercially.

In relation to context, popular dance occupies a range of sites that include stage, screen or 'street' locations (by which I mean common public spaces such as municipal halls, clubs, ballrooms, village greens, high streets and leisure centres), and can be performed by amateurs or professionals, depending on the 'performance context'. Although I would argue that it is generally positioned as distinct from 'art culture', it can occupy 'art spaces' such as galleries, museums and subsidized performance venues. While the legacy of the high–low divide continues to inform the economic, intellectual and contextual distinction between art and popular dance, each can influence and be influenced by the other. Indeed, the continued critique and destabilization of the high–low divide is summarized by Collins (2002, p. 6) who refers both to the 1960s 'Pop Art' movement, in which artists drew upon popular forms in the context of galleries and museums, and the 1990s 'high-pop' which 'represents the reversal of that flow by transforming *Culture* into mass entertainment [original emphasis]'. Storey (2003, p. 95) also identifies attempts by intellectuals to approach popular culture through the same values of artistic worth attributed to high art in what he describes as an 'aesthetics of popular culture'.

While it is necessary to consider popular dance in relation to the local sites that it occupies, it is equally important to reflect upon its global context from a geopolitical perspective. There is clearly an underlying assumption that 'the popular' is a Western phenomenon. In music and cultural studies, definitions of and research into the popular idiom reflect an imperialist position in their focus on forms located in Western Europe, North America and Australia (Aharonian, 1983; Burnett, 1999; Middleton, 1997; Shuker, 1998). Yet, in dance terms, there are practices that exist both in vernacular settings and other popular fora that would oppose this ethnocentric reading: the Cuban rumba (Daniel, 1995), the Brazilian samba (Browning, 1995), the Argentinian tango (Savigliano, 1995) and the screen dance performances of popular Bombay cinema (Shresthova, 2004). Therefore I would want to promote the potential for a more geographically inclusive understanding of popular dance. Given the expeditious transmission of popular dance practices through global mass communications systems, there is certainly opportunity to examine the tensions between the transnational character of popular dance and its reception in local contexts.[13] Indeed, Storey (2003) reflects on how current understandings of popular culture conceive it in relation to globalization. Although he critiques accounts of globalization that read it though the lens of a homogenizing socioeconomic phenomenon, he highlights how areas of this scholarship have usefully conceived the global transmission of popular culture through perspectives of hybridization and locally situated values and meanings.

I argued at the beginning of this chapter that the popular is more usefully understood as an approach. As I demonstrated above, different intellectual paradigms have produced distinct understandings of the popular and each of these reveals different value systems: a form with a low level of cultural worth; a form with a high level of consumption; and a form that either maintains the dominant ideology or articulates expressions of resistance. Building on the ideas explored in Chapter 2 regarding the popular as a site of contestation, I choose to approach popular dance with this in mind. Central to my understanding of popular dance are the contesting of power relations between the commercial industries that seek to produce and disseminate popular dance and the participants in popular dance who create locally articulated practices. While I dispute the notion of a dominant power model that leaves no opportunity for resistance, I acknowledge the capacity for social, economic and political structures to act as regulating and restraining forces.[14] It is the interface between production, mediation, transmission and consumption of popular dance that is key to developing a richer understanding of the distinctive characteristics of movement practices located within the popular domain.

4
Writing Popular Dance

The emergence of popular dance studies

In the past decade or so, popular dance scholarship has rapidly expanded through a much more visible presence in academic journals, anthologies and monographs dedicated to popular dance topics. The institutionalization of this area is further evidenced through the development of degree-level studies on popular dance,[1] the inclusion of a Popular, Social and Vernacular Dance Working Group within the Society of Dance History Scholars, and the provision of a specialist training workshop titled 'Teaching Popular Dance in Higher Education' by Palatine in January 2010.[2] I therefore suggest that, within the broad domain of dance studies, the burgeoning interest in the popular marks out an emergent subdisciplinary research field of 'popular dance studies'.

My aim in Chapter 4 is to provide a mapping of this nascent research field and to reflect on the intellectual apparatus that it brings to the study of popular dance. In turn, I reflect on how these approaches inform my own intellectual directions within the context of this book. I therefore undertake a literary critique of selected monographs, peer-reviewed journal articles and conference papers to elucidate how popular dance is constructed textually within dance scholarship.[3] While I accept that this is not an exhaustive literature survey, I provide a sufficiently broad sweep of the field to begin to identify emergent directions in dance studies regarding its approaches to popular dance. In Chapter 4 I consider the following: how scholars classify the dance practices to which they refer; the research topics and foci that occupy scholarly interest; the types of methodology employed in studies of popular dance; the extent to which this research addresses contexts of production, circulation and reception; and how the writing attends to the corporeality of popular dance. In conclusion I seek to demonstrate that popular dance possesses its own set of characteristics that position it as distinct from other forms of dance. Consequently, it demands an intellectual treatment particular to its own conditions of creation, performance and consumption.

Naming popular dance

In Chapter 3 I positioned the popular as a historically contested term and highlighted some of the values and critiques underpinning its various definitions. As part of this discussion I also reflected on how dance scholars have conceived classifications of 'vernacular', 'social' and 'popular' dance. Although none of the scholars directly below present an extended consideration of terminology, it is worth examining their forms of categorization as this further contributes to understanding how labels operate discursively. Within the literature reviewed, the term 'vernacular' is used widely and several scholars explain its usage within the context of their work.[4] In a study of American jazz dance, Stearns and Stearns (1994, p. xvi) describe vernacular 'in the sense of native and homegrown'. Yet they offer case study examples that occur in professional film and theatre contexts, in addition to bars, clubs, dance halls and other 'street' settings. Furthermore, the concept of 'native' enters into a problematic duality that produces the notion of 'outsiders' or 'others', while also failing to recognize the transnational character of popular forms. De Frantz (2002a) comments on the Stearns's misuse of the term 'vernacular' through their inclusion of stage performances in this category and, in a move perhaps to unsettle the values that underpin different genres of dance, questions why they do not position this dance as 'art'.

In recognition of the interconnecting values of the art canon and intellectual study, Malone (1996, p. 2) conceives African American vernacular dance as that which occurs outside the academy and stresses that it is an 'evolving tradition' and 'process of cultural production'. Her reference to Ralph Ellison's generic understanding of vernacular as 'a dynamic process' (Ellison cited in Malone, 1996, p. 2) suggests a tendency towards evolution and adaptation of the dance over a fixed syllabus or repertoire of steps. The emphasis on modification and innovation is supported by Jackson (2001), whose discussion of vernacular dance foregrounds improvisation and the individual dancer as its key mode of transmission. In turn, Monaghan's (2001) study of the Lindy Hop offers a dual understanding of 'vernacular'. First, he conceives it as 'an indigenous language of the people' to locate it as a dance practice arising from the African American community of Harlem; and second, he employs vernacular in the sense of 'ordinary' to describe the Lindy Hop's marginalization in relation to other prominent dance forms that occupied the 'Broadway and Hollywood' stage (Monaghan, 2001, p. 126).

The category of 'social dance' is also commonplace, although explanations of its application are underdeveloped in comparison to 'vernacular'.[5] For instance, Doolittle (2001) refers to 'mass social dancing' in the title of her article, but makes overlapping references to 'popular' and 'vernacular' elsewhere and George-Graves (2009) describes ragtime both as 'social' and 'popular' dance. Monaghan and Dodson (2000) refer to the Lindy Hop as 'social', but note that it occurs within the contexts of social, stage and competition dance. Indeed, a number of authors observe how dances are transmitted across both theatrical/ performance and vernacular/social contexts, thus illuminating the fluidity of classification (Daniel, 1991; De Frantz, 2002b; McMains, 2001; Penny, 1999). In an article on ballroom dance, Penny (1999, p. 47) offers a definition of social dance as follows: 'people dance for their own enjoyment rather than performing for onlookers'. Although social dance lacks the formal performer–spectator division that characterizes art or presentational forms of dance, Penny overlooks the mutual gaze between dancers and the concomitant sense of display that exists within the context of participatory social dance.

The reason that scholars have perhaps sought to explain the term 'vernacular' rather than 'social' in relation to dance is that the former carries the dual meanings of 'homegrown' and 'ordinary', whereas the latter refers to a common sense definition of 'social' as 'participatory'. Therefore, while 'vernacular' then expresses notions of indigenous or community production, everyday performance contexts, intellectual marginalization and evolving forms, 'social' is simply assumed to mean participatory or recreational. In much the same way that scholars present 'social dance' as a self-evident category, the term 'popular' is employed without necessarily defining its meaning or parameters (Gonzalez, 2003–4; Osumare, 2000; Stanley Niaah, 2004; Usner, 2001). Yet the idea that the popular marks out a framework or context of classification is evident in some of the literature. For instance, Cook (2006, p. 9) locates Master Juba within 'black popular entertainment', Hope (2004, p. 28) describes Jamaican dancehall as a 'popular event', Foley (2001, p. 38) discusses traditional Irish step dance within the context of 'popular culture', and Taylor (2000, p. 415) examines 'popular uses' of ballet. The idea that the popular also serves to mediate and quantify cultural forms is noted by George (2002, p. 77), who describes the stage performance of the Whitman Sisters as 'popularizing black social dance', and McMains (2009), who references the expanding popularity of salsa and DanceSport.

From these multiple usages it appears that categorization continues to be troubling for dance studies scholars. As I suggested in Chapter 3, I do not seek to develop a rigid definition of popular dance, nor do I wish other scholars to abandon the labels 'social' and 'vernacular' in favour of 'popular'. Rather, I am interested in how these classifications reveal significant tensions and values in the way that academics conceive dance practice. While I have already made claim for how I intend to employ the category 'popular dance' in this book, the literature under review usefully calls attention to the mobility and adaptability of these different forms of dance. The popular travels easily across borders and contexts, it is produced within everyday contexts but is then mediated as a presentational form, and is closely tied to the pleasures of participation and consumption. The idea that popular dance cannot be easily contained forms part of its attraction. It is locally produced yet globally transmitted, ordinary yet spectacular, marginalized yet celebrated. Consequently, popular dance prompts scholars to develop research questions and methods that attend to its dynamic and mutable character.

Research clusters and questions

The literature under investigation focuses on a rich array of dances and this diversity relates to historical eras, geographical locations, performance contexts and participant identities. Notably, a number of published monographs have been devoted entirely to selected popular dance subjects: African American vernacular dance (Stearns and Stearns, 1994), ballroom (Malnig, 1992; McMains, 2006), club dance (Buckland, 2002; Pini, 2001), hip hop (Osumare, 2007), rumba (Daniel, 1995), samba (Browning, 1995), tango (Savigliano, 1995), the jazz tap of the Nicholas Brothers (Valis Hill, 2000), the vaudeville performances of the Whitman Sisters (George-Graves, 2000), and African American vaudeville in the swing era (Dixon Gottschild, 2002). In addition, clusters of studies have evolved which examine the following dance practices: ragtime, tap, salsa, hip hop, dancehall, club dance, lindyhop and ballroom.[6] Although the above texts could be classified in multifarious ways and the groupings that I offer are neither fixed nor discrete, that studies of popular dance have begun to develop a critical mass is significant for two key reasons. First, the 'popularity' of a topic reveals a paradigm of value from which it is possible to ascertain those dance forms considered to be of scholarly interest. Second, the transition from isolated studies to wider bodies of research is integral to dance scholarship as the latter opens up academic debate to reveal important confluence and divergence of thinking.

As well as clusters of research that share commonality of dance form, other bodies of work exist that can be grouped according to different interests. For instance, several scholars have chosen to focus on individual dancers or star performers such as Master Juba (Cook, 2006; Winter, 2001), Margot Webb and Harold Norton (Dixon Gottschild, 2002), Jack Cole (Valis Hill, 2009), Buddy Bradley (Valis Hill, 1992), the Whitman Sisters (George-Graves, 2000 and George, 2002) and Cholly Atkins (Malone, 1988). Other work centres on popular representations of dance in film and television, such as film noir (Becker, 1987), the Gap clothing advertisements (Dunagan, 2007), Hollywood musicals (Becker, 1989; LaPointe-Crump, 2000), Jamaican dancehall docu-videos (Wright, 2004), hip hop film (LaBoskey, 2001), the *Mad Hot Ballroom* documentary (Dodds, 2008), pop music video (Dodds, 2009), and the silent films of Douglas Fairbanks (Studlar, 1995). Although far less common, a few studies address popular dance venues or organizations, such as the Savoy Ballroom in Harlem, New York (Hubbard and Monaghan, 2009), the Philadelphia Dancing Assembly of the eighteenth century (Matluck Brooks, 1989) and the provincial music halls of nineteenth-century Britain (Barker, 1987).

Although this literature review indicates that a diverse range of dance practices and representations are examined, a number of omissions exist. For instance, with the exception of Young's (1999) analysis of gothic club dancing, there is a dearth of research on the dance styles of 'youth subcultures'. This absence may partly be due to the transient character of popular youth forms. Unlike the art dance canon, which is preserved through a performance repertoire, popular dance within a vernacular context undergoes a constant process of innovation and modification by those involved. Thus short-lived 'dance fads' or those situated in 'underground' communities and contexts are easily overlooked. In an isolated study of the social dance practices of people in the 'third age', Thomas and Cooper (2002) reveal that the 'older dancer' forms an absent subject in dance scholarship.[7] In light of these two areas of neglect, Chapter 6 focuses on the subcultural dance styles of punk, heavy metal and ska fans, and Chapter 8 centres on the dance practices of a British Caribbean club for the over-40s.

In addition to mapping how topics of investigation can reveal particular values and interests, an analysis of the research questions or issues
examined also produces significant findings. With the exception of a
few studies that primarily seek to provide a historiography of a specific dance or collection of dances (Stearns and Stearns, 1994; Szwed
and Marks, 1988), the literature can largely be divided into two broad
categories of research: identity politics and cultural analysis. The relationship between dance and identity is pivotal to a wide range of texts,
and I include only a small selection of examples here: the European
embodiment of 'blackness' in ragtime (Robinson, 2009); articulations of
transnational and local identity in mambo (Gonzalez, 2003–4); female
pleasure and self-regulation in salsa (Skinner, 2008); masculinity in hip
hop films (LaBoskey, 2001); gender and sexuality in Jamaican dancehall
(Cooper, 2000); age, gender and class in competition ballroom (Penny,
1999); queer performativity on the dance floor (Bollen, 2001), race, gender and nationality in country western dance (Ponzio, 1996); and combat and spirituality in krumping (Zanfagna, 2009).

The other branch of research is characterized by research questions
that examine how the dance participates in the creation, maintenance,
modification and transgression of cultural values and meanings. Again,
just a few examples of this are as follows: how vernacular dancing can
'construct culture in black communities' (Jackson, 2001, pp. 41–2);
how social dancing enacts 'choreographies of community cultural values' (Doolittle, 2001, p. 11); the social meanings of dance for participants in the 'third age' (Thomas and Cooper, 2002); how underground
house dancing creates a 'communitas' (Sommer, 2001); the globalization of hip hop and its interface with local indigenous interpretations
(Osumare, 2000); 'how an historical inheritance of imagery and metaphor from literary romance informs the position of ballet in popular
culture' (Taylor, 2000, p. 415); exotic dance and censorship (Hanna,
2000); and the commercialization and theatricalization of social dance
in the dance marathons of the Great Depression (Martin, 2009).

It is important to note that these are not absolute categories and that
many of the texts cited above span both questions of identity and issues
of cultural meaning. What is paramount, however, is the emphasis on
wider cultural concerns in this literature, which substantiates the argument in Chapter 1 that an area of work has developed in dance studies
that calls upon issues, theories and methods from cultural studies as
tools of intellectual enquiry. 'Identity politics' and 'cultural analysis'
are key to cultural studies, in particular the way that culture constitutes
a site of contested meanings and values that reflects different models of

power (Barker, 2000; During, 1993). Evidently, popular dance studies appears attentive to the complex social, political and economic meanings invested in popular dance practice. In view of this, I seek to demonstrate in Part II how the popular dance case studies articulate distinct cultural values and identity positions.

Notably within the literature, issues of aesthetics tend to be awarded less attention. While there is a well established tradition of scholarly work that deals with methods of dance analysis and criticism and classifications of genre and style in theatre dance (Copeland and Cohen, 1982), this kind of schematic approach may be less appropriate given the dynamic and mutable character of popular dance that I discuss in the previous section. Furthermore, I heed Storey's (2003) concern (cited in Chapter 3) that an 'aesthetics of pop' is simply an attempt to legitimate popular forms through criteria of worth that reproduce the values of the art canon. Yet some consideration of aesthetics would begin to acknowledge the complex codes and values that underpin popular dance practice and reconceive the 'performance' of social or vernacular dance as 'choreographic' and intentional rather than random and spontaneous.[8] In summary, although I would fully endorse the attention devoted to matters of cultural expression in popular dance, I would also argue that questions of aesthetics that acknowledge the multiple and evolving character of popular dance would offer a deeper understanding of corporeal expression.

Popular methodologies

From the literature review, three key methodologies come to the fore. The two most common are ethnography and historiography, but I turn first to textual analysis, which has been highly influential across the arts and humanities. This methodological approach is primarily used for the study of representations of popular dance, such as LaBoskey's (2001) analysis of masculinity in hip hop films, Malnig's (1998) research on images of dance in women's journals, and Cooper's (2000) study of song lyrics and media texts in relation to Jamaican dancehall.[9] This focus on 'textual sources' is perhaps not surprising as textual analysis forms a problematic strategy for the study of popular dance within its live participatory setting. Whereas there is a relatively constant repertoire in theatre art dance that constitutes the subject of examination, popular dance that exists as part of a dynamic social context is subject to perpetual evolution and modification and personal interpretation of the dance is permitted and encouraged. With theatre art dance, the notion of a 'text' exists in the form of the dance work itself and, although theatre dance choreographies undergo subtle variations, a vocabulary exists that is comparatively fixed. In the case of popular dance within live participatory events, it is difficult to delimit a discrete text as such since the dancing often takes place over several hours and recurs across weeks, months and possibly years. There is obviously an option to study the dance synchronically; however, any sense of its dynamic and evolving character is then lost. Even with such a 'snapshot' approach, the process of identifying which or whose version of the dance should be examined raises complex questions of authenticity and authorship that are problematic in their desire to fix popular dance practice in a way that fails to recognize its fluid and multiple character.

It is perhaps for these reasons that ethnographic fieldwork and historical studies form the major methodological approaches to the study of popular dance.[10] Arguably, ethnographic methodologies facilitate a rich and evocative picture of popular dance events. For example, Skinner (2008, pp. 65–6) commences his article on salsa dancing in Belfast with a detailed description of his participants: 'Christina wants to forget the illnesses and stresses back home', '[Annabel] is fearful that she might appear single' and '[Leanne] had a salsa love child'. Consequently, the salsa community under investigation becomes particular and individualized rather than homogeneous and abstract. Similarly, Stanley Niaah employs a dense account of the visual and sensory stimuli that form the backdrop of a Jamaican dancehall:

> clouds of smoke, cigarette lighter salutes, market trucks passing, the bright light of the moon, Labba Labba the dancer, music pumping, soldier lorries passing, children playing, male youth showing off their motorcycling skills, drinks galore, sugarcane and jerk chicken on sale, elders 'dropping legs', Japanese tourists, the Guns & Roses Girls, school uniforms, 'batty riders', video cameras, Rastafari brethren, and gangsters! (Stanley Niaah, 2004, p. 9)

In some instances scholars combine fieldwork data with other research tools. For instance, Browning's (1991) analysis of samba employs ethnographic methods in conjunction with historical and semiotic analysis, Taylor's (2000) examination of ballet in popular culture utilizes field interviews and textual criticism, and Hanna's (2000) work on exotic dance incorporates field visits with textual analysis. What is most significant is the way that these studies have adopted methodologies drawn from anthropology and ethnology in order to deal with the constantly evolving popular dance practices located within a live social setting. It is also notable that, in line with cultural studies, there is a preference for qualitative research, whereas quantitative data is rare.[11]

The other way in which scholars have approached the fluid character of popular dance within a live context is through historical methodologies. For instance, Wall (2009, p. 183) offers a historiography of 'teenage dance fads' from 1955–65 through 'drawing on secondary accounts, an analysis of dance as represented in contemporary media sources, as well as film and fan web sites that help re-create the time' and Cook (2000) presents a historical analysis of record catalogues, trade journals and advertisements to examine ragtime music and dance. Stearns and Stearns (1994) conducted extensive interviews to trace the history of African American jazz dance and Doolittle (2001) combines archival research, interviews and 'embodied histories' to interrogate the mass social dancing of the 1930s and 40s in Alberta, Canada. In her commitment to constructing an 'embodied history' Doolittle (2001, p. 19) invited participants to recall dance memories through the activity of dance itself, which allowed her to examine 'experiences of vanished dancing through actual experiences of dancing with older people. This text is embodied and remembered rather than written down.'

Another historiographic strategy for addressing the transience of popular dance is adopted by Robinson (2009, p. 98) who uses primary source materials to produce a fictive account of ragtime dancing: 'I borrow from dance reconstruction's close examination of movement and reliance on embodiment as a research tool and historical ethnomusicology's use of everyday texts to imagine the past'. Robinson notes (2009) that reconstruction is generally employed in relation to the set repertoires of court and concert dance, whereas twentieth-century social dance is rarely addressed. Significantly, while this is in part due to the multiple representations of social dance and its absence of strict codification, Robinson (2009) also suggests that it lacks the high levels of value awarded to other forms of dance.

The prevalence of ethnographic and historiographic studies of popular dance practice clearly attends to its proclivity towards innovation and modification. While there is not the scope within this book to undertake both approaches, I employ a fieldwork apparatus since my research enquiry seeks to examine how value is produced within the live dancing moment. In the Introduction to Part II, I reflect more fully on this methodological approach.

Dance in production, circulation and reception

I suggested in Chapter 2 that a key concern within cultural studies is the contextual framework of 'cultural expression'. Agger states:

> cultural studies, in its emphasis on culture as practice, helps us situate the creation of cultural artifacts in complex social and economic spaces within which creative activity is conditioned, even determined. (Agger, 1992, p. 13)

Cultural practices and representations are clearly shaped by and responsive to the social, political and economic framework in which they evolve and this context similarly impacts upon how cultural expression is circulated and subsequently consumed. Hence the context of production, modes of distribution and experiences of reception and consumption are fundamental to understanding the meanings and values that surround cultural practices and products. Significantly, several dance scholars also highlight the importance of examining dance within the context in which it is produced and practised. Rooted in an idea derived from dance anthropology and performance theory, Thomas and Cooper emphasize the importance of examining the whole 'dance event':

> rather than restricting the focus to particular dances or dancing, that is the dance forms, the dance event takes into account the social context in which the dancing is practised and performed. In this way form is not separated from context. (Thomas and Cooper, 2002, p. 56)

Similarly, in a study of the swing revival, Usner (2001, p. 90) comments: 'the historical moment and sociopolitical context in which neo-swing arose in southern California seems also singularly significant to understanding it'. I therefore seek to examine how scholars within popular dance studies choose to reflect on and interpret the conditions in which popular dance is produced, how it is subject, and adapts itself, to processes of mediation and transmission, and how it is received and practised.[12]

In the literature under review, the majority of studies address the production of the 'dance event'. As indicated earlier in the chapter, this may well result from the predominance of research on questions of identity formation and cultural analysis over those of aesthetic criticism. These wider issues of social production potentially require a greater level of contextual framing. Some research directs close attention to the 'performance context' or the organization of the whole 'dance event'. For instance, Penny (1999) details the infrastructure of competition ballroom, Stearns and Stearns (1994) relate the structural and economic organization of jazz dance within a variety of performance contexts and Young (1999) considers the subcultural field of goth club dancing. Yet these examinations of the immediate performance context remain discrete from the sociohistorical and politicoeconomic frameworks in which the dance is situated.

Other studies offer a more sustained consideration of the broader context in which the dance evolves and identify links between how these circumstances affect and shape understanding of the dance practice. In a study of krumping, Zanfagna (2009) conceives the dance through the metaphor of the circle to examine how the dance calls upon the 'ring-like contexts' (2009, p. 338) of battle and spirituality and how it has been commercialized through the 'mainstream circles' (2009, p. 347) of music video and popular documentary. Hope (2004) draws links between the 'violent masculinity' that is symbolically represented through Jamaican dancehall and the poor socioeconomic conditions of inner-city Kingston. Wagner (1986) details how processes of industrialization and urbanization produced anti-dance sentiments towards the taxi dancers in American dance halls in the early twentieth century. In her study of the dance marathons of the Great Depression, Martin (2009) traces the shifting legislation that altered perceptions of competition dancing from celebration to offence and Hanna (2000) surveys how the discourses of the 'Religious Right' and the legal framework of the First Amendment are employed to censor erotic dancing.

With the increasing emphasis on cultural analysis, it is not surprising that contexts of production are integral to understanding the dance. Likewise, processes of circulation and distribution are also awarded considerable attention. Desmond (1997) notes how dances are modified and how the meanings and values that surround them alter as they migrate from one social group to another. Meanwhile Buckland (1983) and Malnig (2009) identify how the print and visual media play an instrumental role in the dissemination of popular dance. Therefore, since notions of transmission and mediation are key to understanding popular dance, several authors consider processes of circulation, which reveal a diversity of apparatuses at work. For instance, Cook (2000) identifies the use of technology in the dissemination of ragtime dance; Cooper (2000) focuses on the broadcast of Jamaican dancehall through media texts; Jackson (2001) foregrounds the distribution of African American vernacular dance through oral and visual devices; and Szwed and Marks (1988) note the transformation of European set dances through the migration of peoples.

Other authors focus more specifically on how popular dance is shaped and modified by modes of transmission and the meanings that are produced as part of this process. For example, Daniel (1991) addresses the influence of the Ministry of Culture on the distribution of rumba as a means to produce a Cuban national identity; Usner (2001, p. 89) looks at the relationship between internet sites, as a 'primary place for discussion about music and dance', and the neo-swing revival in Southern California to examine issues of nostalgia and race; and Valis Hill (1992) details the impact of Buddy Bradley's Broadway style of jazz tap on British ballet and the West End stage. Banes and Szwed (2002, p. 170) address how the 'dance instruction song' is an apparatus by which social dance and 'bodily knowledge' is transmitted. Through their textual analysis of lyrics and music they conclude that this mode of dissemination 'has served crucial aesthetic, social and political functions' (Banes and Szwed, 2002, p. 170). This tracing of how popular dance migrates across different contexts and the impact this has on its meanings and values clearly attends to its dynamic and evolving form.

In Chapter 2 I commented on how studies of consumption dominated the cultural studies scholarship of the 1980s and marked an intellectual shift from the notion of culture as a force of domination to the idea that consumers could articulate a negotiation of the cultural hegemony through engaging in the pleasures of the popular. In view of this, for much of the literature under review issues of consumption and experiences of participation are key. This is particularly evident, though not exclusively, in work rooted within ethnographic or historical methodologies. Research that employs participant interviews potentially offers rich data that can convey experiential accounts of popular dance. For instance, Young (1999) draws upon interview material, fanzines, databases and internet discussion groups to give voice to the participants of goth club dancing and Stearns and Stearns (1994) employ interview data to present an oral history of African American jazz dance. Consequently, bearing in mind the critiques of textual analysis and consumption studies raised in Chapter 2, experiences of consumption are rooted in the participants' embodied knowledge rather than in the abstract speculation of the scholar.

With the literature under review, notions of participation and reception are read in localized and individualized ways. Gonzalez (2003–4) presents a detailed study of a mambo performance by young Guatemalans in Disney-style dress, which formed part of a Corpus Christi festival. In terms of reception, she details her 'inappropriate' rocking of the hips in response to the event as an African American woman familiar with the mambo in a social context, the reserved contemplation of the local *mestizo* town residents and visiting Mayan merchants, and how the event shatters illusions of authenticity and exoticization from the perspective of the tourist gaze (Gonzalez, 2003–4). With a similar attention to localized interpretation, García (2009) examines the contrasting reception of mambo in New York and Havana, and Osumare (2002) addresses the global transmission of hip hop within localized contexts in Hawai'i. For Osumare, the consumption of this transnational form within selected Hawaiin communities facilitates a performative engagement with breakdancing that allows participants to articulate their own identities through an 'Intercultural Body':

> against the rubric of the imported hip hop vernacular, continuing Polynesian-Asian indigenous styles are also embodied in gesture and posturing, such as martial arts gestures and local Hawaiian gates. (Osumare, 2002, p. 38)

Indeed other scholars draw close links between notions of reception and identity. For example, Cook (2000) investigates the private participation in ragtime dance in the domestic setting and the impact of this on cultural anxieties about class, race and gender and Stern (2000) examines the codification and standardization of Latin dance to suit different consumer groups. What is evident from all of these studies is the capacity of the dancing body to articulate a complex set of meaning and values through its reception of, and participation in, popular dance forms.

In contention with the theories of mass culture discussed in Chapters 2 and 3, the dancing body is not a passive recipient, but actively engages in popular dance as a means to negotiate, resist and re-inscribe cultural meanings. This is supported by Cohen-Stratyner (2001), who traces a shift in the theoretical framing of popular dance. First, she identifies a model of popular dance that has a social function, such as the maintenance of social norms. This perspective echoes the manipulationist paradigm discussed in Chapter 3, which assigns to the popular a regulatory role. Yet she suggests that in more recent scholarship there has been a move towards understanding popular dance as a vehicle through which to challenge regulatory norms and offer alternative models of existence

(Cohen-Stratyner, 2001). The notion that the popular dancing body constitutes an active agent, which responds to and potentially resists the conditions under which it exists, is explored by several scholars. In their study of the dance instruction song, Banes and Szwed offer an extended critique of the mass culture thesis:

> far from assuming a docile listener, it galvanizes audiences into action with both its swinging beat and its lyrics. It is a dialogic form, requiring interaction between artist and auditor. Thus, even though the form of dissemination – especially after the invention of the phonograph – has been mass production or broadcast, the dance instruction song does not promote passivity. Rather, it provides a means for individual agency and creativity, especially with its improvisational component. (Banes and Szwed, 2002, p. 198)

Through a different line of argument, Wall (2009) also critiques the mass culture thesis in relation to the teenage dance fads of the 1950s and 60s. He argues that, while these dances tended to emphasize collective or 'mass' participation over the individual, they were not simply a media creation that demanded little dancing skill. He traces how, instead, they were appropriated from the 'black adult jook joint, via black teenage disc hops, to white high schools' (Wall, 2009, p. 191) and that their rapid turnover was rooted in the 'modernist' desire among teenagers to pursue the latest trend, rather than in manipulative marketing by the recording and television industries. Furthermore, far from lacking in skill, he describes the Madison as

> a communal and individual display of cultural competence achieved, in part, through a mastery of the figures, the unconventional timing, the knowledge of the cultural references in the narration, and their interpretation as stylized movement imbued with the insolence and understated swagger of youth. (Wall, 2009, p. 194)

Clearly, the historical reading of the teenage dance fads attributes agency to the participants, while also acknowledging the important role of the media in transmitting popular dance.

Given that popular dance scholarship demonstrates a commitment to cultural theory, it is not surprising that attention is devoted to the contexts in which dance is produced, the means by which it is transmitted, and how it is then consumed and/or participated in. In light of ideas raised in Chapters 2 and 3 which foreground the capacity of popular forms to express, negotiate, challenge and reinvent power relations, this sense of agency clearly emerges in the popular dance scholarship under investigation. It is these contested meanings and values that I seek to explore through my case study examples in Part II.

Embodying popular dance

I suggested in Chapters 1 and 2 that cultural studies is remiss in its neglect of the dancing body. Although several studies of dance events exist, the dancing body marks a notable absence; there is little sense of what the body is doing and how this signifies meanings and values. Within popular dance studies, there are different degrees to which the dance itself is textually constructed. In some instances there is a detailed examination of the dance event, but no movement analysis or description (Cooper, 2000; Hanna, 2000; Ponzio, 1996; Taylor, 2000). In such instances, the author possibly assumes that the reader will have a knowledge of the dance under discussion, or the article seeks to address the meanings and values that surround the dance practice rather than interrogate the movement itself. Yet, as with those cultural studies texts that neglect to discuss the dance, I would argue that a sense of corporeality is vital to understanding the dance practice. The embodied actions of a moving agent in time and space appear to be fundamental to interpreting the social meanings and values in circulation at a dance event or within a representational form. Since research in popular dance is a relatively recent subject of enquiry with dance studies, it would appear that a clear delineation of what the body does and how it moves is paramount to illustrating and animating the dance practice.

In view of this, a substantial proportion of the literature in question provides a detailed movement analysis and addresses a wide range of components. Despite the transient and elusive character of many popular dance forms, the authors have sought to comment on issues such as key movement characteristics, the spatial organization of the body, speed, rhythm and dynamics, physical demeanour and attitude, structural components, improvisational possibilities, stylistic variations, levels of technical expertise, the relationship between the dance and music, codes of conduct and relations between fellow dancers. From this, a cogent sense of physicality begins to emerge. This level of analysis is particularly beneficial for those dance forms that are relatively new or that are situated on the margins of 'mainstream culture'. For instance, in a study of underground house dancing, Sommer (2001) provides a detailed description of movement dynamics, spatial arrangement, improvisation and its structural organization, the presence of physical humour and popular sources of movement content. It is this level of detail which reveals some of the meanings and values that reside in this popular form:

> among Househeads, humor is most pointedly made by mimicking and commenting, in dance, on the other guy's style. Yet, because of the overriding sense of inclusion, the quality of the humor can be wickedly accurate but rarely rancorous and cruel. Humorous exchanges often involve props – a roll of toilet paper, a balloon, and so forth. For example, someone's shirt gets swiped and is passed around in a contest of 'keep away.' It becomes a handkerchief to blow the nose on, a dress, a wig of long hair tossing in the breeze, a waiter's towel. (Sommer, 2001, p. 83)

Similarly, in a study of goth club dancing, Young (1999, pp. 81–2) offers a close reading of movement style and content in order to illustrate 'recurring traits that mirror the politics and aesthetics of Gothic subculture':

> constituting a sort of *danse macabre*, it is flamboyant and theatrical, generally presenting a deadpan-serious figure who resembles the tormented or dying. A signature Gothic move is executed with the dancer bent forward from the waist with hands held behind the back in an expression of bondage. Convulsive movements are also common, suggesting that the dancer is crying, in severe pain, or in the last throes of death. Dancers often bring to mind images of Frankenstein awakening, condemned prisoners being electrocuted, or victims of electroshock treatment. Alternately limp and rigidly erect, they jerk their torsos and limbs as if convulsed with high voltage. (Young, 1999, p. 82)

While Sommer (2001) and Young's (1999) descriptive accounts are rooted in ethnographic field notes, other scholars have adopted different kinds of writing strategy as a means to embody the dance. I recounted earlier in this chapter how Robinson employs reconstruction as a method by which she brings archival research into motion through a fictional description of ragtime:

> Lillian's partner reaches for her waist, she grasps his shoulder, and their hands lock. After bouncing and rocking in place to the music,

waiting for that ever-elusive beginning of the next phrase, they are off. They sway their shoulders and hips, left then right, in unison as their feet brush past one another, trying to keep up with the rag-time pianist's fingers. Step-together-step, step-together-step they go, barely landing on the pulse before the next bar begins. (Robinson 2009, p. 100)

Savigliano (1995 and 1996) adopts a performative style of writing in her ethnography of tango which seeks to complicate the multiple voices that constitute its form. As Thomas eloquently describes:

the presentational format draws on a range of writing styles, personal, polemical, performative: introductions and reintroductions and different conclusions are offered; political debates and theories are set up and immediately deconstructed; descriptions of tango dance are set out like performance scripts, with stage directions and so on. Savigliano is clear that the study is not just about tango; rather tango *is* both the project and the methodological tool. (Thomas, 2003, p. 152)

These approaches adopted by Robinson (2009) and Savigliano (1995) bring to light important questions regarding the textual strategies through which popular dance is animated and mobilized.

From this literature survey, it appears that popular dance demands an intellectual approach that responds to its dynamic and mutable character. Although scholars have traditionally devoted little attention to the study of popular dance, an increasing cultural relativism has impacted on dance studies, which now engages with a plurality of popular dance enquiries, and marks out a new domain of 'popular dance studies'. Not surprisingly, a considerable degree of intersection exists between approaches to popular dance within dance studies and some of the core intellectual principles of cultural studies. Given the interest of cultural studies in the processes and practices of popular forms, scholars within the field of popular dance studies have adopted approaches developed in cultural studies.

The authors in question interrogate popular dance practices and representations through key research questions and methodological frameworks that focus on how broader cultural issues are inscribed within, enacted and negotiated through the dance. As popular dance constantly undergoes processes of transmission, mediation and reinvention, research in this field requires a wider frame of analysis.

Consequently attention turns to how the context of production, modes of distribution and experiences of consumption or participation impact on the meanings and values that underpin popular dance practice. Yet whereas cultural studies is myopic in its neglect of the dancing body, the research here awards the movement content far closer analysis in recognition that the dancing body is a critical site of agency and power in the domain of cultural production. I therefore employ this strategy in Part II as I seek to locate the case study examples within a framework of analysis that both considers how the social, economic and political conditions inform the dance practice, and how the popular dancing body rearticulates itself within those given constraints.

5
Embodiments of Value

Given that I aim to interrogate how concepts of value can be read through the popular dancing body, in Chapter 5 I seek to construct a theoretical apparatus to illuminate 'values in motion'. While dance scholarship constantly exposes and references questions of worth in its work, to date there are no sustained studies that seek to theorize the ways in which value operates through dance practice. I therefore turn to specific models of value through which I can develop the notion of 'embodied value'. Initially, I look to philosophy, economics and sociology to examine how scholars within those disciplines have formulated paradigms of value.

First I consider the question of economic value, through the work of philosopher Karl Marx (1867; ed. 1957). In Chapter 3 I identified how popular dance frequently lends itself to commercial exploitation, making it important to examine how the popular is located within specific contexts of production. Second, I focus on class value, as specifically articulated by sociologist Pierre Bourdieu (1984) and then reconceived through the work of sociologist Beverley Skeggs (2004). The strength of Bourdieu's work for this study is that it brings economic capital into dialogue with social and cultural capital, which usefully addresses the multiple value systems and taste cultures that shape popular dance practice. Furthermore, Skegg's (2004) understanding of class as a form of inscription that exists in relation to other identity positions feeds into my examination of how popular dance articulates values of class, gender, race and nation. Third, I look to the matter of artistic value, primarily through the work of several economists (Abbing, 1996; Klamer, 1996; Van den Braembussche, 1996) who illustrate the close ties between economic and aesthetic value. Overall, I seek to show how these values are not distinct, but constantly set in negotiation with each other. This allows me to conceive popular dance through a tension between how the body is constrained by frameworks of value and the extent to which it reproduces, challenges and destabilizes these interacting systems of worth.

I then locate three further approaches to value that attempt to move beyond the limitations of the absolutist and relativist position through reinstating the question of worth. First I examine English literature scholar John Frow's (1995) 'regimes of value', which I employ in Chapter 6 to consider how the neo-burlesque striptease community articulates its own measures of worth. Second, I summarize economist Michael Hutter's (1996) 'theory of play', which I draw upon in Chapter 7 to illuminate the contingent and contradictory values that characterize the dance practices of punk, metal and ska fans. And third, I look to anthropologist David Graeber's (2001) 'visibility of value', which I call upon in Chapter 8 to reflect on the explicit and hidden values of Sunday Serenade, a British Caribbean dance hall. In conclusion I construct a model of 'embodied value'; that is, the multiple enunciations of significance, judgement and worth that come into play within the field of popular dance.

Economic values

In Chapter 2 I touched briefly on the work of Karl Marx in relation to questions of culture, ideology and the political economy, but I want to return to questions of economic value in this chapter, given the propensity of popular dance to attract commercial interest. Economic theories of value can be traced back to the work of Adam Smith, David Ricardo and Karl Marx (Fekete, 1987). For the purposes of this chapter, I want to draw attention to the work of Karl Marx since his economic theory of value and critique of the capitalist political economy has proved so influential on the field of cultural studies, which in turn informs the intellectual focus of this book.[1]

In Chapter 1 of *Capital: Vol. 1* (1867; ed. 1957, p. 7) Marx focuses on the 'commodity', which he describes as 'an external object, a thing whose qualities enable it, in one way or another, to satisfy human wants'. Graeber (2001) explains how the Marxist conception of value does not conflate its price, that is its monetary worth, with its actual worth. Instead, an object's value is dependent on the cost of producing it, which is tied to the relationship between labour and production costs (Fekete, 1987). Thus, in Marx's terms, there is a separation of use-value from exchange-value with an emphasis on the latter (Fekete, 1987). Marx (1867;

ed. 1957, p. 4) describes 'use-value' as the 'utility of a thing', which thus only comes into being though consumption. Hence the use-value of an object relates to the human needs or desires that it satisfies and can range from a material entity to something that takes a more abstract form, such as a song (Suchting, 1983). It is 'exchange-value', however, that marks a common currency between objects:

> Exchange value shows itself primarily as the quantitative ratio, the proportion, in which use-values of one kind are exchanged for use-values of another kind. (Marx, 1867; ed. 1957, p. 4)

Thus, while commodities may have different material properties, the exchange-value is the universal system by which the 'value' of an object is measured (Suchting, 1983). For Marx (1867; ed. 1957), the value of a commodity, which is expressed through exchange-value, is determined by the amount of labour required for its production. Elster (1986) usefully exemplifies this in relation to a basic barter system: if a mat takes six hours to make and a worker catches a fish every three hours, the exchange rate would be one mat equals two fish. Thus Marx calculates the time spent making a commodity in proportion to the total amount of labour in the system and this marks its exchange-value (Graeber, 2001). Exchange-value is then expressed through the common currency of money (Marx, 1867; ed. 1957; Suchting, 1983). This basic economic model is complicated, however, by the notion of 'surplus value'. In Marx's (1867; ed. 1957) 'theory of labour', while the labour of the worker is embodied in the commodity, the commodity itself belongs to the capitalist owner. Yet if the value of a commodity equals the labour that goes into its production, then there is no opportunity for profit. Thus Marx conceives the notions of 'surplus value' to describe the way that workers labour beyond their own exchange-value to produce profit (McLellan, 1975). In other words, while it may take the labourer only two hours to produce his or her wages, s/he is required to work an eight-hour day; this 'surplus-labour time' therefore creates 'surplus value' (Marx, 1867; ed. 1957; Suchting, 1983).

Yet there are a number of limitations to the Marxist economic model of value, in particular its tendency to conceive production in the abstract (McLellan, 1975). Elster (1986) suggests that the more products a company wants to sell, the lower it has to set its price. Concomitantly, price is affected by how keen consumers are to purchase a particular product, whereas Marx posits that price is determined by cost rather than demand (Elster, 1986). Elster (1986) goes on to argue that an additional worker, or an increase in other factors of production, makes it possible to use machinery or raw materials more effectively, thus yielding higher productivity. Again, Marx did not allow for the possibility that entrepreneurs have the capacity to manipulate rates of production in a number of ways (Elster, 1986). Indeed, Marx crucially ignores any sense of agency on the part of the worker. As Graeber (2001) notes, it is difficult to measure labour value precisely, since one needs to take into account the length of the working day in relation to the pace and intensity of output. He points out that people are never stretched to their absolute physical and intellectual limits, which clearly affects rate of production (Graeber, 2001).

Elster (1986) also contends that Marx's theory of labour value rests on some simplistic suppositions: that raw materials are freely available, that all work is equally (un)pleasant and that all skills are equivalent. Instead, it is necessary to consider such factors as the scarcity of materials required to produce the commodity, how bearable the work is and the rarity (or otherwise) of the worker's skills, along with how desperate the consumer is to purchase a particular product (Elster, 1986). All of these components clearly affect exchange-value. Connor (1992) proposes that exchange-value produces an alienating effect in its dissolution of use-values: it is only through the common currency of money that relative value can be measured and that use-value becomes visible again. Yet the stability of money as a unit of measure is called into question. Economist David Harvey identifies how the value of money is put into doubt by its unreliability in relation to unpredictable financial frameworks such as currency exchange or the stock market (Connor, 1992).

Although I would argue that, for the purposes of any discussion around value, the economic construction of worth should not be overlooked: there is a danger that value exists only in economic terms. Fekete references a branch of philosophy known as utilitarianism which focuses on personal morals and public choice but specifically in relation to questions of the economic:

> as a theory of preference-based valuation, modern utilitarianism analyses the choice of actions in terms of consequences and evaluates the consequences in terms of the satisfaction of needs and desires and the advancement of general welfare. (Fekete, 1987, p. viii)

Utilitarianism is primarily a cost–benefit model that reduces personal pleasure and benefits to being the only criteria for value (Fekete, 1987).

Generally, traditional economic theory focuses on the 'logic of choice' and assumes that consumers make the best available choices under given preferences and limitations (Van Heusden and Klamer, 1996, p. 47). Yet in reality, social subjects do not always follow a rational course of action in their consumer choices, otherwise producers would be able to predict consumer needs and take ultimate control of the market.

While the Marxist theory of value is overly abstracted and locates worth in the object of exchange rather than in relation to 'how' consumers value commodities, the importance of this work is that it raises significant questions regarding worth and in so doing provides a critique of the capitalist model of production and its desire to make profit. In light of some of the arguments raised in Chapter 2 that call for a need to return to matters of the political economy, I would concur that it is equally important to read the popular dancing body through questions of economic worth. From the entrance fee of a club through to the multinational companies invested in the promotion of popular entertainments, dance is inextricably linked to the financial market. Access to dance events carries an exchange-value and the dancing body constitutes a form of labour power. I therefore conceive the commodification of popular dance as an embodiment of the economic; dancing costs and sells. In the following two sections, in which I respectively examine class value and the value of art, issues of the economic continue to inform this thinking.

Class values

The work of sociologist, Pierre Bourdieu offers an interesting model of class in that he moves beyond a purely economic understanding. Consequently, class is not expressed simply through monetary wealth, but through an entire 'symbolic economy' (Skeggs, 2004, p. 15). In his seminal work *Distinction: A Social Critique of the Judgement of Taste* (1984), Bourdieu develops the notion of 'taste' as a marker of class. For Bourdieu (1984, p. 6), 'taste' is a system of classification that both classifies objects and 'classifies the classifier'. Bourdieu employs the economic metaphor of 'capital' to refer to the ways in which the body is invested with different kinds of resources (Skeggs, 2004). For instance, 'economic capital' refers to salary, inheritance and property; 'cultural capital' alludes to education and background; and 'social capital' is rooted in contacts and networks (Shilling, 1993). Thus, through expressions of 'taste' individuals reflect particular class lifestyles facilitated by their *habitus*; that is, the particular dispositions to which they have access as a result of their knowledge, assets and upbringing (Frow, 1995; Skeggs, 2004). The *habitus* is therefore delineated through different classifying practices and class lifestyles are a product of the *habitus* (Bourdieu, 1984). From our commodity choices through to our cultural interests, we articulate a distinctive set of taste preferences. Whereas some practices are considered 'vulgar', other are perceived as 'distinguished' and it is these articulations of value that create class division (Bourdieu, 1984).

John Frow (1995) argues that Bourdieu constructs a fixed and essentialized reading of class in which bourgeoisie and working class taste cultures are respectively rooted in the high art/low culture divide.[2] Further to the ideas raised so far, I want to introduce the work of sociologist Beverley Skeggs, who also tackles questions of value in her monograph *Class, Self, Culture* (2004). Skeggs (2004) describes how bodies are inscribed with class and other identities and while for some groups class is a mobile resource, for others it is fixed. She continues that different systems of exchange place worth on these characteristics, which produce values that are read by others and through which relations are formed. She is interested in the conditions that create class, rather than in how it is lived (2004). She observes how the classification of class supports the interests of particular groups: it offers a 'knowledge position' that views others in particular ways to produce singular perspectives that deny alternative representations (Skeggs, 2004, p. 6).

Drawing on the work of C. A. Gregory, Skeggs (2004, p. 13) suggests that value serves to 'describe and prescribe' so that we are both subject to value and the producers of it. Thus the act of legitimization mobilizes value and 'the moral evaluation of cultural characteristics is central to the workings and transmission of power' (Skeggs, 2004, p. 14). Consequently, different representations of class produce different inscriptions of the self that are situated in a set of power relations. Skeggs (2004) argues that, whereas the middle classes are deemed rational, constrained, moral and reflexive, the working class are characterized as primitive, degenerate, lascivious and in need of reform. Hence the classes are rhetorically inscribed with values of 'good' and 'bad'. For Skeggs (2004) class is located discursively and performatively.

In light of Frow's (1995) critique of Bourdieu (1984), I would not wish to associate a particular class with popular dance practice. Yet it would be foolish to ignore the ways in which popular dance is articulated through different class groups. To return to the ragtime dance introduced in Chapter 3, Rust (1969) identifies that, although ragtime was danced across different class strata, in its British context class position was reinforced through the contexts in which people danced: whereas the wealthy danced in smart hotels and restaurants, the lower classes attended dancehalls. I recalled in Chapter 3 how ragtime dance was modified as it moved from African American, working class bodies to the white middle classes and this usefully illustrates how popular dance can be an expression of class interests. On one hand, the 'refined' version of ragtime as adopted by the white middle classes allayed their racial anxieties through distancing the dance from its African American origins; yet it also gave licence to the illicit pleasure of temporarily occupying a 'black' physicality (Cook, 2000). This latter point clearly speaks to Skeggs's (2004) observation regarding the mobility of class inscription for some groups; hence the white, middle class consumers of ragtime dance occupied a privileged power position that allowed them to act out a black working class identity (Cook, 2000). Drawing on Bourdieu's (1984) thinking, I would argue that different dancing communities express distinct taste cultures, although they may not be as class-bound as Bourdieu suggests.

The value of art

> Cultural elitism is built on the critical ability to trash that which is popular and whose popularity is 'reflected' (so it is believed) in the relatively higher economic value it may command. (Ruccio et al., 1996, p. 67)

Although I suggested in Chapter 1 that the hegemony of the Western art canon rests on a precarious value system that is biased, elitist and ahistorical, I want to return to the matter of art and value. First, as the above quotation would suggest, some of the ideas covered earlier regarding the economic system filter into questions concerning the value of high art. Whereas I have already illustrated how the popular frequently behaves in a highly commercialized way, art occupies a particularly troubled relationship with the economic. Second, art is always a useful counterpoint to understanding perceptions of the popular. Again, the above quotation describes how art seeks to denigrate that which is popular, so in examining how art is valued, it serves to reveal how the popular is devalued.

Several scholars suggest that 'art' purports to deny economic influence. Abbing (1996) describes the romantic view of the artist as an autonomous and selfless individual who is concerned purely with the integrity of the work rather than economic reward. Similarly, Klamer (1996) supports this notion that artists refute remuneration as the prime motive for creating work and that art described as commercial is typically a pejorative assessment. Consequently, there is always a certain anxiety around art that is developed within a capitalist framework (Van den Braembussche, 1996). Indeed, this sense of tension produces a distinction between what is considered 'high art' and that which is 'mass-produced'. High art is viewed as independent of the market and created purely for its own sake, unlike mass or popular art which is driven by capitalist production; in value terms, the former is the ideal and the latter is inferior (Bernstein, 1987; Frow, 1995).

Yet this humanist vision of an autonomous artist creating purely from an internal aesthetic impetus has been seriously challenged, since art constantly interfaces with the economic. Van den Braembussche (1996) notes how art interrelates with the culture industry and its personnel, in the form of managers, producers and marketing people, and Klamer (1996) identifies how some artists command high fees for performances or for the sale of their work. Indeed, Frow states that

> all cultural production is dependent on the market, not simply in an economic sense but in the broader sense that it is in principle subordinated to a common standard of value that allows the difference between cheap and valuable art to be determined. (Frow, 1995, p. 19)

Klamer (1996) describes how an economic view of art sees it purely in terms of self-interested behaviour in the market and that price indicates value. To illustrate this, Klamer (1996) uses the example of Van Gogh's *The Portrait of Dr Gachet*, which has commanded the highest price ever for a painting, but at the time of creation could not be sold by the artist. Klamer (1996) explains how the economic interpretation is that, currently, demand is high for Van Gogh and supply is fixed and very limited, hence the inflated price. This position primarily sees the picture as an investment that will yield an even greater sum of money when resold (Klamer, 1996). The economic perspective conceptualizes art as a commodity situated in a basic supply-and-demand market; yet as Klamer (1996) identifies, this presumes that people are rational about how much they will pay for art and that the price represents its aesthetic worth. Ruccio et al. (1996) concur that people expect a correlation between aesthetic and economic value, hence the high price of 'good' art, although the two are not always commensurate. As they note, this legitimizes the purchases of art collectors (Ruccio et al., 1996). The whole notion of commensurability is problematic, however, as it presupposes an intrinsic worth in art; that, on some occasions, price may fail to reflect this true worth and, in other instances, price may be vastly higher than the actual quality of the art. Indeed, Klamer (1996) also conceives art from a romantic perspective in his articulation that the act of measuring art in economic units potentially manipulates and alters the character of a work. He comments on how the economic often usurps the aesthetic: 'the money measurement usually intervenes in the art form and devalues the experience' (Klamer, 1996, p. 22). Again, this is clearly an absolutist perception of art that assumes an inherent artistic value that precedes economic worth.

There are ways of conceiving art, other than in its relationship to the market. Van den Braembussche (1996, p. 33) asserts that artists are motivated through 'value rationality' rather than 'economic rationality', which explains why many choose low-wage artistic careers to pursue their personal interests. He teases this out further in a discussion of the economic versus the aesthetic value of art. He commences with the supposition that one can value art, although not own it in an economic sense (Van den Braembussche, 1996). Whereas economic discourse is located in terms of calculations, costs and benefits, aesthetic discourse is discussed in terms of inspiration, discrimination, the test of time and value; while the former deals with utility theory and rational choice, the latter is concerned with humanism and value rationality (Van den Braembussche, 1996). Yet again this falls into a problematic binary in which the economic only conceives art within a cost–benefit model, whereas the aesthetic perspective provided by Van den Braembussche (1996) assumes that art possesses an intrinsic worth.

There are ways of conceptualizing aesthetic worth outside the absolutist paradigm. Fekete (1987) argues that no one interpretation can encapsulate a piece of art; thus a plurality of evaluations constructs value so that it is located in social ontology rather than epistemology. He describes how aesthetic value derives from aesthetic competences and not all readers possess the same level of competence (Fekete, 1987). Similarly, Klamer (1996) acknowledges that taste, and therefore aesthetic value, is not a given in that artistic communities promote certain taste values and, from this, one learns how to appreciate art by reference to specific criteria. Although aesthetic validity is often universalized within the domain of value, it can be localized, challenged and destabilized in different historical contexts (Fekete, 1987).

Whereas art demonstrates an uneasy relationship with the economic, in that it appears to deny it but also relies upon it as a measure of value, popular culture operates far more commercially through its close alliance with mass production and the mass media. Thus on the surface it might appear that popular dance has a far less troubled relationship with the economic. Yet, in a study of krumping, Zanfagna (2009) comments on the difficult relations between participants and the commercial mainstream and I have analysed the documentary feature film *Mad Hot Ballroom* to demonstrate how the capitalist economy seeks to shape or re-imagine popular dance as a means to target a mass audience (Dodds, 2008). Thus many of the concerns regarding the interactions between economic and aesthetic value also apply to popular dance.

Another apparent division between art and popular practice arises in relation to matters of aesthetic value. As art culture is historically valued, it is constituted through a well established set of aesthetic discourses that range from absolutist beliefs of inherent value through to taste values that are contingent and localized. In contrast, since popular culture is awarded little or no value, its aesthetic discourse is underdeveloped in comparison to art. In spite of this, as Fekete (1987) suggests in relation to art, artistic communities possess clear ideas about the aesthetic codes and conventions that structure their practice and it is these localized articulations of value that I aim to examine in relation to popular dance. In Part II, I observe how particular communities employ distinct value systems that award meaning and worth to their dance practice. I therefore move on to consider three theoretical frameworks, that I respectively call upon in Chapters 6, 7 and 8, which offer strategies for the analysis of value.

Regimes of value

[T]he analysis of cultural texts must be set in relation to the institutionalized regimes of value that sustain them and that organize them in relations of difference and distinction. (Frow, 1995, p. 87)

John Frow is an English scholar who writes from the perspective of cultural theory. While he is particularly concerned with refuting the high/low culture correlation with class position, he nevertheless recognizes that labels are awarded to certain groups of cultural artefacts that express concepts of value. As a means to expose these mechanisms of value construction, Frow (1995, p. 144) proposes a 'regime of value': that is 'a semiotic institution generating evaluative regularities under certain conditions of use, and in which particular empirical audiences or communities may be more or less fully imbricated'. He takes the notion of a 'regime of value' from Arjun Appadurai, who suggests that frameworks of value alter radically across different sites and commodities. This allows commodities to move across cultural boundaries, by which means different communities share certain meanings (Frow, 1995). Appadurai conceives a 'regime of value' as a broad agreement regarding what is desirable and what constitutes a fair exchange (Frow, 1995). In a denunciation of inherent value, Frow favours a socially contingent notion of value as such:

> the concept of regime expresses one of the fundamental theses of work in cultural studies: that no object, no text, no cultural practice has an intrinsic or necessary meaning or value or function; and that meaning, value and function are always the effect of specific (and changing, changeable) social relations and mechanisms of signification. (Frow, 1995, p. 145)

Thus, the regimes of value that constitute high culture produce educational frameworks, art institutions and specialist journals to support it, while regimes that constitute popular culture are equally involved in producing formal training, discourses of interpretation and the codification of cultural practices. Frow (1995) then asserts that value judgments take place within a particular regime; this is not a deterministic position, but a set of possible judgements shaped by specific regimes.

Frow's concept of 'regimes of value' is not without its epistemological limitations. Although Frow (1995) himself sees the difficulties of the relativist position, in that the idea that all values are equally valid is both a fiction and a trivialization, he recognizes that the acceptance of 'locally valid' constructions of value is just as problematic in its inability to explain how and why values are formed. He argues that if regimes of value are incommensurate, then how can value judgements be applied consistently in terms of what is shown in galleries or taught in schools, for example?

In response, I would argue that values are inherently inconsistent and contradictory and that commensurability is only a temporary phenomenon. In his critique of Appadurai Graeber (2001) queries how such regimes operate, in that it is not apparent 'what' constitutes these regimes. Whether they are produced at the level of the individual, the institution or within society as a whole is certainly not explicit. Graeber (2001) also notes that one could trace the history of a commodity across different value contexts, but that this history does not contribute to its value. Indeed, one of the shortcomings of Frow's work is that he does not offer any case study examples to demonstrate specific regimes of value. I would argue that Frow's work is useful in acknowledging the socially situated position of value, without falling into an extreme domain of relativist equivalence or absolute stasis, but that it fails to track how specific communities articulate value and how those articulations both shape and are shaped by other value economies, such as the marketplace, cultural institutions, political factors, sociohistorical contexts and so on. In Chapter 6, I seek to show how neo-burlesque striptease produces a regime of value that is responsive to the social, economic, political and artistic framework in which it exists.

The value of play

Michael Hutter is an economics scholar who has developed a theory of play as a means to explain the creation of value as part of the self-organization of the social world. Hutter (1996) suggests that 'play' is a useful metaphor in economics in which there are rules, moves and players. His notion of play is characterized by three key components: 'closure', which creates self-meaning; 'contingency', which occurs within a specific set of rules; and 'chance', which derives from the agency of the participants. He suggests that play is an act of communication rather than an articulation by an individual, and that a 'move' in play is only recognized if someone else understands the rules and can continue the play (Hutter, 1996). A play can range from a one-on-one encounter to a vast, crowded performance, which is clearly relevant to dance. Hutter (1996) details how the economy could be conceived as play. Its 'closure', or self-meaning, is actioned through money, in the sense that money only has meaning within the framework of a particular currency. The economy has an element of 'contingency', in that it is constituted through certain rules and practices, while there is also an element of 'chance' through people's interactions with the economy and with money (Hutter, 1996). The creation and articulation of value through play is as follows:

> plays consist of moves, the moves need rules, and rules need a context. The context is the borderline or frame of the play, and yet an element of it. The context can be alluded to in the play by referring to something called quality or value. In any case, that value is not discussed (or 'compromised') in the play. Yet, the play would be non-existent without it. Values, then, are the medium in which players observe themselves. (Hutter, 1996, p. 128)

Thus value is the creation of a particular social play or 'play of meaning' (Hutter, 1996, p. 129).

Hutter (1996) goes on to suggest that, in addition to economic value, there are other kinds of play of meaning, such as the play of art. Whereas in economics, play is carried out through an abstract monetary currency, Hutter (1996) asserts that in art play is expressed through visual, aural or linguistic means. Indeed, I would add the kinetic to this to acknowledge the corporeality of dance. Given his economist perspective, Hutter is particularly concerned with the interrelation of play with the economy and with art. He argues that art depends on economic value in order to survive. Yet the economy is not simply a financial pool that art can draw upon, but rather is a play that is organized through chances, contingencies and closure. For instance, publishers and producers take chances in backing work and, although these individuals rely on economic skills, they are also required to enter into an aesthetic play in which they must evaluate the potential of a new script, book or programme (Hutter, 1996). Although there are certain contingencies in the play of art, these are not fixed, in that people playing with the rules of the artistic game, for instance by trying out new products or offering existing products to new markets, can result in the development of new art forms and aesthetic values (Hutter, 1996).

Although Hutter is deeply preoccupied with the play of the economic domain of artistic production and the creation of value within that interaction, what is useful about his concept of play is its acknowledgement of both contextual factors that shape value formation, as well as the opportunity for individual agency that facilitates changes, developments and modifications to existing value patterns. In Chapter 7 I draw on Hutter's (1996) 'theory of play' in my examination of youth subcultures to suggest that the live music gig can be conceived as a site of rules, chance and moves through which the dancing interactions of participants in this space construct, destabilize and renegotiate subcultural values.

The visibility of value

> Value, I'll suggest, can best be seen in this light as the way in which actions become meaningful to the actor by being incorporated in some larger, social totality – even if in many cases the totality in question exists primarily in the actor's imagination. (Graeber, 2001, p. xii)

The anthropologist David Graeber (2001) has developed a theory of value based on the notion of action and is particularly concerned with the expression of visible and invisible value. His theoretical conception of value contains metaphors of movement, vision and performance which clearly lend themselves to the study of dance. Graeber (2001) initially draws on the work of fellow anthropologist Nancy Munn, who proposes that value emerges through action rather than residing in the object. In Munn's terms, commodities are produced and circulated, while social relations also have to be maintained; she explains that this process requires 'human investment', and hence value is rooted in the distribution of that time (Graeber, 2001, p. 45). Graeber's (2001) 'theory of action', however, is specifically located in Marxist thinking. He asserts that it is people who produce objects and commodities and that these are not simply physical entities, but are the consequence of a subject's action. In order for this to occur, there must exist a system of social relations in which people manage production. People are then defined and identified through what they produce and, consequently, acquire power and agency through these identities. For Graeber (2001), value requires some degree of public recognition and acknowledgement. Indeed, he argues that economic models that favour individual gratification fail to see that values are collectively generated and acknowledged. It is this sense of social cognizance of value that allows Graeber to develop links between value and vision.

Graeber (2001) recognizes that, although value can be expressed through economic price structures, it can also be tied to notions of desirability and the latter is often apparent in non-market-based communities or in domains outside the marketplace, such as the home, the church and so on. Although money represents a value object that can be collected, stored and exchanged, some value objects/events can not be manipulated and consumed in this way, such as chanting or a performance (Graeber, 2001). Graeber (2001, p. 81) argues that such artefacts or actions are often seen as 'sources of value' rather than simply the vehicles through which value is transmitted. He suggests that exchange or performance are creative actions which have a role in producing values and that specific objects and actions sometimes become representative of broader creative actions and the values that they encompass (Graeber, 2001).

Graeber (2001) identifies that many forms of 'currency' tend to be for adornment, and so issues of visibility and invisibility are key to value. He suggests that money cannot be worn as adornment and therefore cannot act as a mark of a person's distinctiveness; instead it is linked to an individual's 'hidden capacities for action' (Graeber, 2001, p. 94). Indeed, Graeber's (2001) theory of power is tied to two kinds of social power: the power to act on others and the power to present oneself so as to persuade others to act in a particular way towards you. Whereas the former is tied to invisible mechanisms, the latter is associated with visible forms of display. Thus, in Graeber's (2001) terms, on one hand the money that one owns is not visible but does constitute a capacity for action; on the other, valuable objects are tied to the social identity of the owner and are made highly visible. Monetary wealth allows the owner to act upon others, but the visibility of objects or adornment of great value demarcate how others should treat the owner.

Although Graeber's 'theory of action', particularly in relation to notions of visibility, is significant in placing the concept of value within a dynamic framework of recognition and exchange between subjects, rather than as a fixed worth attributed to particular objects – and although it allows him to theorize value within communities that do not use capitalist markets of monetary exchange – there are some inconsistencies. While Graeber mentions performance, in particular chanting, as a phenomenon of value and exchange, the majority of his discussion is rooted in commodities produced in factories (or by craftspeople) that are concrete in form. Thus ephemeral markers of value, such as performance, are not fully addressed. However, I would argue that there are certainly useful ties here between popular dance, visibility and power. In Chapter 8 I therefore draw on the 'visibility of value' to explore how the explicit and hidden values of Sunday Serenade, a British Caribbean dance club, complicate questions of race, age and national identity.

Embodying value in popular dance

I suggested in Chapter 4 that within dance studies there exists a privileging of the moving body and its capacity to articulate complex social meanings. As part of this expressive capacity I wish to argue that it is a 'body of value' that signals intellectual worth, economic exchange, taste preferences and measures of aesthetic discrimination. Yet the popular dance body has been culturally and intellectually subject to elitist judgements that position it as marginal, low, frivolous and lacking in worth. Along with many of the scholars I highlighted in Chapter 4, I want to participate in the reinstatement of its value through reclaiming it as a body that is rich in aesthetic and cultural meaning. However, this is not simply a strategy for an inverted elitism or a free-floating relativism that seeks to value the popular as an end in itself. I have no desire to convince readers that popular dance is inherently good. Rather, I want to demonstrate how values are formed through its embodied practice. I therefore focus on the participants of popular dance to interrogate how they construct their own systems of classification and criterion of worth. In other words, how is value danced?

While I focus closely on how popular dance communities express values in the moment of dancing, I attempt to resist the humanist compulsion to portray these participants as free agents able to create value systems independently of other institutions and frameworks. Instead, I seek to acknowledge that corporeal experience is produced under specific and localized conditions. Therefore I take into account how popular dance practice is both shaped by and responsive to the networks of aesthetic, social, and economic value surrounding the dance event. In recognition of the centrality of the dancing body within this investigation, I employ the notion of 'embodied value': that is, the multiple enunciations of significance, judgement and worth that are expressed through the movement practices of different communities engaged in popular dance forms.

Part II
Dancing Values

Introduction

In Part II: Dancing Values, I set out to examine how three dancing communities produce localized expressions of value through their embodied practice. Chapter 6 focuses on neo-burlesque striptease; Chapter 7 looks at the dancing experiences of punk, metal and ska fans; and Chapter 8 deals with Sunday Serenade, a British Caribbean dancehall. In approaching these three case studies I do not intend to produce a systematic model of value that can be applied to all forms of popular dance. Rather, in recognition of the dynamic and mutable character of the popular, I seek to give voice to the way that the participants place value on their specific area of practice and to illustrate how these measures of worth are articulated through the body. However, I also acknowledge that the dancing participants are dialectically situated within existing value frameworks. In my analysis of each case study, I therefore draw on the apparatuses of value that I introduced in Chapter 5. I consider how each of the dancing communities are produced within and responsive to different economic structures; I explore how the taste cultures of each community mobilize questions of identity, in particular positions of class, race, gender and nation; and I observe how each community produces an aesthetics of worth that is expressed through their movement choices.

Before focusing on the three dancing communities under investigation, I would like to reflect briefly upon the qualitative approach that I employ. Gray (2003) identifies how the cultural studies research of the 1970s, which drew on qualitative research methods from sociology

and ethnographic methods from anthropology to examine lived experience, has been subject to critique. Sociologists argue that cultural
studies research lacks the necessary scale and breadth required of qualitative data and anthropologists suggest that cultural studies scholars do
not engage in an extended period of in-depth fieldwork (Gray, 2003).
In response, Gray (2003) argues that cultural studies must be understood within its own intellectual tradition. First, she comments that
sociology's method of large-scale sampling is primarily concerned with
an entire 'population' and therefore its results are more generalized,
unlike cultural studies which promotes a deeper engagement with how
individuals use and understand cultural texts and how this produces
a particular sense of self. Second, she notes that the anthropologist's
'total immersion' in the field has traditionally focused on 'other' cultures, whereas cultural studies research tends to take place within the
researcher's own cultural framework. Furthermore, cultural studies
research is primarily interested in 'meaning making', which demands
in-depth interrogation of consumers and participants rather than
extended periods of observation (Gray, 2003).

While I would not claim that the research methods I adopt for the
purposes of this book constitute the level of sustained study that is
typical of anthropology, I would argue that I employ qualitative methods typical of the ethnographic research that Gray (2003) describes in
cultural studies. Indeed, I would suggest that a qualitative approach
acts as a robust apparatus for the study of popular dance practice and
the value systems that circulate in response to it. Participant observation techniques facilitate the documentation and analysis of the social
dynamics of the live dancing moment and participant interviews offer
a means to understand how those who actively engage in the dancing
make sense of their embodied experiences. Although the number of
participants interviewed in each case study was relatively small, and
the field visits would not amount to what could be described as a 'deep
immersion', I nevertheless produced a rich set of data from which I
could make an in-depth interpretation of how value is constructed
and circulated within different dancing communities.[1] Equally, I do
not wish to suggest that my field research forms a definitive study of
value.

Clifford (1986) reflects on how the practice of writing is key to ethnographic research; yet it is not a neutral recording but a fictional construction that reveals the partiality of truth. Thus, as a researcher, I have
the capacity to place value on whichever material I choose to include
or deny in my findings and my writing on the field is created from

multiple value choices, rather than existing as a singular truth. This understanding of ethnographic writing as mediated, constructed and rhetorical in character is supported by Atkinson (1990), who argues that the ethnographic text seeks to convince the reader of the existence of a specific social field through the plausible evidence of field notes and interview data. This material, however, has been filtered, analysed and interpreted from the subject position of the researcher (Atkinson, 1990). Consequently, the dancing values that I write about in Part II cannot claim to be absolute truths; rather, they are partial constructions mediated by myself as the researcher and presented through the codes and conventions of dance studies research.

This attention to the power relations between the researcher and the researched has brought about a need for self-reflexivity (Clifford, 1986; Gray, 2003; Thomas, 2003). This raises some key questions about who the researcher is in relation to the research subject, how the researcher conducts the research and for what purposes (Clifford, 1986). Gray (2003) describes how the 'experience' of both researchers and informants occupies a central role in cultural studies research, in that such research is not the reflection of a free-thinking agent, but is produced through a matrix of social, political, intellectual and economic structures. Consequently, my research cannot be divorced from the subject position from which I speak and my ontology produces knowledge from a particular set of power relations. In the following chapters I therefore detail aspects of my personal self that are likely to shape how I read the values of the dancing communities under investigation. As I explained in Part I: Introduction: Let's Dance!, my relationship to each dancing community shifts across the positions of performer, enthusiast and outsider. I suggested in Chapter 1 that cultural studies has traditionally sought to mask the researcher's tastes and values in a bid to produce objective forms of analysis; however, this contradicts the stance of value-forming communities who constantly express measures of worth and judgements of significance. While I do not seek to be wilfully subjective and biased in the findings of this research, it should be evident by now that I value and am committed to the study of popular dance and that, in choosing to present the three case studies that form the following chapters, I demonstrate an investment in them as dance practices.

6
'Naughty but Nice': Re-Articulations of Value in Neo-Burlesque Striptease

With dazzling red hair and air of cool, she saunters to the stage area with microphone in hand. Unmistakably Jessica Rabbit, in a vermilion satin dress that clings over every curvaceous inch of her delicate frame, her breathy vocals drift effortlessly along with the refrain 'Why don't you do right, like other men do'. She eases over to a table, leaning forward to display her small, yet plump cleavage to an anxiously grinning young man. Back to the centre, commanding attention with her ruby brilliance, she flashes her thigh to reveal a small soft toy Roger Rabbit tied to her leg. She smiles cheekily as images of rabbits and sex collectively flit through our minds. Knowing precisely where our thoughts lie she interjects in pithy Northern accent, 'like a good Rogering?'[1] With barely time to register her play on words, she straddles a man, while happily chatting on. Upright once again, she deftly throws her leg on the table, to give us another shot of Roger. She struggles to untie him, mops her forehead, then throws him away knocking over a couple of glasses and a candle on a nearby table. Unfazed by the chaos, she slowly removes her skirt, bluntly suggesting 'this is where you cheer'. Immediately we whoop, but she turns her back while sending her bottom into a wild shimmy of soft undulating flesh. Hand on table, she breaks back into a grand arabesque as she slowly, slowly, slowly removes a delicate silk stocking. One moment coy, the next pissed-off, she yanks it away from her foot. Leg now by ear, she removes the other stocking, pulling a face of mock pain at her hyper-extended leg. Centre-stage again, she whips off her large red knickers to reveal a sliver of bright red

G-String. All that is left is the corset. She smiles. We smile. She gestures for applause. We whoop and off it comes. She looks shocked, then smiles knowingly. We want more. She shimmies her breasts, red sequinned pasties flying round like little windmills. We applaud, we cheer, but still want more. She nods to her breast and twirls a single pasty tassel. Blown away by this technical mastery, she repeats her clever trick with the other breast. One final shimmy and this scarlet spectacle has gone.

Amber Topaz performing at Volupté,
London (13 September 2008)

In this chapter I present an Anglo-American study of female 'new' or 'neo'-burlesque striptease, a performance genre that re-emerged in the 1990s, in which performers remove clothes to a state of partial, and very occasionally total, nudity.[2] I situate neo-burlesque as a form of popular dance in that, although it is theatricalized and presentational in style, it occurs within the popular entertainment context of cabaret and the body is choreographed according to a movement repertoire rooted in striptease performance, which historically occupies a position of low art. Integral to neo-burlesque performance is the notion of tease, which plays upon a delicate matrix of wit and seduction: it is 'naughty but nice' (Blanchard, 2003, p. B01); 'erotic, not blue' (Athorne, 2005, p. 25) and 'good, clean, British fun' (Shepard, 2005, p. 26). Indeed the introductory description of Amber Topaz's 'Jessica Rabbit number' illustrates the critical components of neo-burlesque striptease: the presence of humour, an erotic play, a solicited audience interaction and the desire to tease.

I therefore set out to explore how female neo-burlesque striptease discursively and performatively re-articulates a framework of value in relation to the undressing of the female body in performance. I commence with a history of burlesque striptease to trace the values that underpin the staging of the female body in late nineteenth- and early twentieth-century performance. I then move on to examine how current neo-burlesque striptease creates a 'regime of value' (Frow, 1995) that calls upon the traditions of classic burlesque performance to produce a distinct striptease body inscribed by its contemporary politics of production. First, I consider the discourses of autonomy, inclusivity and empowerment that are articulated through and in response to neo-burlesque performance. As part of this discussion, I consider how these political claims are situated in relation to the neo-burlesque economy

Figure 6.1 Amber Topaz performs at Café de Paris. Photo copyright © Alex Simmons. Used with permission.

and the extent to which they mobilize questions of gender, class and race. Second, I explore the notion of 'tease' as a critical performance strategy and methodological apparatus. I reflect upon how tease operates both as a performance of seduction and as a playful critique, which affords a performative space through which to express and comment upon female sexuality in the act of disrobing.

For this research I documented 25 burlesque shows across London and New York between October 2005 and November 2008.[3] I participated

Figure 6.2   Little Brooklyn at Starshine Burlesque. Photo copyright © Don Spiro.
Used with permission.

in two burlesque workshops, led by Jo King from the London School
of Striptease, and I conducted semi-structured interviews with six burlesque performers: Amber Topaz (12 August 2008), Kitty Bang Bang (20
October, 2008) and Fancy Chance (16 December 2008) in London and
Little Brooklyn (8 November 2007), Creamy Stevens (8 November 2007)
and Darlinda Just Darlinda (8 November 2007) in New York. In addition
to the qualitative dimension of the research, I call upon scholarly literature on burlesque[4] and humour,[5] along with critical press reviews to
interrogate how neo-burlesque produces a discourse of value in response
to the striptease body.[6]

I have also choreographed and performed neo-burlesque striptease
under the guise of Scarlett Korova from the Korova Milk Bar and
Emmental La Bouche from La Bouche Burlesque. Although infrequent,
I have produced my own shows, performed at specific burlesque events
and featured at private parties. While this dimension of my burlesque
experience is primarily recreational and therefore not part of a practice-
as-research methodology, this performance work undoubtedly feeds
into my critical and embodied knowledge of neo-burlesque striptease.

My commitment to the politics of neo-burlesque clearly shapes how I read the values that circulate within this performance scene. To make sense of the meanings and values currently in operation, I now look to the historical lineage of burlesque striptease to reflect on how this has informed contemporary practice.

The rise and fall of tease

The etymology of burlesque derives from the Italian term *burla*, meaning a joke or farce, and originated as a sixteenth-century European literary tradition that satirized the poetic and narrative works of the period (Hanna, 1998; Willson, 2008). As a performance genre, it took the form of travesties and pantomimes, and continued until the mid-nineteenth century to incorporate all kinds of comic and inverted musical theatre (Allen, 1991). The beginning of burlesque as a platform for female spectacle, however, is marked by the arrival of music hall performer Lydia Thompson, and her troupe the British Blondes, for her 1868 debut in New York (Allen, 1991).[7] Thompson starred in *Ixion*, a lampoon based on classic mythology, in which she played a king; the narrative was loosely strung together through dance and popular songs and included a mockery of the cancan and a satirical take on some high-profile divorce cases of the time (Allen, 1991). Initially the shows, which toured the United States, were received by enthusiastic middle class audiences and awarded critical acclaim, while any shock factor was linked to the topical content (Allen, 1991). Yet the feminine spectacle that characterized this genre soon provoked social anxieties concerning normative representations of womanhood:

> what audiences saw on this stage full of male-impersonating, revealingly attired, slang-spouting, minstrel-dancing women was a physical and ideological inversion of the Victorian ideal of femininity. (Allen, 1991, p. 138)

While the aesthetic of the Civil War privileged a slim, asexual body and a pale, natural face, Thompson and her troupe flouted these conventions with their voluptuous frames, dyed blonde hair and gaudy make-up (Allen, 1991; Willson, 2008). During this period, women were traditionally silenced within the confines of the domestic space, so the public domain of theatre offered Thompson a site through which to express her sexuality (Buszek, 2006).

Acceptable representations of gender were further troubled as Thompson displayed both a masculine image in her cross-dressing roles and an excessive femininity:

> costumed to highlight her legs, hips and bosom, Thompson revealed far more of her body than fashionable dress allowed and put her secondary sex characteristics on stunning display. (Pullen, 2005, p. 94)

What is most significant is that Thompson exerted control over and evinced pleasure at her sexual representation, in what Buszek (2006, p. 43) describes as an 'awarishness'. This knowing and overdetermined female sexuality is evidenced through the 'even gaze and smirking expression' of the British Blondes depicted in the fashionable *cartes de visite* (Buszek, 2006, p. 53), and prompted British women's rights activist Olive Logan to decry their 'self-conscious winks and leers' (Allen, 1991, p. 123) as offensive.[8] Later in this chapter, I argue that it is precisely a 'choreography of facial commentary' that allows female burlesque artists to produce, critique and negotiate representations of the erotic body in performance.

Burlesque became a staple of American show business and by the 1890s was a well established theatrical tradition, although its cultural status had shifted (Allen, 1991). In response to some of the social sensitivities that surrounded it, burlesque was reconceived as the lowest of the arts and therefore only suitable as a form of male working class entertainment (Allen, 1991; Buszek, 2006; Shteir, 2004). Whereas the popular vaudeville theatre of the era was characterized by morally upright acts, carefully controlled audience behaviour and theatres that were decorated to bourgeois tastes, burlesque houses lacked these middle class values (Allen, 1991). By the early twentieth century, references to satirical humour and sexual transgression disappeared (Allen, 1991; Buszek, 2006) and, instead, 'burlesque of this era boiled down to gags expressing class and sexual anxiety and to a brand of female sexual display that was essential and crude' (Shteir, 2004, p. 54).

From the late nineteenth to the early twentieth century, there were increasing opportunities to witness displays of the female body in the context of the romantic ballet, *tableaux vivants*, concert saloons and dime museums (Shteir, 2004).[9] By the 1920s, in tandem with the decadence of the jazz age in which women were keen to explore both their sexual and their economic power, burlesque performance became increasingly *risqué* (Shteir, 2004). Although it was not until the 1930s that women would undress down to pasties and g-strings, the

1920s saw an important division emerge between the 'teaser' and the 'stripper'. Whereas stripping involved a more abrupt and straightforward removal of clothing, 'the teaser undressed with a lot of sashaying, winking, and cavorting in between dressed and union-suit states' (Shteir, 2004, p. 80). Out of this 'tease' tradition celebrated burlesque performers, such as Ann Corio, Gypsy Rose Lee and Sally Rand, came to prominence (Shteir, 2004). The 1950s, however, provided easy access to images of the naked body through adult movie houses and pornographic magazines, which demanded that strippers perform increasingly explicit acts (Shteir, 2004). Thus with the introduction of topless bars and peep shows, notions of tease were no longer required or valued (Shteir, 2004).

The ultimate demise of the striptease act occurred with the sexual revolution of the 1960s: the rhetoric of 'free love' prompted nudity to lose its cachet of an illicit thrill, while factions within the burgeoning feminist movement denounced it as an androcentric objectification of the female body (Shteir, 2004). For several decades after, the 'tease' disappeared and stripping slipped into the realm of pornography. During the 1990s, however, the striptease body re-emerged. One development was through the creation of relatively upmarket corporate venues, such as Stringfellow's Cabaret of Angels and the Spearmint Rhino Gentlemen's Club, which feature topless lap, table and poledancing.[10] The other is through the burlesque revival, described as 'new' or 'neo'-burlesque (Gumbel, 2003; Harris, 2004; Shepard, 2005), which took place across London, New York and other key cities.[11] In light of this history, I now consider how neo-burlesque produces a 'regime of value' (Frow, 1995) that calls attention to its performance heritage, but which comments upon its contemporary political position.[12]

Exercising creative autonomy

In a sharp rebuff against topless dancing, early twentieth-century burlesque impresario Harold Minsky asserted 'femmes on the bump and grind circuit do not merely expose themselves. There is drama and interest in what they do, how they do it' (1965, Minsky cited in Shteir, 2004, p. 322). Similarly, Roach (2007) argues that neo-burlesque is also characterized by its commitment to an artistic autonomy evident from the way that performers design, produce and choreograph a diverse range of acts.

On a chilly autumn night, much later than advertised, Grandma Nasty (Hot Box Burlesque, 14 October 2005) bursts out from the faded velvet curtains of the Slipper Room; an 'old woman', complete with grey wig, lines crudely drawn on her face, sensible hat, green corset, frilly bloomers and enormous false breasts in a matronly white bra. A huge cheer rises from the hot and crowded bar. A drink or so later, Cleo Cutthroat emerges in pink Cleopatra wig and white vest emblazoned with 'Fuck Bush' scrawled in marker pen.[13] She rips off her wig to reveal a jet black Mohican and swigs from a bottle labelled with the skull and cross bones. Immediately blood spills out of her mouth and the crowd goes wild as she struts out towards them wearing two slits of tape across her nipples. The following night, Creamy Stevens (*Mr Choade's Upstairs/Downstairs*, 15 October 2005) plays the naughty mortician. Dressed in a white lab coat she attends to a corpse, draped in a sheet on the 'slab'; she powders his face, kisses him and cheekily touches him up. Underneath the coat she wears a leopard-skin dress and as she slowly disrobes to expose her pink corset and fishnet stockings, the corpse appears to have an erection. The audience whoops in encouragement as she whips a large rubber penis out from beneath the sheet.

Figure 6.3   Creamy Stevens as a 'naughty mortician'. Photo copyright © Norman Blake. Used with permission.

Neo-burlesque striptease offers performers a multitude of creative possibilities through which to present the act of undressing and performers clearly welcome this opportunity for artistic freedom:

> nobody told me that I'm not quite the right height, not quite the right look, or not quite the right sound. I can sing any song I like, I wear any costume I like and I'm perfect for the role. (Amber Topaz)[14]

> I really like the autonomy of it. I get to come up with a theme, I get to come up with my own choreography, I get to pick my own music, I do my own costumes... it's really nice to do something where you can decide exactly what you want to do. (Kitty Bang Bang)

Neo-burlesque performers evidently experience a sense of agency in how they choose to express the erotic self and this emerges from the diversity of acts on display. Yet constraints exist in that the striptease routine is rooted within particular performance conventions tied to the act of undressing that I will come to later in the chapter. Furthermore, given that audiences enter into an economic exchange, since they pay a fee in return for the neo-burlesque performance, they undertake this transaction with expectations of striptease in mind. Indeed, the relationship between exchange-value and creative autonomy is closely linked. For instance, commercially successful and media-celebrated performers, such as Dita von Teese and Immodesty Blaize, perform at high-profile events and adopt a conservative image of burlesque that utilizes the glamorous markers of feminine display with little reference to wit, humour and critique.[15] In contrast, the neo-burlesque artists who form the focus of this research perform in small-scale cabaret venues, such as the Slipper Room and the Bethnal Green Working Men's Club, and prove far more radical in their performative construction of the striptease act. Thus, while creative autonomy is both valued and realized within neo-burlesque striptease, the degree of performance radicality is circumscribed by the tightly bound relationship between commercial opportunity and consumer demand; the less the performance disturbs, the wider the audience it attracts.

The politics of inclusion

In addition to a creative autonomy, neo-burlesque striptease promotes an inclusive ethos that celebrates a wide spectrum and representation of body types. This echoes the values of late nineteenth- and early twentieth-century burlesque: Lydia Thompson and her British Blondes were famed for their voluptuous bodies (Allen, 1991) and burlesque performer May Howard would employ no woman weighing less than 150lb (Shteir, 2004). With her hair set in 1950s-style peroxide curls and dressed in a glamorous white evening gown and feathered hat, Dirty Martini (Koko, 19 March 2008) strides across the vast stage of a former London music hall. As she disrobes to a raunchy bump 'n' grind number, we cannot fail to see her bodily spectacle; substantial flesh, generous thighs and soft round belly. She celebrates her excessive sexuality without apology: she outlines her *décolletage* cheekily, sneaking a finger down her cleavage, juggles her plump breasts, plays at mock coyness, then executes lewd pelvic thrusts. Before the late-night crowd of the Slipper Room, Little Brooklyn (*Mr Choade's Upstairs/Downstairs*, 15 October 2005) takes on the role of disgraced television entertainer Pee Wee Herman.[16] Initially, her broad curvaceous frame remains masked under the Herman-esque tweed suit, red bow tie, white gloves, black and white brogues and socks with suspenders. During the course of her strip, she whips a rubber chicken from beneath her crotch and her pasties spring forth as goggly eyes on coils. This playfully unsettles a normative feminine corporeality as she allows her ample breasts to become a site of comedic spectacle rather than erotic pleasure.

Although I have seen performers whose bodies range from extremely thin to generously overweight, idealized and unattainable bodies are a notable rarity. Indeed, the multifarious bodies situated on the burlesque stage most frequently reference the foibles of a quotidian physicality: thus pot bellies, droopy breasts, cellulite and wobbly bottoms and thighs are both welcomed and celebrated. This excess of imperfect flesh suggests an unruly body; one that cannot be controlled or contained by the disciplinary frameworks of modern capitalism that seek to delimit and regulate the female body through a wealth of cosmetic and physical regimes (Featherstone, 1991). That many types of physique are visible on the burlesque stage clearly resonates with performers:

> You know, I'm like 160lb, I'm 5'4', I'm actually that American average... You open any fashion magazine and you'll see a woman who's a zero and like 6' tall and it looks like a boy, it has no curves... I think that's why I really love it. I feel like I'm making a contribution to a new sort of idea of what beauty is and I really hope that changes women. (Darlinda Just Darlinda)

Figure 6.4 Little Brooklyn as Pee Wee Herman. Photo copyright © Ed Barnas. Used with permission.

The women who you see in burlesque you are not going to see in a more commercial stripping club or large theatrical dance piece. So I think what's so attractive about burlesque is the permissions, you have permission to [...] look at someone, to stare at a stranger, to watch them take their clothes off and to see a body shape that you're not gonna see almost anywhere, and all types. (Little Brooklyn)

This celebration of body sizes that operate outside the dominant cultural aesthetic extends to audience members who take affirmative pleasure from the diversity of bodies on display. A female spectator at the Slipper Room commented 'this gives me such confidence, I have cellulite' (14 October 2005), which suggests an identification with the quotidian bodies that refuse to be sanctioned by a feminine ideal. In addition to the broad range of physiques embraced and applauded, other types of body that resist the commercial imagery of advertising, fashion and celebrity culture have also taken to the neo-burlesque stage: pierced and tattooed bodies (The World Famous Pontani Sisters and Fancy Chance), queer bodies (Bearlesque), disabled bodies (Matt Fraser), transgender bodies (Lazlo Pearlman) and 'older' bodies (Jo 'Boobs' Weldon and Jo King).

Although neo-burlesque appears to endorse social and corporeal inclusion, other areas of diversity are less apparent. While I have witnessed performances by African American, American Korean and Latin American artists and two black British performers, burlesque tends to be dominated by white British and American artists. In terms of class position, with one exception, all of the women I interviewed were educated to degree level (or had completed a three-year performance training that included related academic studies), which suggests a relatively high level of social and cultural capital. Furthermore, out of the six performers I interviewed, only two could rely on neo-burlesque as a full-time occupation, one had a part-time job to build upon her neo-burlesque income, and three had full-time jobs which allowed them to support their neo-burlesque performance interests.

The lack of racial and class diversity within the neo-burlesque community relates back to Skeggs's (2004) assertion that some identities facilitate mobility while others are fixed. As predominantly white, educated women, neo-burlesque artists occupy a position of power that offers access to alternative subjectivities. Their social and racial inscription allows them to act out a striptease body that, on one hand, is a site of sexual pleasure and autonomy, but on the other has been stigmatized as disreputable and immoral. Ultimately, their white, educated status gives them temporary licence to perform this marginalized body, but with the assurance that they do not retain its abject associations. Roach suggests that when performers are not dependent on striptease as a means of income, this gives licence to explore the erotic body in alternative ways: 'when you take capitalism and economics out of the equation – when the motivation is no longer trying to earn money – sex-positivity starts to become more radical and more interesting' (2007, p. 111). As I suggest in the previous section, the less that neo-burlesque artists are driven by commercial imperatives, the greater the opportunity to dramatically negotiate and re-imagine the female striptease body. Yet this reveals a class privilege, since neo-burlesque artists exercise the choice to strip for reasons of creative autonomy rather than economic necessity.

Discourses of empowerment

Although the claims of autonomy and inclusion are not as extensive as the neo-burlesque community might suggest, these political aims are clearly valued. Another area of value lies in the notion of empowerment and this sense of agency relates both to audiences and to artists. Contemporary audiences are typically mixed-sex and Willson (2008) suggests that neo-burlesque performance welcomes a transgressive spectator-and-performer relationship. For instance, Lola Pearl (*Hot Box Burlesque*, 20 October 2006) plays a 'birthday girl' with a large iced cake and, as the climax to her act, she lights a couple of candles on her pasties and selects an audience member to blow them out; and in a 'bunny girl' routine, Crimson Skye (*Ska Burlesque*, 9 May 2008) invites a male spectator to the stage and then cheekily whips his face with her gloves. The option for audience members to 'become' the performance is even further extended with the inclusion of audience participation slots at *This is Burlesque, Starshine Burlesque* and *Mr Choade's Upstairs/Downstairs* in which spectators come on stage to dance sexily and strip a little or enter into drinking competitions with bottles of lager placed provocatively between performers' legs. The enthusiasm with which audience volunteers enter into this impromptu performance space certainly suggests that spectators at least feel sufficiently empowered to cavort and preen before a public audience, even if this is positioned as a light-hearted send-up. Yet evidence suggests that neo-burlesque offers more sustained opportunities for audience members to enjoy and flaunt their own sense of sexuality.

The desire to pursue the neo-burlesque experience beyond the position of spectatorship is evident from the multitude of classes, workshops and competitions that seek to meet this consumer demand. Across London and New York there are numerous burlesque training and performance events aimed at both the general public and either amateur performers or novice professionals, such as the courses run at the London School of Striptease and the New York School of Burlesque, or burlesque competitions, such as Tournament of Tease in London and Miss Exotic World Pageant in Las Vegas. This reveals the way that popular dance offers commercial opportunity within the context of the free market economy as entrepreneurs devise ways for audiences to access neo-burlesque commodities and experiences. For instance, burlesque accessories, such as corsets and boas, are sold in high-street retail outlets and the Women's Burlesque Institute promotes classes on burlesque hair and make-up styles.

Yet aside from this economic intent, Willson (2008) argues that burlesque striptease classes offer women a sense of empowerment in their affirmation of female sexuality and this sentiment resonates across these workshop environments in their acceptance, celebration and display of bodies irrespective of age, size and physique. At one of her burlesque workshops, Jo King (Tournament of Tease Burlesque Class, 15 February 2007) asks whether we 'love our bottoms' and not everyone responds positively. She asks: if we do not love ourselves, then who else will? and states that she has worked with people who have had mastectomies or amputations and 'those are the people who have good reason not to feel satisfied with themselves'. In conclusion she tells us that we have no right to complain and should 'get over it!' The class spontaneously applauds, convinced by her rhetoric. Indeed, the kind of empowerment that Jo King seeks to offer women, particularly in relation to body image and sexuality, not only speaks to the dimension of neo-burlesque that validates corporeal inclusivity, but also to the blurring of the spectator–performer divide. The relatively easy transition from audience member to burlesque performer is evidenced by The Tease Maids, a group of 'graduates' from one of Jo King's burlesque courses, who have performed at *Hip Hip* (2 December 2005) and other neo-burlesque events.

The idea of neo-burlesque as transformative also emerges from the audience–performer exchange whereby the sense of energy and spectacle produced through the performers' striptease act galvanizes audience response, which in turn fuels the performers' confidence and esteem. Already, I have referenced multiple examples in which audience are encouraged to whoop and applaud as a means to encourage the performer to reveal or do more. In this way audience members are motivated to express agency through their aural and kinetic feedback at the performance event and, on occasions, through the passage from spectator to performer within a range of pedagogic and performance contexts. Equally, performers identify how they experience neo-burlesque performance as a site of personal change:

> I think it improves this whole confidence in how you treat yourself in life, you put yourself out there, you're on stage naked, you can do anything, you could jump off a cliff or fly, you're like: what else can I do? (Little Brooklyn)

> When you're on stage, though, it's like it's a fantasy land. You can kind of have a play and do whatever you want. So for me, it's like I want to be funny and foolish and because having an audience that is laughing is just about the best response and I get the most amazing feeling when the audience gets it. (Fancy Chance)

> I suppose the fact that I'm doing this on my own terms, that it's 100% my choice to be there…that's a powerful thing when people are saying I think what you do is great. (Creamy Stevens)

Although I would not want to assume that neo-burlesque provides transformation outside the performance context, it is evident that a sense of validation, agency and esteem can affect performers' experience on the neo-burlesque stage, and therefore change and empowerment occur at least at the level of the personal. Thus far, it appears that the neo-burlesque scene propagates a popular dancing body valued for its creative autonomy, corporeal diversity, and strategies for audience access and inclusion. The second set of values I now seek to explore are located in the concept of 'tease'.

A tease of seduction

In the historical development of burlesque striptease, Roach (2007) identifies a distinct separation in the 1920s between the 'stripper' who removed clothes in an almost perfunctory fashion and the 'teaser' who was far more playful in her act of undressing. Within the neo-burlesque scene, the notion of 'tease' is central to the way that performers disrobe. In my examination of 'tease' I argue that it can be understood within the context of neo-burlesque striptease in its dual sense: that is, to tempt without returning the object of desire and to make fun of or provoke someone through jest. In this current section, I therefore examine tease as an art of seduction, to demonstrate how neo-burlesque artists seek to defer and play upon their performance of undress, while refusing to satisfy the desire aroused. I reflect upon the construction of the sexualized body in neo-burlesque and how performers simultaneously comment upon their erotic display. In the following section, I then interrogate how neo-burlesque uses 'tease' as a strategy that allows performers to play comedically, and sometimes disconcertingly, with the codes and conventions of striptease.[17] This form of mockery allows performers both to advocate and to critique the striptease body. Throughout these two sections, I also appropriate tease as a methodological tool. The notion of teasing out or disentangling usefully illuminates how I seek to grapple with the research data, untangle its meanings and flesh out a set of ideas. Therefore tease operates both as a system of value and as an intellectual apparatus.

In the opulent décor of a chic Mayfair club, burlesque artist Lily White is a model of 1940s feminine style and decorum (Volstead Club, 2 October 2006). With her cream complexion and long red hair, she enters to the strains of *La Vie en Rose* in a tight pink bodice and feather skirt, carrying large feather fans. She poses, twirls and swirls her feathers, pulling animated Monroe-style facial expressions that flicker back and forth from modesty to pleasure, chastity to desire. Some sassy music then takes over as she flashes her buttocks behind her feathers. She unpeels one glove and gives it to a female spectator, followed by the second, which she provocatively hooks around a man's neck. Slowly she edges down her skirt an inch or so at a time, then swirls it above her head before discarding it on the floor. She playfully teases with the slightest 'suggestion' of what she might do; a raise of an eyebrow or a look of shock creates a thrilling sense of anticipation followed by one revelation after another. She removes her bodice and briefly flashes her breasts only to hide them behind her sweeping pink fans. The music climaxes and we are treated to her breasts while a generous smile lights up her entire face.

In classic burlesque of the early twentieth century, there was clearly an impetus for women to acknowledge and explore their sexuality on the performance stage. Shteir (2004) recounts how the striptease of the jazz age provoked a challenge to Victorian sexual mores as women moved beyond coy stereotypes to sexual pleasure as an audacious form of self-expression. Willson (2008, p. 139) suggests that in neo-burlesque performance, although there is still opportunity for the performer to explore her sexuality, it is enacted through a position of self-reflexivity: 'the woman embraces and enjoys her sexual power, spinning a web of seductive manipulation with her erotic energy, but also puts question marks around the whole interchange'.

In contrast to Lily White, Miss Gertie (*Hot Box Burlesque*, 14 October 2005) offers a much more unorthodox performance in relation to traditional models of female sexuality, but tease is still paramount. She appears, dressed as an old woman in orange 'County Jail' overalls, with grey wig, lines inscribed on her face, handbag and cigarette in mouth. She executes some press-ups, typical of the hyper masculine body in the male penal system, but then repeatedly applies lipstick and kisses various audience members like a 'batty old aunt'. After some time, she removes her overalls in a perfunctory fashion to reveal tight blue shorts with Jersey Girl written across the buttocks and a big black bra. Beneath the bra she exposes American tan tights slung around her neck with large balls at the end, which swing around like a pair of saggy old breasts. Suddenly, the music cuts to *The Times They Are A-Changing* by Bob Dylan and she begins to clean off her make-up with a wet wipe and removes her grey wig. She then takes off the false breasts and an austere white bodice underneath. As she undresses her movement is increasingly sexy as her body enjoys both the liberation of discarding the multiple layers of clothing and responding to the enthusiastic whooping of the audience each times she removes another item. Slim, with jet black hair, richly coloured tattoos of a naked woman and vine leaves undulate across her back and torso as she twists and spirals in time to the music.

Within neo-burlesque performance, performers and audiences share a mutual pleasure in undressing and calling attention to the naked body, with erotic display as an important component of this. Interestingly, how this eroticism is played out in movement terms operates in diverse ways. Whereas Lily White enacts her sexuality through an alluring, traditional female glamour, Miss Gertie presents an idiosyncratic model of eroticism through introducing a grotesque female body, which she then takes pleasure in dismantling to reveal her distinctly individualized sense of self. The idea that tease is central to neo-burlesque is clearly acknowledged by performers:

> I think the tease harks back to burlesque's roots when it was burlesque striptease, but you didn't show that much...It's like everybody says, it shouldn't be about the strip, it's about the tease. It's about promising the audience something and it's about the journey getting there. (Kitty Bang Bang)

In my traditional act I take my stocking off really, really, really slowly…I've got my leg by the side of my head and I'm pulling my stocking off really slowly, and there's humour in it as well. The tease is, is she gonna get it off? They're out of their seats waiting. You know, it's provocative, isn't it! (Amber Topaz)

It's not necessarily people are waiting for the person to get naked, people are kind of wondering *how* [interviewee's emphasis] they're going to take their clothes off. You know, and what's going to be underneath that's going to be a surprise. And that's a nice part of the tease, I guess. (Fancy Chance)

Although neo-burlesque offers a broad spectrum of sexual display, it employs codified dance movements that recur as part of the act of undressing and these are often located within a slow, deliberate tease: gloves eased off a finger at a time, sometimes through small biting actions that conjure up notions of oral fixation or fellatio; stockings gently peeled back to allow the spectator to luxuriate in a length of naked leg; bra straps flicked off shoulders as a cheeky step towards total removal; and corsets delicately unhooked inch by inch. To add to the tease, performers find inventive ways to extend the moment leading up to the 'big reveal'.[18] For instance, they remove bras with their backs to the audience and breasts are masked with fans, boas and other props to suspend the tease even further. Frequently, the pelvis is accentuated (through sensual gyrations of the hips or protruding buttocks) as another signifier of the sexualized body.

Celina Vixen (*Starshine Burlesque*, 8 November 2007) stages a Restoration number, complete with powdered wig, white gloves, corset and pearls. Set to a piece of chamber music, she appears the epitome of gentility. Initially, she poses demurely with a small fan, but pulls a saucy face to signal her potentially licentious nature. Slowly, she bites at the fingers of her gloves and removes them with a 'naughty' wink. With her back to the audience she drops her skirt to reveal a thong and then undoes her corset in a slow and teasing manner to show us a glimpse of her gold, glittery nipples. Retrieving her fan, she uses it to 'pleasure' her genital area. Finally, she fakes an orgasm and ends collapsed on a chair in a state of ecstatic bliss.

Yet erotic tease seems not only to operate through slow, seductive undressing, but can also call upon a playful element and this is probably best epitomized through the tassel twirling and bottom shimmies that are key features of burlesque performance. Miss Trixie Malicious (*Hip Hip*, 25 May 2007) plays a 'hula girl' archetype with sarong skirt, black polka-dot bikini and flower garland around her neck. On a nearby table sits a small gold volcano surrounded by flowers. She performs hula hip-gyrations, pulls a 'cocktail umbrella' from her bra, puts a pineapple on her head and sets the volcano alight. As a new piece of Dick Dale 'surf music' comes on, she goes into a frenetic hip-wiggling and circles the garlands around her neck. As she undoes her sarong and shimmies her bottom in the direction of the audience, the crowd whoops wildly at this spectacle of dynamic flesh. Her articulate facial commentary involves several shocked 'ooh' expressions to punctuate key moments of her undress. Finally, she removes her bra and rapidly twirls her pasties, at which point the audience (and her volcano) explode with delight.

While tassel twirling and bottom shimmies do not sit comfortably with a traditional model of erotic display, in that they are playful and comedic in style, they clearly produce a high level of performance spectacle located in the mutual excitement generated at the performer–audience interface; the crowd applauds enthusiastically as the burlesque stripteaser twirls and shimmies in a perpetuating circuit of pleasure. Indeed, for tease to operate it requires the mutually validating presence of performer and spectator. Both enter into a contract of exchange as the spectator pays for the pleasure of the tease and the performer provides this through her striptease performance. Demand is articulated in performance as the audience whoops for more and supply is enacted each time the performer removes an item of clothing. Yet tease constantly threatens to defer the moment of supply.

Tease, as an erotic expression and articulation of femininity, operates in multiple ways as burlesque performers call upon the glamorous and the grotesque, pleasure and spectacle, and comedy and critique to comment upon female sexuality. In a study of postwar burlesque films, Schaefer (1997, p. 53) describes the burlesque body as 'uncontained' and 'undomesticated' and I have already commented on how Buszek (2006) refers to an 'awarishness' to explicate how burlesque photography depicts an overt and self-conscious sexuality. In line with these arguments, the neo-burlesque body in performance expresses a similar kind of excess in its unruliness. Performers boldly expose their sexuality in a manner that is knowing, provocative and playful. This excessive spectacle of the erotic refuses to be disciplined by feminist or moral voices that seek to contain the undressed female body as erotic entertainment. Instead artists and audiences take mutual pleasure in this decadent corporeal display. While articulations of the erotic are expressed through diverse means, what binds these multiple representations is the use of facial expression as a critical performance commentary.

In a description of beauty pageants, Foley (2005, p. 62) asserts that the smile is both a theatrical tool and a construction of Western femininity that signifies a benign, pleasing, passive and available being. In response, I suggest that neo-burlesque performers consciously sabotage the passivity of the feminine smile through a 'choreography of facial commentary': they wink suggestively, flick their eyes to heaven, pull coy faces, fabricate mock shock, and offer smiles of pleasure and collusion as a self-reflexive performance strategy.[19] In a conscious rejection of the fixed smile of feminine passivity, artists in the neo-burlesque scene employ facial expression to direct audience gaze, to foreshadow what is to come, to comment upon what has happened and to relay complex positions (such as commitment, detachment and enjoyment) concerning their performative relationship to the act of undressing before a public audience.

As Willson (2008, p. 4) suggests, 'the burlesque performer looks back, smiles and questions her audience, as well as her own performance, a performance that is comic, outlandish and saucy'. The excessive sexuality employed by artists and the employment of tease as a means to control the act of undressing through a self-reflexive critique suggests a powerful sense of agency on the part of the performer. In the following section I therefore explore further the idea of tease as a critical performance strategy.

The tease of a knowing wink

While all of the performances include aspects of the erotic, particularly through a tease of seduction, rarely is this the only dimension of the act. As Willson (2008) suggests, neo-burlesque performance also operates through humour and I now explore this dimension of the tease. For the performers I interviewed, humour disrupts the erotic display of the body as the sole *locus* of attention:

> I think [the humour] makes it a disarming thing and I think it makes a more immediate connection with the audience – I don't think that it's possible for them to make judgements about you, about what you're trying to do [...] I mean, you know, in our culture in general women taking off their clothes in public is relegated to traditional strip clubs and there's really nothing ever remotely funny about that. (Creamy Stevens)

I think burlesque really should contain an element of humour otherwise it's just stripping. I mean, you know, it can be stripping very gracefully, not quite as Spearmint Rhino and gratuitous as it could be, but without that element of humour and appeal to the audience and sense of character, then I think it is just stripping. (Kitty Bang Bang)

Thus in these terms humour facilitates a shift in value systems that legitimates and distances the burlesque body from perceptions of contemporary striptease culture. For Amber Topaz, it is employed as another means to efface the performer–audience divide and to break down potential taboos regarding public nudity:

Humour connects you to the audience, humour makes them feel less uncomfortable to the fact that you're, you know, partly naked and if you're sending yourself up, again that connects you to the audience, 'cause they don't feel like I'm some untouchable kind of erotic dancer – I'm a showgirl. (Amber Topaz)

Fancy Chance and Little Brooklyn meanwhile see humour as a vital means through which to make social commentary, whether it is light-hearted sexual commentary or a more probing polemic:

the name burlesque [is] loosely rooted to the idea of a *burletta*, which was a piss-take of operas, and it was like pinch-and-tickle piss-takes, so there was like *double entendres* and lots of little adult jokes and everyone had a good laugh to it and burlesque was basically pinch-and-tickle adult humour. (Fancy Chance)

I mean, burlesque actually means to make fun of, so people would go to a burlesque show, the idea is making light of everything. You know, you go to burlesque shows now and they make light of either our physicality, or of politics, or the act of disrobing. And there are serious acts as well, but even in those there's a wink and a nod. (Little Brooklyn)

Humour can be understood as a binding mechanism that facilitates expressions of social cohesion and a means to affirm human relationships (Palmer, 1993; Ross, 1998). Thus, in neo-burlesque performance humour potentially opens a site for a shared exploration of eroticism and sexuality. Notably, humour can also serve to dissipate embarrassment (Simpson, 2003) which, as Amber Topaz indicates, is relevant here as public nudity and sexual display are potentially sources of social anxiety. Yet Palmer (1993) suggests that humour can also be a vehicle through which to confront the taboo and therefore functions as a 'safety valve'. For instance, he uses the example of saucy seaside postcards of the early twentieth century to illustrate how they provided licence to engage in mild sexual humour in a society which had strict sexual codes. This idea can be extended to burlesque: while early twentieth-century burlesque allowed audiences to access a sexual thrill from female somatic spectacle, the 'taboo' in neo-burlesque is, perhaps ironically, the celebration of women's sexuality. The overt representations of the female as 'erotic spectacle' clearly unsettle those feminist discourses which have sought to 'unburden' women from these normative gender constructions. Humour also operates as a form of prestige or social power and is frequently positioned as a masculine trait (Palmer, 1993, p. 72). Hence female burlesque performance enters a critical space wherein women explore an autonomous female eroticism through comedic representation.

In one of her acts, Dirty Martini (Koko, 19 March 2008) plays a 1940s starlet. She wears a clingy pink dress and behind her hangs a giant spider's web that conjures up notions of film noir and the *femme fatale*. Initially she walks around seductively and twirls centre-stage to reveal a little leg. She then raises her arms to expose her curvaceous undulating body and seductively glances around with her eyes. She teases off her gloves and slowly undoes the zip to allow her dress to slip down to her ankles. Without warning, she suddenly gets trapped in the web, from which a pair of black arms grab her and play with her breasts. While the hands remove her bra to reveal a pair of spider-shaped pasties, her look of outrage and alarm signals a comical register of facial commentary. Although she employs traditional representations of femininity in her glamorous attire and her role as the helpless female, I would argue that tease functions here as a form of critique.

Mulkay (1988, p. 71) defines tease as 'to say or do something that is intended light-heartedly to make fun of someone else's words or actions'. Neo-burlesque performers use tease to make humorous comment upon constructions of femininity and eroticism. Indeed, Mulkay identifies how teasing significantly contributes to social discourse that combines serious and humorous elements. He suggests 'teases are recognisable as humorous because they are constructed with certain distinctive features which serve as signals of the speaker's humorous intent and as cues that the apparent message should not be taken literally'

(Mulkay, 1988, pp. 75–6). He further describes teasing as an exaggerated response to an existing statement or action and while his research focuses specifically on verbal discourse within everyday social contexts, the notion of teasing lends itself well to the burlesque artist's performative response to existing models of female sexuality. Notably, in line with Mulkay's thinking, neo-burlesque performers often employ exaggerated images of femininity, either through the personas they adopt or through the spectacle of seduction; however, this is not to suggest that audiences should take them at face value. Instead, I suggest that part of the tease, the humorous play on female representation, is located in the complex way in which performers simultaneously embrace and critique the images that they employ.

Palmer (1993) describes how paralinguistic cues, such as light-hearted tone or exaggerated facial expression, signal when a speaker intends to be humorous. In neo-burlesque, the same kind of performative framing devices are employed to demonstrate that the erotic imagery and female representation are in jest. In one number, Little Brooklyn (*Starshine Burlesque*, 8 November 2007) is dressed as a 1950s housewife with a large beehive hairdo and rubber cleaning gloves. Before her is a table with a washing-up bowl and she begins furiously to clean a glass. She plunges her cloth into the glass, in a slightly manic style, suggesting a sexual frustration which is all the more comical as she begins to produce lots of soap suds that call to mind images of ejaculation. She then bites at the fingers of her gloves, in typical burlesque fashion, although the sexual allure that comes from the removal of satin evening gloves is turned on its head as she wrestles with these yellow rubber fingers. She removes her black polka-dot dress, pulling a series of enormous smiles and looks of shock, almost as if her strip remains slightly beyond her control. In a clever inversion of the glamorous fan dance, she uses her two washing-up bowls to mask her breasts and pose in an alluring burlesque style. In keeping with her 'desperate housewife' persona, the audience laugh and whoop as she lathers up her breasts and bottom as the climax to the act.

While it appears that satire was an important component of late nineteenth-century burlesque, parody is more commonly identified with neo-burlesque humour (Roach, 2007; Willson, 2008). Dentith (2000) describes parody as an imitation and transformation of someone else's words and Ross (1998, p. 48) suggests that 'parody is a parasitical form, which cannot exist without its "host", but this need not mean that it cannot be original or creative'. In the two examples outlined

Figure 6.5   Little Brooklyn as a 1950s housewife. Photo copyright © Ed Barnas. Used with permission.

above, Dirty Martini and Little Brooklyn clearly reference female stereotypes, but find ways to comment upon these images through humour; Dirty Martini has no choice but to comically succumb to being stripped, although she acknowledges that she is in on this joke with her themed pasties and exaggerated looks of horror, and Little Brooklyn escapes her position as sexually frustrated housewife when she indulges in her erotic lathering. Ross (1998) usefully likens parody to retro fashions in which consumers choose perhaps to reclaim a style that has been unfashionable, but now wear it in 'quotation marks'. Although, as Shteir (2004) notes, burlesque lost its social value towards the end of the 1950s and was denounced both in some feminist quarters and by the Christian moral right, respectively, for its sexual objectification and licentious representations of the female body, it has since been reclaimed but in 'quotation marks'. The 'choreography of facial commentary' that I suggest is a vital dimension of neo-burlesque performance allows artists to comment self-reflexively on the striptease act.

The concept of parody has been employed by several theorists as a means through which to complicate gender identity. Schaefer (1997, p. 56) describes how female performers in postwar burlesque films 'made a spectacle of gender' through their hyperfeminine costumes, which served as a parodic 'masquerade'. For Schaefer (1997) the exaggerated feminine dress offered a transgression of normative gender identity. The notion of 'masquerade' is developed in Joan Riviere's reading of femininity as an excessive or 'exaggerated playing up' as a means to critique biological conceptions of gender (Harris, 1999, p. 60).[20] Yet for Riviere there is no distinction between the masquerade and real femininity, which limits its transgressive potential:

> if any version of gender mimicry or masquerade is to be effective as a resistant or subversive strategy, at some point or on some level it must be clearly legible as differing from the norm. (Harris, 1999, p. 62)

The other scholar most closely associated with the link between gender and parody is Judith Butler (1999) who conceives gender as 'performative'. For Butler (1999) gender is constituted through a series of stylized gestures and acts; it is a parodic imitation and repetition of everyday enactments, that collectively regulate a binary gendered order, although she views it as a failed copy since an original (biological) gender does not exist. Although Butler (1999) recognizes that not all parody is subversive, she looks to drag performance as a means to trouble or disrupt gender identity:[21]

> if that anatomy of the performer is already distinct from the gender of the performer, and both of those are distinct from the gender of the performance, then the performance suggests a dissonance not only between sex and performance, but sex and gender, and gender and performance. (Butler, 1999, p. 175)

In a rich discussion of the performance of 'effeminate gestures' that enters into dialogue with Butler's reading of drag performance, Gere (2001, p. 375) argues that, whereas drag is essentially a 'choreography of fashion' characterized by 'cross-dressing', effeminacy is an embodied subversion of gender, which is far more troubling. While drag reinstates heterosexual norms through the materiality of dress, effeminacy disrupts gender at the level of bodily inscription. Although neo-burlesque artists occasionally cross-dress, the majority of performers could not be described as drag artists. Yet the kind of masquerade to which Schaefer (1997) refers is evident in the excessive display of sexuality, the teasing erotic vocabulary and the stylized feminine dress. This spectacle of normative femininity, however, is unsettled through the 'choreography of facial commentary' that exists in tandem. Consequently, neo-burlesque employs a double articulation of gender in which dress and gesture might signify normative gender identification, while facial expression might convey ridicule, frustration or anger at these feminine ideals. This slippage or disjunction is then the point at which humour comes into play and allows neo-burlesque striptease to make fun of itself, to work through jest, and to tease the very practice through which it operates.

Several scholars also see parody as inextricably linked to questions of value. Hutcheon (2003, p. 90) challenges the view of parody as a dehistoricized quotation and instead positions it as a 'value problematising' means through which to comment upon history. Dentith meanwhile suggests that parody is a discourse that assumes evaluation:

> while all language use certainly involves imitation, the particular inflection that we give to that imitation (and parody is one possible inflection) indicates the extent to which we have adapted language to occasion, transformed the value given to the utterance, and thus redirected the evaluative direction in that chain of utterances. (Dentith, 2000, p. 4)

In relation to parody, the value position that it adopts is not always one of mockery and ridicule, but can also engender a fondness, respect and affection for the original (Hutcheon, 2003; Ross, 1998). This nuanced understanding of value surfaces in the neo-burlesque scene whereby performers both value the pleasure of the erotic body (even within normative models of feminine sexuality) and playfully comment upon those images. Thus female stereotypes are both embraced and challenged. For instance, Darlinda Just Darlinda comments on how she welcomes the opportunity to express a normative femininity:

> You know, women used to wear corsets and pretty gloves and do their hair every day and wear make-up every day and now it's not the norm. It's not really necessary, which is good, which is like we talked about, it's feminist, we can do whatever the hell we want, which is great, but I think that like getting to be extra-beautiful, extra-feminine, hyper-feminine, it's amazing, it's really good. (Darlinda Just Darlinda)

Yet Creamy Stevens explains how she likes to undercut gender expectations:

> I use a very classic kind of set-up for a striptease burlesque act where there's a voice that says, 'bye honey, I'll be home at six, have dinner ready' and I've got a fluffy nightie and a baby and smiling and from out of the cooking pot I take a martini and a bottle of pills so at the end I bite the head off the bird in the bird cage and drown the baby in the pot, so you know, I think that's the tease. It's sort of like people might want you to be really pretty and do nice things and do exactly like they want you to do but I really relish in not doing what people want me to. (Creamy Stevens)

The suggestion is that performers relish both occupying and subverting the female images that have shaped their understanding of femininity. They therefore enter a critical performance site that allows them to take excessive pleasure in and actively reject images of femininity located within the patriarchal paradigm.

While some humorous commentary in neo-burlesque striptease centres on the negotiation and reinvention of representations of the female body, other performers enter into a broader social and political critique. For instance, Nasty Canasta (*Mr Choade's Upstairs/Downstairs*, 21 October 2006) performs a number under the guise of Tonya Harding, the ice skater whose former husband hired an assailant to attack Harding's rival Nancy

Kerrigan. Dressed in ice skates, black skater dress and gold gloves she earnestly commences with a mock skating routine. As the music shifts to a raunchy rock track, with the refrain 'Get me with your best shot', she begins to strip with attitude. A man enters the stage with an iron bar as his penis and she whips it from him in a triumphant moment of empowerment. While Kerrigan was feted as the middle class 'golden girl' of ice skating, Harding was positioned by the press as 'white trash' for her criminal associations and poor social background. In Nasty Canasta's performance, however, it is Harding who is celebrated for her gutsy reclaiming of the phallic iron bar to the delight of the audience.

In one of her acts, Darlinda Just Darlinda (*Feminist Neo-Burlesque Symposium*, 26 October 2007) appears in a red sequinned dress waving the national flag, but to her disgust pulls from her vagina a neatly folded picture of President George W. Bush, which causes much amusement in the audience. Fancy Chance (*Burly Q*, 12 July 2006) is even more audacious, as she strips before a large photographic portrait of the North Korean leader Kim Jong Il that would undoubtedly be viewed as a mark of disrespect to this national dictator. Acts such as these allow performers to engage with social and political issues that lie beyond the realm of popular entertainment and are perhaps closer to the satirical dimension of nineteenth-century burlesque, since their positions demonstrate a more attacking or critical edge. In conclusion, the neo-burlesque body

Figure 6.6   Darlinda Just Darlinda at the beginning of her George Bush number. Photo copyright © Linus Gelber. Used with permission.

PHOTO BY STACIE JOY

Figure 6.7 Darlinda Just Darlinda at the end of her George Bush number. Photo copyright © Stacie Joy. Used with permission.

perpetually stages itself in a playful spectacle of protest. Whether it is in reclaiming the abundant sexuality of the female body, disrupting the gender representations to which women have been assigned or in speaking back to a wider social politics, neo-burlesque artists employ the trope of undressing as a means to perform, negotiate and transform their lived experience.

Teasing out values of distinction

It is evident from this chapter that artists and audiences within the neo-burlesque scene discursively and performatively construct a localized 'regime of value' that references the traditions of late nineteenth- and early twentieth-century burlesque, but also produces meaning within the context of its contemporary performance practice. First, the neo-burlesque stage offers a creative autonomy that allows for a distinctive range of performance personae and *mises-en-scène*. Yet it is important to acknowledge that this sense of liberation is constrained by the conventions of the striptease repertoire and the commercial aims of different artists, producers and venues. Second, the neo-burlesque community promotes social and corporeal inclusivity so that marginalized female bodies are both welcomed and celebrated. In spite of this negation of an idealized feminine physique, neo-burlesque striptease is less inclusive in its racial and class diversity. Furthermore, its performers have the necessary income, through either their neo-burlesque work or entirely different careers, to enable them to produce performances that challenge, negotiate and re-imagine the striptease body. Third, the neo-burlesque event facilitates a performer–audience interaction that generates an intense and mutual validation and affirmation of the erotic in performance, and which can offer opportunities for personal transformation. Clearly the neo-burlesque community makes a powerful claim to values of autonomy, inclusion and empowerment. Although evidence of this exists within the context of neo-burlesque striptease, these utopian ideals are delimited by economic structures and dominant social codes of race and class. In terms of gender, however, neo-burlesque performers offer a potent political commentary on the female striptease body through an 'aesthetics of tease'.

In one sense tease functions as a mode of erotic exploration achieved through somatic sexual conventions, such as the slow unpeeling of a stocking and the seductive undulation of the hips, or through the playful spectacle of bottom shimmies and tassel twirling. In another sense, tease operates as a form of humour through which performers comment on the act of undressing as erotic entertainment, through devices of masquerade, exaggeration, parody and satire. This breadth of approach allows performers to embrace, reject or renegotiate images of femininity, and a 'choreography of facial commentary' is key to this self-reflexive critique. Whether it is a wink of collusion with the audience or mock horror in the face of nudity, neo-burlesque artists construct a metacommentary that can signal both pleasure in and criticism of the images of femininity through which they choose to work. This contestation of the striptease body marks a teasing-out of its potential for erotic pleasure through deferred sexual gratification and a synergistic celebration and destabilization of the female body as display. The teasing of a body of ideas enables the neo-burlesque artist to re-articulate the values inscribed in the production and consumption of striptease through the complex politics of a small but knowing wink.

7
Pogoing, Headbanging and Skanking: Economies of Value in Dancing Subcultures

> The next day I woke up and my neck was just in agony, I was literally, like, just holding my head up, going what's wrong, why did I do that?
>
> (Interview with Aimee, 25 October 2005)[1]

Aimee, a 23-year-old metal fan, relaxes in the lounge of a city hotel. Dressed entirely in black, with a skull and bat wing motif emblazoned on her T-shirt, she smiles softly as she recalls her headbanging debut. Irrespective of this harsh corporeal initiation into heavy metal music, she has fervently continued to headbang at gigs for the past eight years. Although there exists a wealth of academic research that attends to subcultural music, dress, language and behaviour, the subject of dance within youth subcultures forms a serious area of neglect. Using interview data from a selection of punk, metal and ska fans, I set out to examine the complex matrix of value systems that both inform and express participant experience of subcultural dance.[2] I draw upon subcultural theory (Hebdige, 1979; Muggleton, 2000), popular music studies (Bennett, 2001; Berger, 1999) and fandom studies (Hills, 2002; Sandvoss, 2005) to explore how the interrelationships between social, aesthetic and economic values play out through dancing at live music gigs. Before analysing the participant data, I examine how subcultures and fans are conceived within scholarly research, present my research design and reflect upon my ontological position within the study.

Figure 7.1   Aimee the metal fan. Photo copyright © Sherril Dodds.

Subcultures, fans and academics

In Chapter 2 I outlined a body of work that developed in the 1970s through the Centre for Contemporary Cultural Studies (CCCS). This research employed semiotics and Marxism to describe the way that youth subcultures used 'spectacular' forms of dress, language and behaviour to position themselves as oppositional or resistant to 'mainstream' or 'parent' culture (Hall and Jefferson, 1976; Hebdige 1979; Mungham and Pearson, 1976; Willis, 1978). This work has been subject, however, to a number of critiques.[3] With the exception of Willis (1978), who employed ethnographic research, the other scholars' findings are based on textual interpretations of visual signifiers, so symbolic meaning takes precedent over participant experience (Muggleton, 2000; Stahl, 2003). Another criticism directed at the CCCS is its positioning of subcultures as white, young, working class and male (Bennett and Kahn-Harris, 2004; Weinzierl and Muggleton, 2003), which I will return to later in this chapter.[4] The idea that a subcultural group is a fixed and homogeneous collective with a unified ideological stance of resistance is now largely discredited. Such a perspective fails to acknowledge the potential for participants to move across groups, for local variations and for membership simply to be 'fun' (Abercrombie and Longhurst, 1998; Bennett and Kahn-Harris, 2004; Muggleton, 2000).

In response to these critiques of the CCCS model of youth subcultures, in the 1990s a new body of subcultural work developed. Influenced by postmodern thinking, 'post-subculture theory' conceives subcultures as fluid entities in which participants indulge in an apolitical play of surface styles and need not express any degree of authenticity or commitment (Bennett and Kahn-Harris, 2004; Muggleton, 2000; Stahl, 2003).[5] Stahl (2003, p. 27) suggests that the concept of a 'spectacular subcultural style' barely registers in postmodern culture with its emphasis on image and consumerism. Whereas the CCCS interpreted subcultures as politicized in their resistance to mainstream media and consumer culture, post-subculture theory comments upon the media literacy of subcultures and their willingness to produce identities through consumer choices (Weinzierl and Muggleton, 2003). Yet the emphasis on post-subcultures as transient, superficial and occupied only with surface style implies a moral relativism and denies the opportunity for a radical politics (Stahl, 2003). Thus, while the CCCS afforded subcultures too much political agency, post-subcultural theorizations have tended to undervalue their trangressive potential in reading them as consumerist and individualized (Weinzierl and Muggleton, 2003). In light of this, Muggleton (2000) argues for a middle ground. While he acknowledges that subcultures do facilitate some level of individuality, transience and heterogeneity, he observes that members also demonstrate a degree of commitment and depth in their involvement (Muggleton, 2000). Thus, although subcultures are not the unified and homogeneous groups identified by the CCCS scholars, there is undoubtedly worth in continuing to work with the concept of a subculture as it points to 'an identifiable, knowable and researchable space' (Bennett and Kahn-Harris, 2004, p. 15).

Whereas the concept of a subculture is a typology created by academics (Abercrombie and Longhurst, 1998), the notion of a 'fan' exists in common currency and offers another lens through which to interpret the dance practices of participants committed to specific popular music cultures.[6] Even more pertinent to the interests of this book, the concept of the fan is positioned within a paradigm of value. Jenson (1992) asserts that, in spite of considerable overlap between academics, aficionados and fans, the fan is conceived as Other. The aficionado dwells on high art, whereas the fan engages in popular forms; and while the aficionado and the academic are believed to occupy a rational and objective distance from their object of interest, fandom displays an excessive and obsessive infatuation (Jenson, 1992). Indeed, fans are frequently read through negative frameworks of value; their pleasures lie in mass-mediated forms that lack cultural legitimacy (Fiske, 1992); they are conceived as 'cultural dopes' (Grossberg, 1992); and the popular stereotype of fans depicts them as deviant, excessive and abnormal (Jenson, 1992). Yet in spite of these value judgements, a rich body of work exists on fandom which can offer a theoretical apparatus through which to interpret the values that inform popular dance practice (Hills, 2002; Lewis, 1992; Sandvoss, 2005).

My objective for this study, therefore, was to design a small-scale qualitative research project that would allow a selection of participants to voice their experiences of subcultural dance practice at a level of depth previously unexplored in subcultural research. To provide some degree of diversity, I chose to investigate three dance styles – pogoing, headbanging and skanking – which are respectively associated with punk, metal and ska subcultures. I gained access to participants through posting messages on bulletin boards, approaching contact names on music websites, attending gigs and word-of-mouth searches. From this preliminary enquiry I invited four individuals per music style to participate in a semi-structured interview that lasted approximately 45 minutes. My interviewees came from a range of geographical bases, held a variety of occupations and ages ranged from 23 to 47.[7] The four punks I interviewed were Mikey, an unemployed 38-year-old from Burley Park, West Yorkshire; Pete, an unemployed 41-year-old from Ashton-under-Lyne, Greater Manchester; Vince, a 38-year-old logistics manager from Brighton; and Melanie, a 38-year-old from Leeds who worked in information technology.[8] The four metal fans I interviewed comprised Aimee, a 23-year-old student from Chester; Sienna, a 32-year-old advertising manager for a rock venue in London; Max a 35-year-old ICT technician from London; and Kate, a 28-year-old support worker from Borehamwood, Hertfordshire. Finally, the four ska fans I interviewed were Jamie, a 25-year-old games tester from Woking; Stuart, a 41-year-old tyre fitter from Aylesbury, Buckinghamshire; Sonny, a 47-year-old builder from London; and Chris, a 45-year-old barrister from Ruislip, Middlesex.[9]

It is also important to situate myself reflexively within the research project as this undoubtedly affects the collection and interpretation of my research findings. In the early 1980s, I discovered the Sex Pistols' back catalogue and began to consume both old and contemporary punk and new wave bands. While I doubt I would have described myself as a punk at that time, I dabbled in a punk look with spiky hair, a dog collar, band T-shirts and fishnet tights. Yet barely within the space of a year, I then became very interested in the 1980s mod revival and, in addition to buying retro and current mod music, I also dressed in popular mod styles and attended live music gigs. Thus to some extent I typified the transient subcultural member who moves across different affiliations and buys into different styles, although I was heavily invested in the music and its associated political views. During my mid-20s I became a keen follower of the early 1990s grunge music and dressed and danced accordingly. Consequently, my own fandom clearly shapes the importance I award to dancing at live music events.

Although in doing this research I wish to give voice to the dancing participants, I acknowledge that they too carry biases and may contrive their answers for a variety of reasons. As Hills (2002) notes, fan discourse cannot be taken at face value, nor can fans offer an unproblematic interpretation of their own fandom. Harris goes so far as to suggest that

> fans are also motivated by self-invention, in which fandom provides an opportunity to live in and through a set of symbols that are expressive of one's aspirations rather than 'reality'. (Harris, 1998, p. 6)

In this chapter I am particularly concerned with how participants imagine and reflect upon their dancing experiences and how different systems of value both inform and express subcultural worth. I consider how aesthetic, social and economic values produce discursive tensions that are paradoxically played out in the dancing moment. Although my focus in this chapter centres primarily on the interview data, in the following section I provide a description of the dance practices under investigation as derived from my own observations and from explanations offered by the informants. The aim here is to illustrate the diverse and nuanced character of subcultural dance.

Pogoing, headbanging and skanking

The dance style predominantly associated with British punk music is the pogo and it comprises a repetitive and explosive style of jumping on the spot with the arms held close to the body. Nursing a pint, hungover and huddled in a thick leather jacket, Vince (6 January 2006) describes the pogo as 'people basically packed together like sardines jumping up and down'. While the pogo demands no codified gestural action, the upper body and arms come into play through crowd interaction. With her jet-black bob and tight leather mini skirt, Melanie (20 February 2006) recounts how punks often hang on to each others' shoulders and Mikey (13 October 2004), slight and covered in tattoos, talks about a 'grappling action' with nearby dancers. Although 'slam dancing' developed initially though the US punk scene, it also features at British punk gigs.[10] Mikey and Vince picture it as an equally high-energy style of movement in which participants intentionally crash into each other whilst shooting out their arms with clenched fists.

Headbanging is associated with heavy metal music and principally consists of the feet rooted to the spot to enable a vigorous shaking of the head. With his black cowboy boots and mane of dark brown hair, Max (24 April 2006) states 'headbanging is throwing your head backwards and forwards as ferociously as possible'. In addition to headbanging on a vertical plane, Aimee also describes a lateral action in which participants move their heads in a u-shaped trajectory, and 'whirlwinding' in which the head whips round in a circular action. Although the feet are often stabilized to provide balance while headbanging, Max recalls leaping up and down at particularly crowded shows in which spatial limitations automatically preclude the expansive headbanging action. Sitting in a smart coffee shop, wearing little to reveal her metal affiliations, Sienna (18 January 2006) talks about the practice of 'windmilling'

Figure 7.2   Melanie the punk fan. Photo copyright © Sherril Dodds.

at metal gigs in which participants kick forwards and back using their arms like planes and 'work themselves up into a frenzy where that turns into a cartwheel'. Max, Aimee and Sienna also reference gestural actions prevalent at metal gigs, such as the 'devil horns' salute (in which the index and little finger point upwards) and pumping the fist into the air. The other identifiable movement practice closely tied to the metal scene is 'air guitar' in which participants enact the experience of playing an imaginary electric guitar to, at times, a sophisticated level of verisimilitude.

While pogoing and slam dancing are typically associated with punk rock, and headbanging and air guitar are specifically linked to heavy metal, several movement practices cross punk and metal events. For instance, Aimee and Sienna refer to 'circle pits' at metal gigs, in which audience members race around the venue in a collective circle (with an additional group sometimes heading in the opposite direction), and Vince and Mikey reference them at punk shows. Another group activity that features at both punk and metal gigs is the 'wall of death'. In a metal context, Aimee suggests that 'the crowd separate into two halves of the room and basically run at each other', while Mikey explains that at punk gigs 'about three people just charge into the audience and knock everyone flying'. Further shared practices are 'stage diving', in which audience members climb on stage and dive off into the crowd; 'crowd surfing', in which a participant is carried over the heads of the audience; 'human pyramids', in which participants mount each other while balanced on arms and knees; and 'moshing', which carries many similarities to the jostling and barging actions typical of pogoing and slam dancing.[11]

Pogoing and headbanging are relatively straightforward to characterize and describe; however, 'skanking' is a more difficult dance to pin down as it refers to a range of dances linked with first-, second- and third-wave ska music.[12] Here I briefly outline forms of skanking or 'ska dancing' as identified and practised by the informants under discussion. Sonny (13 February 2006) reclines on his sofa, surrounded by his vast record collection, in red trilby hat and stylish leather shoes. His interest lies in first-wave 1960s Jamaican ska music, to which he performs 'shuffling', a dance that rapidly shifts from the ball of one foot to that of the other.[13] Although this basic action forms the core of the dance, a series of flamboyant additions, which Sonny describes as 'flash moves', can be incorporated to demonstrate individuality and expertise.

Figure 7.3 Sonny the ska fan. Photo copyright © Sherril Dodds.

Stuart (23 January 2006), who I first met at a ska gig dressed in the standard Two-Tone style of 'suedehead', polo shirt, turned-up jeans, braces and Doc Martens, is a 1980s Two-Tone ska fan. For him, skanking constitutes a low-level twist in which snake-like arms provide balance while the legs are alternately raised with flexed feet. Jamie (18 December 2005), with his baggy jeans and mop of blond hair, dances to third-wave ska punk, and demonstrates skanking as a basic 'cancan' step with the upper body thrown forwards or backwards and a rapid jogging on the spot. Chris (3 March 2007) sees me in his study, the walls lined with hard-backed books and rows of vinyl. In his cushioned leather chair he conveys a wide interest both in first- and second-wave ska, and a concomitant knowledge of various skanking styles. First he describes a quintessential ska dance that accompanies 1960s Jamaican ska, in which the arms either cross back and forth or swing in opposition directly in front of the torso, while the body sways from side to side with flexed knees.[14] He also spoke of 1980s Two-Tone dancing which would involve 'exaggerated body movements' that were characterized by a stiff torso and 'clenched fists'; sometimes the dancers would remain firmly rooted to the spot, executing a rapid series of 'freeze-frame' poses in a jerky and rigid phrase of movement, and on other occasions would perform a 'running on the spot'.[15]

From these descriptions it is evident that the movement vocabulary is more nuanced and diverse than it might initially appear. In the following sections I set out to explore how the informants value their dancing experiences and how this embodied value has the potential to shape and be shaped by the gig event.

Aesthetic evaluations of music and dance

Measures of aesthetic judgement form a key value framework at the live gig event. This can be expressed as a somatic evaluation of the band's performance and many of the informants describe dancing as a means of enunciating affirmation. Aimee suggests 'when you go to a gig you want to in a way show the band that, you know, I am really into your music'; Jamie reflects 'if you are going to go for it then you really have to throw yourself into it... It is a good way for the band to know that they are doing well'; and Mikey explains 'you hear a good band, fast powerful, heavy music and you wanna get in there and jump around and also you know it shows appreciation to the bands'. Berger (1999, p. 44) conceptualizes this performative relationship between audience and musicians as 'the sociology of attention' and Fonarow (1997, p. 365) refers to

Figure 7.4 Chris the ska fan. Photo copyright © Sherril Dodds.

it as 'a visible signifier of an assessment' to delineate the way that audiences articulate approval by their presence on the dance floor. As Berger (1999, p. 44) indicates, a 'successful' or 'valued' performance is only evident through the audience's audible approval or 'body motion'.

A dynamic power play exists between audiences and bands, not only rooted in aesthetic concerns, but also shaped by economic drivers. Several informants commented on how audiences will automatically dance as a sign of respect for well known, commercially successful bands. Jamie notes that 'if the band is quite popular then quite a lot of people would [dance]' and Sienna talks of how bands with a 'big following' will play some 'crowd pleasers and as soon as it's something the crowd know then they start dancing'. Pete (9 January 2006), with his shock of bleached hair and Union Jack T-shirt, positions this uncritical celebration of established names as unnecessarily sycophantic through suggesting that audiences get 'infected with the big band bug'. Less established bands on the other hand must court audience interest and several of the informants describe how band members will solicit an embodied response. Stuart states 'certain bands shout out "Come on, why aren't you lot dancing"' and Pete recounts 'if there is not many people up dancing, the singer will just [say] "Come on, are you not going to get moving or what?"' This type of plea marks a power imbalance between band and audience that can obviously lead to frustration. Max recalls 'I've been at some shows where the lead singer has got very upset' and Sienna explains 'well they swear at you'. Yet on some occasions the band can produce a change in audience energy through its own embodied performance. Melanie remembers a gig in which

> one of [the band] was just running round the crowd and getting mauled and stuff and...that was amazing. Well, they were really going for it and everyone fed off it and everyone was like 'yeah!'

Thus subcultural members are keenly aware of both the economic motivation and the social kudos for bands that can encourage audiences to offer an embodied affirmation of the gig event through their dance practice. In relation to heavy rock music, Berger (1999) comments at length on the significance of audience approval. He suggests that bands constantly monitor audience reactions and responses and this will affect, for example, whether a song stays in the repertoire or not. In this respect, the audience possesses a corporeal power in relation to whether it chooses to dance as an expression of taste value.

Figure 7.5   Pete the punk fan. Photo copyright © Sherril Dodds.

As Berger (1999) identifies, the audience expects certain standards and if people are not impressed they will leave the dance floor. Yet the dancing can also produce a mutually validating relationship. Berger (1999, p. 156) describes this as a 'feedback loop' in which the band will incite dancing through the energy of its performance and the dynamics of audience dancing will further galvanize the band. Thus the intention is not simply to 'grasp' audience attention, but to perpetuate this reciprocal performative experience, which compels the audience to retain its interest (Berger, 1999, p. 156). Many of the informants identified this connection or dynamic between band and audience through which the energy of the performance arises. Sienna states:

> I suppose there is something in wanting to feel that you are part of the performance... you do feel a great affinity with the band, especially if you're a fan of the band, and there is this thing going between you and the band... they're like, 'we love you guys and you know it's really important that you show up for us', and so you are doing your thing for all the band and you feel that you are part of the whole experience.

Melanie meanwhile proposes:

> for me a good concert isn't always about the band playing the best, it's about the atmosphere in general and when there is a good atmosphere there usually have been a lot of people dancing, but... which comes first: the people dancing or the good atmosphere?

This idea that the audience dancing and the quality of the gig are mutually generative acts is also recognized by Max:

> I went to see Marilyn Manson a few years ago at the London Arena and it was an amazing show: it was absolutely fantastic, everybody was dancing and there was enough room to actually dance about and, you know, jump up and down. And the last time I saw him it was a great show but it just didn't have that buzz, the band just seemed to be missing something.

I would therefore argue that the construction of the 'performance' occurs at the audience–band interface and the presence of dancing bodies signifies both aesthetic and economic worth. Sandvoss suggests that 'fan performances are always constituted between text and context by turning the object of consumption into an activity with a given micro field of social and cultural relations' (2005, pp. 44–5). This performance metaphor to describe fan activity offers a useful approach to subcultural dance as it suggests that the consumption of music at the gig event con- stitutes an 'embodied performance' in itself. Likewise, Berger describes heavy metal fans' behaviour as a 'performance' not only in the sense of dressing in particular ways, but also in terms of 'their comportment and body stylistics that pushes their behaviour from mere socializing into performance' (1999, p. 39). Kahn-Harris also regards subcultural activity as a 'performance' in which 'scene members "perform" trans- gression to each other' (2004, p. 110).

The concept of 'subcultural performance', then, relates not only to the 'official' performance of the band on stage, but to the movement actions of audience members that both express and respond to the quality of the gig in a complex power play informed by aesthetic, social and economic values. Significantly, Sandvoss (2005) also refers to fan 'performance' as an act that draws attention to behaviour which is scrutinized by others and this leads to the second area in which values are played out at the gig event. The sense of 'perform- ance' comes into play, not only at the intersection of band and audi- ence, but also between participants who observe and, in Sandvoss's terms, 'scrutinize' each other. This scrutiny frequently takes the form of an aesthetic evaluation directed at the dancing skill of other par- ticipants since, without exception, all of my informants spoke of how they examine the movement capabilities of other subcultural members at live music events. On one hand, several informants stress the simplicity and accessibility of the dancing, thus emphasizing its egalitarian role: Pete suggests that pogoing is 'so simple you know a three-year-old child could do it', Max notes 'nobody worries if you are a good dancer or a bad dancer' and Melanie insists 'it's about taking part rather than being perfect'. Yet the dancing can also be a means to express ability and esteem: several informants explained their awe at particular dancers. Melanie (7 March 2006), dressed in a long gothic skirt and blood-red lipstick, recounts her first impression of metal fans headbanging:

> it was when I was 18, not long 18, started going to this Astoria club and started seeing people headbanging there properly. To me, at 18 years old and very green and inexperienced with these very scary looking people headbanging and just thinking, wow, they look so cool.

Chris meanwhile identifies his impression of a particular dancer:

> I can remember watching his body movements ... and thinking 'man that looks cool' ... his body looked to be completely syncopated to the rhythm of the music and it was a very fluid movement.

Thus, although informants position the dance as potentially accessible to all, this does not prevent dancers rating each other on their technique and expression. To some extent, this stands in contrast to Thornton's (1997) findings in relation to dance music subcultures. Although she does not directly address the dance practice, she argues that 'subcultural capital' is predicated on oppositions of inclusion and exclusion or hip versus uncool. In respect to the informants studied here, dancing serves as a means to foster accessibility and respect, although in the following section I illustrate the fragility of this sense of 'subcultural community'.

The interest in individual style articulated by the participants even extends to a competitive element whereby dancers enter into a display of showmanship. Sienna explains:

> you see the guys all sort of watching one another and then sometimes watch one person at a time which is kind of weird ... they do it in a round, so one person jumps into the centre, does his thing then comes out, and then another person moves in.

Stuart recalls entering into 'dance-off contests' with people in which 'the last one dancing' is champion and, as a ska music promoter, Chris explains how he used to give away prizes for the best male and female dancer. Likewise, Sonny talks about winning several shuffling competitions in which the winner is recognized by 'people backing down, showing appreciation by bowing their heads'. He recalls how 'it became very competitive' in terms of assessing 'who could dance the best and the quickest'. Both Stuart and Sonny obviously relish a sense of personal achievement in winning 'dance-offs': Stuart describes feeling 'proud' and Sonny 'elated'.

Although the dancing offers opportunities for democracy and accessibility, and several informants spoke of its inclusivity, individual proficiency and distinctiveness are privileged, aspired to and, in some cases, rewarded. Yet this idea of individuality and showmanship appears to sit in tension with the concept of 'community', which forms the second area of value that I seek to explore in relation to subcultural dance.

An expression of community values

Several of the informants spoke of experiences of alienation or derision because of their subcultural affiliation. For instance, Aimee recalls:

> when I went to school, [there] were mainly the sort of people wearing tracksuits and into dance music and some of the grief I used to get off them was just unbelievable...I dyed my hair black and started listening to all this music and like they were 'ooh you're a freak now'.

Likewise Kate states:

> the amount of hassle I've got from people for absolutely no reason whatsoever...grown men standing in their circle calling me Morticia Adams. It just really wound me up because if you get to know me I wouldn't hurt a fly, but just because I look differently...yeah, it does annoy me, it really does wind me up.

Other references to marginalization emerge in the interview data, whereby the informants position their subcultural peers as a community of outsiders. Stuart says of ska fans, 'I think it was a lot of people at one point who were downtrodden, or felt that they were not within a group'. Sienna says of 'metallers', 'people outside that group think they are aggressive, but they're not. They tend to have been loners when they were younger.' Kate even suggests that they are 'people that have been the rejects of society, like have either been the kids that've been bullied at school or, you know, kids that have had family problems and stuff'. Thus within the subculture a sense of alienation or marginalization may be the norm.

Irrespective of these perceptions concerning the outsider status of individual members in their everyday lives, many of the informants argue that a feeling of community emerges through their subcultural affiliation. Indeed this seems to echo the inclusionist philosophy of the neo-burlesque community as discussed in Chapter 6. Kate insists, 'being a metaller...sometimes gives you a little bit of identity and a little bit of community and a sense of belonging'; Mikey recalls 'the ethos of punk for me back then was just like...our little secret society'; and Sienna states 'you do feel you're in a subculture, in a tribe and there aren't too many people out there so you have to do something to collect them together'. Significantly, several informants spoke of how this sense of community is constituted through dancing. In relation to ska,

Figure 7.6 Kate the metal fan. Photo copyright © Sherril Dodds.

Chris proposes 'a collective spirituality sort of descends onto the dance floor'; Pete explains that pogoing is 'like a communal thing; all your mates are there and they're all having a good time…it comes back to the punk ethos, everyone's doing the same basically'; and Sienna says of headbanging, 'when you are dancing you have this sense of being part of the collective…[there's] something really important about all being together and all dancing'. Indeed, within the gig event there are multiple opportunities for expressing communal participation and these range from simple acknowledgements, such as smiling at other participants and placing arms around each other's shoulders, through to complex movement interactions such as stage diving, human pyramids, circle pits and walls of death. Stuart notes 'I've been…in the middle of the dance floor and you have people tap on your shoulders and you start dancing with them'; Aimee suggests that 'lots of people put their arms over each other and like all sort of stand in a line head banging in tandem'; and Mikey states 'people will get in a grapple, you know, where people get in a line and you'd be going up and down and jumping'.

The theme of community articulated by the informants in relation to their subcultural affinities also emerges in subcultural, fandom and popular music research. Hills (2002) describes how fans interpret texts in a communal, rather than isolated, fashion and one only has to think of internet discussion groups, the production of fanzines, casual conversations at gigs and the presence of dancing as a positive evaluation of performance quality to see how fandom simultaneously creates and responds to collective dialogues and interactions. Abercrombie and Longhurst (1998) note that fans are often situated within communities that are located in opposition to other kinds of groups or institutions. Although the notion of 'opposition' is complex to deduce across diverse individuals whose interests and values potentially lie beyond their selected subcultural affiliation, a strong sense of being an 'outsider' certainly emerges in the interview data. Bennett (2001) identifies similarities across punk and extreme metal in the physical layout of gigs; the small venues and proximity of the stage to the dance floor creates a sense of community and solidarity. He goes on to suggest that this 'closeness' is manifest in stage diving which, although it might appear as a feat of daring, instead relies on a mutual trust between audience members and operates as a bonding phenomenon. Likewise, Fonarow (1997, p. 362) asserts that dancing close to the stage in packed venues produces 'intimate physical contact with strangers'. Indeed, the shared visual and physical movement activities that cross all three subcultures clearly speak to notions of community.

This model of a unified sense of membership echoes the 1970s CCCS studies of subcultures (Muggleton, 2000). Yet in spite of the insistent community rhetoric, evidence from the interview data offers examples of how participants can choose to distance themselves from or become marginalized within the scene. For instance, several of the informants spoke disapprovingly about particular movement practices, thus intentionally creating a divide between themselves and other subcultural members. Jamie notes 'there is a lot of pushing and shoving and some kids skank really with their elbows...and that really annoys me'; and Mikey recounts 'punks used to spit at the bands...I find that sort of behaviour a bit moronic actually'. Members can also experience a sense of alienation within their subcultural group. Sienna remembers 'there was one point where I hadn't been to a club for a while...and I saw all these people dancing in a way that was quite strange to me...I felt "shit", I'm not part of the scene anymore because I don't know this dance'.

Thus although the informants all emphasized notions of community within their experiences of subcultural life, there are clearly competing social values in circulation that are located in a tension between outsider and insider, communality and individuality. Tsitsos (1999, p. 399) comments 'members of the scene confront the paradox of being part of a scene (and, therefore, a community) which endorses individuality'. Likewise, Muggleton states 'subcultures are, paradoxically, a socially shared means of expressing an *individualistic* sensibility [original emphasis]' (2000, p. 163). Yet this contradiction is not necessarily problematic. Hills describes it as

> a 'dialectic of value' in which personalised, individual and subjective moments of fan attachment interact with communal constructions and justifications without either moment over-writing or surmounting the other. (Hills, 2002, p. xiii)

Similarly, Sandvoss (2005, p. 55) refers to fans as 'imagined communities' that share certain symbolic and mediated activities. For him, whether this community exists is not the real concern; more pressing is that this perception of shared experience has actual 'social and cultural impact'.

In light of Sandvoss's point, the informants clearly perceive their subcultural affiliations within the context of an identifiable community paradoxically constituted through outsiders. Yet this rhetoric of inclusion mobilizes a complex politics of gender, race and class. From my interview data, it appears that the subcultures under investigation are

accessible to both male and female participants and, while some movement vocabulary such as headbanging and crowd surfing has typically
been represented through a masculinist paradigm, the informants suggested that both sexes take part in the dance styles under discussion. Yet
the subcultures I investigate demonstrate far less diversity in terms of
race. Certainly, punk and metal music subcultures are racially inscribed
as 'white' and this is supported by my small sample of informants and
observations at gigs. This is not, however, to suggest that subcultures
are distinctly monocultural. In spite of Hebdige's (1979) characterization of subcultures as white, male and working class, there are plen-
tiful examples in the United Kingdom of popular music subcultures,
such as hip hop, bhangra and bashment, that are produced and consumed within black British and British Asian youth cultures. Although
my sample of ska fans was made up of white, male informants, given
the Jamaican heritage of this form, the consumption of first-wave ska
in particular is far more racially diverse.[16] This is clearly evidenced in
my study of Sunday Serenade, the British Caribbean dance club where
Jamaican ska music is played, which forms the focus of Chapter 8. Yet
given the appropriation of this form by white British Two-Tone bands
such as Madness and its third-wave incarnation as 'ska punk', it is not
surprising that these genres of ska are now consumed by a predominantly white audience base.

The troubled notion of community also raises interesting questions
of class. In terms of economic and social capital, the informants I interviewed occupied significantly divergent subject positions: from one
who was unemployed, in receipt of government benefits and living in
rented accommodation, through to a senior barrister who owned a large
detached property in a leafy north-west London suburb. Yet while my
sample of informants shared little commonality of class status, within
the political arena all of the informants voiced a broadly liberal ideology and a clear sense of left-wing politics emerged. Although none of
the informants passed comment on the current political situation, a
strong anti-Conservative stance was voiced.[17]

Aimee states 'you wouldn't get many Young Conservatives getting
into metal'; Sonny feels that ska and reggae fans 'tend to be a bit more ...
on the left'; and Pete suggests 'there wouldn't have been a punk in the
country who liked Margaret Thatcher'. These sentiments surrounding
party politics also extend to the contemporary capitalist framework.
Jamie explains that 'anti-capitalism is quite strong within the whole
[ska] scene' and Pete insists that 'there's like a punk ethic, you should
be doing it for the music and not the money'. These fundamental belief

systems then inform other liberal values and practices. Mikey recalls 'I was quite left-wing and I still am...I was a member of CND, I was going into the whole anti-vivisection, animal rights thing. That all came from punk.' Chris comments 'ska music was the epitome of everything that was great about Jamaica, and it's full of hope and it's full of the voice of the young'. This is reinforced by Sonny in relation to the lyrics of Jamaican music: 'there's a lot more spoken about life than there is in commercial pop music...the transition of the slave trade and how the world moves round and whether the political leaders of the world have got it right or not'.

Although there is not scope within this chapter to tease out the specificities of political allegiances, bearing in mind Sandvoss's (2005) assertion that the 'imagined community' produces material realities, codes of behaviour at the gig event form the third set of values I seek to explore. Thus it would be fitting to examine whether the liberal sentiments articulated above are played out at the gig event.

Codes of behaviour on the dance floor

I stated in Chapter 1 that popular dance traditionally lacks cultural value through its lowly status in relation to the Western art canon. Given this position of derision, that all of the participants partake in dance potentially signals a liberal attitude in their commitment to dance *per se*. Yet the codes of behaviour articulated on the dance floor suggest a far more nuanced and paradoxical play of liberal values, which goes beyond the simple will to dance. Many of the informants acknowledge a degree of violence that arises through the dancing; yet all expressed reproach at this practice:

> I think the kids are a lot more violent-minded...they're all smashing into each other and punching each other and stuff like that. (Pete)

> I've been to shows where kids have deliberately just bashed into people, knocked people over and stood at the sides and knocked their drinks over and that causes all sorts of problems. (Mikey)

> [N]owadays you tend to get a lot of idiots who go to these shows and just want to run into the crowd, bash into anybody, punch people, it just seems more violent now and more unpleasant. (Max)

In response, a complex corporeal etiquette exists that is managed through group monitoring and self-appointed censorship of the dancing. Mikey outlines the fundamental philosophy of the dance floor as follows:

> treating other people how you want to be treated yourself. Do as I will and there is no law and do as I will is the only law. You gotta respect other people, you know.

Chris concurs that 'there is a kind of respect thing going on...you wouldn't barge another person'. Thus any illegitimate behaviour is challenged. Mikey insists 'you don't punch people in the face, you don't use your elbows, you don't use your fists...but some people do, and if they do, then they're told not to'. Likewise, Aimee reflects, 'there are always just like one or two...who you get the feeling are actually trying to sort of fight with the people a bit, and usually people just say "What's your problem", you know, "Get out of here"'. Yet when the dancing becomes dangerous, a mutual support system comes into play: Vince explains 'you're always looking out for each other, someone goes down, you help them up'; and Max remembers 'I was at one show at Brixton one time and the mosh pit was chaotic, but as soon as someone fell over, everybody was helping that person up'.

Yet in spite of this discourse of collective responsibility, degree and force of physical contact are relative concepts. Sienna states that 'people will kind of fall purposely into one another...in a kind of friendly, aggressive way'; Melanie suggests 'sometimes when you are pushing it can be really quite good-natured and you can deliberately know that you are going to do it'; and although Mikey describes grappling, pushing and crashing into people, he explains that there is 'no intention of violence for us. For me personally, and for most of my friends who go, we just want to have a laugh.' The participants clearly see this intense physicality as an enacted combativeness rather than intentional violence, although physical harm can occur. Mikey recalls 'I nearly got my leg broken at a show by some metal kid'; Kate warns 'my friend has broken his arm through slipping'; and Max notes 'I did [stage dive] once and nearly broke my leg'. Thus while participants disapprove of violence, an excessive physicality and its concomitant degree of risk form a major component of the event.

In reference to moshing, Berger (1999, p. 73) argues that its apparent aggression acts both as a symbol and a reality of aesthetic expression, cathartic outlet, personal and social injustice, a critique of mainstream pop and as a marker of community, and in so doing it 'presents both the reality and the representation of violence'. Indeed, the combination of perceived and actual violence, the related injuries sustained and the frameworks of censorship implemented can be equally applied to pogoing, slam dancing and headbanging. Notably, this appears to be less of an issue with ska, which seems to place greater value on technique and physical prowess than on physical interaction. I would therefore argue that the liberal politics foregrounded by the participants are always explored through a relativist position; thus, while they denounce violence and police aggressive behaviour, these are undoubtedly subjective positions.

Another area in which the dancing both shapes and expresses codes of social behaviour emerges in relation to image management. Many of the informants drew attention to the idea that playfulness informs the dance practice, as terms such as 'silly', 'crazy' and 'daft' are used to describe the dance and the dancers. Mikey states 'I've got mad mates who do all sorts of stupid things'; Jamie suggests 'you can't help but smile really 'cause you are fooling around and having a good time'; and Max insists 'I think the majority of people in the metal scene are absolute nutters...we go way over the top, we jump up on stage and dive into the audience'. Notably the informants tend to reject the notion that their subcultural peers might present some kind of social façade and instead promote the idea that their actions are authentic, uncontrived and organic. Aimee insists 'the majority of people into metal don't really take themselves that seriously...you are just out having a laugh and, you know, you suddenly start doing something stupid and everyone else just joins in'. Likewise, Jamie states:

> [skanking] shows that you're fully letting yourself go and you don't really care what people think of you and it's less about what people see you doing. It's not really about being cool because you look like an idiot when you're doing it most of the time.

Overall, this marks a keen emphasis on play, spontaneity and unselfconscious performance. As observed earlier, this forms a contrast with Thornton's (1997) notion of 'subcultural capital' through which clubbers conceive 'cool' as a mark of distinction.

On one hand, given the cultural status of popular dance that I signalled at the beginning of this section, these references to tomfoolery potentially operate as a devaluation of the dancing. Yet, on the other, I would argue that participant dancing not only expresses inherently serious matters, such as belonging, respect, judgement and etiquette, but also positions the pleasure of play as a value in itself. Hills (2002) conceives fandom as a type of 'play' that is non-competitive

Figure 7.7 A dancer at Club Ska. Photo copyright © Sherril Dodds.

in character, although I would like to explore here a more formal understanding of 'play' as articulated through the work of Michael Hutter. Hutter (1996) proposes that 'play' forms an act of communication between two or more players and that any kind of 'move' within the play needs to be understood by another 'player' who is cognizant of the 'rules' in order to further the play. Hutter suggests that all plays are characterized by three elements: contingency, chance and closure. Contingency is constituted through the rules that construct a particular framework; chance exists through the agency of the participants; and closure is the creation of 'self-meaning' within a particular play. Hutter (1996) describes how play requires moves, which in turn require rules that exist within a particular context. It is the context that both is informed by and creates value; thus value is produced through play.

Hutter's concept of play lends itself well to subcultural dance and I use the example of 'codes of behaviour' on the dance floor to illustrate how 'play' occurs within the gig event to produce particular meanings and values. In Hutter's terms, 'contingency' refers to the rules that inform subcultural dance practice regarding what is deemed appropriate conduct on the dance floor. Therefore, as I highlight earlier, subcultural etiquette demands that intentional kicking, elbowing or barging is inappropriate on the dance floor. 'Chance' is then the extent to which subcultural members observe, police, challenge and destabilize these rules in the moment of dancing, and 'closure' is the meanings or values produced concerning legitimate behaviour on the dance floor. At the gig event the play becomes meaningful through specific 'moves'. For instance, when certain dance movements are discouraged or physically halted through the intervention of subcultural members, this signifies unacceptable dance practice and a 'closure' of values takes place. On other occasions, particular dance moves may remain unchallenged even though the rules of behaviour are flouted in some way by the 'chance actions' of a few participants. It is this embodied play that meaningfully demonstrates what is permissible or otherwise on the dance floor and thus produces values of etiquette at the gig event. This is not to suggest that these values become fixed but that they are constantly destabilized and renegotiated through moves and play at future gigs. Thus while informants perceive the dance in terms of playfulness, there also exists a more serious play in which codes of conduct are constructed, negotiated, transgressed and reinforced. This reveals a complex value system in which participants espouse the freedom to express unselfconscious behaviours but within a bounded framework of corporeal regulations.

Economic exchange and the consumption of dance

The final set of values I wish to examine is tied to dancing and economic exchange. As Sandvoss (2005) notes, fan 'performances' take place within specific socioeconomic frameworks and, given that entry to a gig involves payment of a fee, I seek to explore how the participants articulate the use-value of the dancing in their consumption of the event. Dancing clearly plays a central role in the gig experience. Kate states 'if I haven't danced that night, I don't feel that I've had a good time' and Melanie insists 'I feel like I haven't been to a gig properly unless I dance'. This raises the question of what the participants 'receive' through dancing in 'exchange' for their financial investment in a gig.

All of the informants referred to an unadulterated sense of wellbeing and used terminology such as 'elation', 'fun', 'great', 'overawed', 'invigorated' and 'happy' to articulate a clear emotional response to the dancing experience: Sienna explains 'I feel very happy, happy to be expressing through movement my love of the music'; Mikey comments 'you want to go mad, you just get such a buzz off of punk bands, there's nothing like it'; Chris reflects 'I feel a sense of elation and oneness'; and Kate describes it as 'totally invigorated, totally just "wow"'. This suggests a profound sense of pleasure, and several participants saw this as a desire over which they can barely exercise control. For instance, Sonny states 'I just can't help myself', Kate reflects 'to stand there and just watch it isn't enough' and Vince describes how 'you just can't help yourself moving'.

Although the way that the participants articulate this almost involuntary desire to dance places embodied consumption as central to the gig experience, this perspective potentially diminishes consumer agency. The idea of the sensory pleasures of the gig event, such as the spectacle of the band, the blasting amplification, the ethereal lighting display and the overwhelming urge to dance, recalls some of the Frankfurt School and mass culture theory arguments of a consumer lost in the passive pleasures of the popular. While I accept that the sensory offers an important component of the gig experience, I do not want to lose sight of other value systems in operation, such as the way that participants exercise critical judgements regarding the quality of the gig through their embodied practice, and how this in turn impacts upon the political economy of popular music, an idea which I will come to shortly.

In addition to concepts of pleasure and desire, the respondents also spoke positively about the physiological benefits of dancing: Stuart notes 'it's like athletics and running, you get all the biological stuff kicking off'; Jamie suggests 'because it's so energetic it gets the heart pumping and I guess maybe releases some chemicals somewhere'; Chris states 'it's healthy and it's good for you' and Sonny observes 'it's like any exercise is therapeutic and your body releases endorphins into the brain and that makes you feel good'. This attention to a health-and-fitness discourse perhaps reflects the broader consumer culture with its interest in the maintenance of the body through diet and exercise regimes (Featherstone, 1991).

The participants also conceive the dancing as a regulated means to manage complex feelings. Vince states 'bad day, pent-up aggression, you want to let it all out, there's no better way of doing it'. Stuart reflects 'I am quite a laid-back person usually and...don't say boo to a goose...on those [ska] nights, this is my turn to let out'. Jamie asserts 'it is a way to go crazy and get all your energy out. And if you are frustrated about things, it's like a way to kind of forget that I suppose and just have a good time.' The idea of dance as a 'safety valve', a regulated site where individuals can express thoughts, feelings and behaviour that may be unacceptable in quotidian public life, forms a common theme is cultural research. Yet Ward (1993) critiques this position as deterministically functionalist in the way that it reduces dance to having a singular social role, in this sense as a form of 'social escape'. Already the interview data suggests that subcultural dancing offers multiple use-values and, in addition to emotional and physiological benefits, it also speaks to notions of agency and empowerment. For instance, Stuart describes how dancing at gigs 'is the biggest feeling...it just builds you up so much'; Mikey notes 'there's nothing like it...you see a good band and you just want to go nuts'; and Sienna suggests 'it is you on the dance floor and it's you against the world'.

The notion of an 'extreme' investment also appears as a central feature of participant experience. As Sienna suggests, the commitment to fandom demands a particular attitude: 'being a fan of metal it's such an extreme, you are quite a fanatic...it's being wholly one hundred per cent into it'. She goes on to note, 'all the people I know who are into metal are geeks of some sort including myself, we're all obsessives'. In addition to the immense commitment required in the act of fandom, the style of music and dance, particularly across punk and metal, suggests a kind of excess. Aimee states 'the music is quite, I suppose, extreme or something. You couldn't really just, I don't know, just tap your foot along to it.' Mikey explains 'I'm more into the more extreme end of things. I got into the more extreme end of punk very early on. It's like find the most obscure, maddest bands you can find.' Max meanwhile recounts 'heavy

metal music can sound very aggressive... and [headbanging] is a very
violent-looking image as you see a hundred people banging their heads
away in just thin air'. Although skanking does not always share the
extreme physicality of headbanging and pogoing, all of the ska informants spoke of an extreme interest in collecting music within the genre
and each demonstrated an impressive knowledge of ska artists and their
music.

The concept of 'extremes' also emerges in the literature regarding
fan practices. Abercrombie and Longhurst (1998) note how definitions
of fans are often articulated as an 'excess of admiration' which is frequently positioned negatively in terms of a 'fanatical' or 'pathological'
interest in their selected cultural texts. Grossberg (1992) sees a similar
framework of excess around fan interest which marks an extreme divide
between the fan's relationship to a cultural form and it merely being
an 'entertainment'. Jenson (1992) comments that, in fan theory, this
notion of the 'extreme' fan emerges as a critique of modernity in which
the fragmented character of mass society produces an alienated and
partial individual: thus the fan seeks to achieve the sense of community and belonging, through attachment to a cultural object that can
no longer be gained through modern existence. Yet rather than seeing
the 'extreme' fan as an alienated victim unable to cope with modern
life, the multiple and often excessive investments in subcultural communities can offer opportunities for agency and choice. Whether it is
in the obsessive interest in the music, the extreme physicality of the
dancing or a radical stylization of the body in terms of dress and image,
the individual articulates an affiliation with selected subcultural values that suggests a strategy for personal empowerment.[18] Furthermore,
I propose that the physical investment and movement extremes that
characterize subcultural corporealities can be conceived as an 'aesthetics of excess'.

The question whether subcultural dance offers opportunities for
agency, empowerment and transformation deserves further probing as
there appear to be identifiable links between the 'excessive investment'
detailed above and notions of personal power and control. In a discussion of the extreme metal scene, Kahn-Harris (2004) argues that the
excessive corporeal performances of subcultural affiliation produce a
potential site of transformation. He conceptualizes this as a 'liminal
space' that 'constantly exceeds the boundaries of the body, revelling in
the pleasures and pains of embodiment' (Kahn-Harris, 2004, p. 109).
Significantly, he uses the example of 'violent moshing' as a kind of
spectacular transgression, in that participants physically exceed the

culturally codified norms of human interaction. Yet he acknowledges that, given that the extreme metal scene is relatively obscure, this spectacular practice goes almost unnoticed. While I appreciate the idea that subcultural dance offers a site though which participants can engage in a spectacular corporeal transgression of socially regulated modes of physicality through these charged and aggressive dance interactions, he does not document how this 'extreme dancing' offers either personal or social transformation, particularly given its niche status. There are no insider accounts to evidence how participants experience a sense of transgression and whether this is maintained beyond the moment of dancing.

Grossberg also sees fan activity as a form of self-generating empowerment:

> the fan's investment of energy into certain practices always returns some interest on the investment through a variety of empowering relations: in the form of the further production of energy (for example, rock dancing, while exhausting, continuously generates its own energy, if only to continue dancing). (Grossberg, 1992, p. 64)

Grossberg (1992, p. 64) describes this as a kind of 'affective investment' which is a self-perpetuating phenomenon. As fans invest energy in their objects of interest, this offers a form of control that gives alternative possibilities in their lives; for instance, experiences of boredom, frustration and alienation are replaced by passion, hope and focus (Grossberg, 1992). Yet as Berger (1999, pp. 74) warns, while pleasures and meanings are constituted through the social actions of participants, this sense of agency should not be misinterpreted as a kind of 'radical individualism'. In my study, the participants perceive the dancing as a transformative experience in that it brings about emotional, physiological and personal benefits, although I would not want to argue that it necessarily produces wider social change. As Mikey notes, 'punk itself doesn't change the world: it changes people. It changed me and I hope it changed me for the better.' Indeed, that the dancing allows participants space to express different degrees of aesthetic judgement, technical prowess, belonging, community, codes of etiquette and emotional and psychological wellbeing is evidence of agency and the positive somatic experiences of dancing as articulated by the informants indicates notions of empowerment and personal transformation.

Yet music gigs are situated within a system of financial transaction and the pleasures and benefits gained through the dancing moment are only one dimension of the consumer experience. The use-values outlined above are acquired through a framework of economic exchange and Kate is keenly aware of this monetary relationship between the music venue and participant experience: 'I've paid this money, I'm with me mates, I'm gonna dance, so I just do whatever I feel like I wanna do at the time'. From this perspective, she maintains power in that she has committed a fee and expects a good dancing experience from this. Yet because the music industry exists in a free market economy that seeks to create profit through the sale and consumption of recorded music, live performance and related merchandise, it is in the record labels' interests to facilitate and encourage an extreme investment in the dancing experience of participants attending gigs. As Fiske (1992) notes, fan culture exists within a commercial industry and the expression of fan tastes gives cultural industries valuable market information. Certainly, all of the informants place considerable financial investment in their subcultural affiliations, which includes buying music, attending gigs and purchasing clothes and merchandise. Equally, the bands see this economic worth through their pleas for audience participation.

The dancing therefore also functions as a means for participants to communicate both to self and others the necessity of consumption in order to maintain and secure future gig events and dancing experiences. Sandvoss (2005) suggests, however, that fandom is situated outside the usual logic of capitalist exchange; due to the fan's extreme emotional attachment to an object, its use-value bears little relationship to its exchange-value. For instance, the cost of a gig does not tally with the immense pleasure that fans experience from attending the event, while fans often invest heavily in travel (sometimes even abroad) to see a band that is far removed from the exchange-value of the ticket (Sandvoss, 2005). Yet through a Marxist lens, this inequity between exchange-value and use-value occurs with any form of commodity exchange, in that it is impossible to quantify and delineate a correlation between 'exchange-value', which is an unstable phenomenon in itself, and use-value, which is an individualized and relative position. Sandvoss equally recognizes that fans cannot exist outside the capitalist framework of their consumption in spite of the significant chasm between exchange-value and use-value:

the escape from the logic of exchange-value in fan consumption is short-lived, as ultimately any use-value is articulated through demand and thus reintegrated into exchange-value. (Sandvoss, 2005, p. 116)

While fans are deeply immersed in the capitalist structure of the sub-cultural economy, they are nevertheless able to operate judiciously in how they choose to invest their money across the multiplicity of gig events on offer. In this respect, they are able to exercise agency, which is evident from the way that bands work hard to encourage dancing and other positive audience responses so as to ensure a satisfied client experience and future consumer commitment. Fans can also enter into the commercial framework of production to create their own dancing experiences. Abercrombie and Longhurst (1998, p. 140) describe these entrepreneurial fans as 'petty producers' and, from the participants I interviewed, Vince, Mikey, Chris, Melanie and Jamie had all arranged their own small-scale gigs. While none of these initiatives produce suffi-cient income to constitute a full-time salary, they allow the informants to participate in and influence the micro-economy of their subcultural affiliation. Thus fans are not positioned simply as passive consumers of the music economy and its related industries, but can exercise control over their subcultural investments and interests.

Dancing paradoxical values

In spite of its neglect within subcultural research, the dancing body proves to play a central role in the performance of subcultural identi-ties and participant experience of dancing constructs a complex reality that is a site of multiple meanings and contradictions. Diverse and com-peting values are produced through the dance activities of subcultural participants that are both shaped by and respond to the socioeconomic framework of the live music gig. Thus value is constituted in a dynamic interplay between the institutional apparatus of the commercial record-ing industry, the live performances of the band members and the corpo-real enunciations of fans at the gig event. Notions of aesthetic judgement, concepts of ability, respect and esteem, positions of outsider and insider, community and individuality, codes of subcultural etiquette and image management, expressions of pleasure, release and transformation, and an 'aesthetics of excess' are all articulated through the subcultural dancing body. These elaborate embodied stagings suggest a sophisticated under-standing and enunciation of value within the gig event.

A strong sense of light-hearted play also emerges from the research data, which contrasts with existing research that emphasizes the importance of 'hipness' and 'cool' in subcultural identity formations (Thornton, 1997). Yet the concept of play can also be read through the frameworks and interactions of value that serve to regulate behaviour at the gig event. Although Hutter's (1996) 'theory of play' is rooted in an economic model of value, its basic principles can be usefully applied to other cultural formations to demonstrate how value is created and contended. In Hutter's terms, the 'contingency' of play is bounded by the rules of the gig event, such as its aesthetic codes, economic structure and dancing etiquette. Value is only produced, however, through the 'chance' actions of its participants. Consequently, the 'closure' of play is meaningfully constructed as participants conform to, negotiate, transgress or reinforce the embodied values of the gig event. In terms of whether they choose to dance as a means to signal respect to a band, refuse to dance to demonstrate a lack of investment in the music, dance in a way that pushes the boundaries of acceptable physical aggression, or make physical contact to show community allegiance, participants enter into a play that articulates serious matters of judgement, investment and worth.

While all of the informants spoke of the notion of community and a sense of unity within subcultural experiences of dancing, ambiguities and disparities in the value systems that individuals hold clearly come into play. While gender inclusivity and class diversity are well represented within the subcultural communities, in the areas of punk, metal and second- and third-wave ska there exist racial exclusion through a predominance of white dancing bodies. Hills (2002, p. xiii) identifies how fandom is characterized by sophisticated 'cultural negotiations' that facilitate an elaborate network of values and contradictions. For Muggleton, however, the paradoxical meanings that inform subcultural practice can comfortably coexist:

> to claim from the outside as it were, that people's indigenous meanings are contradictory is to ignore how such apparent contradictions can make perfect, logical sense to those involved given their own definitions of the situation. (2000, p. 59)

This sense of a coherent paradox perfectly encapsulates the multifunctional role that dance can play for subcultural members. In reference to her tendency to dance throughout a gig, Melanie asserts 'if it's a band I'm really enjoying [dancing is] just the icing on the cake; if it's a band I'm not enjoying so much, well, [dancing] keeps me entertained'.

She laughs, aware of the contradiction. Within the subcultural context dancing carries experiential and symbolic value; participants take pleasure in the act of doing and they articulate meanings in their dancing interactions. And while these values are multiple, malleable and paradoxical, they are bounded through the body in a complex spectacle of subcultural performances of worth.

8

'There's a Land That I've Heard About': Envisioning Value at Sunday Serenade

8.30pm: Mirabelle dances[1]

The thudding bass line of a reggae track booms out. A small scattering of people mills around the edges of the room. An elderly couple sits at a table to one side and a middle-aged chap busies himself at the bar. We are drenched in darkness, save a few strings of neon lights. In one corner, a woman in a pink top and black trousers dances on the spot, stepping from foot to foot with her arms swinging gently in opposition. Suddenly, she shuffles to the centre of the dance floor, arms raised in the air. Her knees are deeply bent and she holds a low centre of gravity that lends itself well to the heavy reggae tone. As the track changes, she introduces a new stepping motion, her weight changing softly as she waves her right arm in the air. Regularly, she returns to the corner and then comes back to centre. At one point she traverses with one step much deeper than the other and almost drags her back foot along the ground. She then uses the same movement to edge sideways with hands on hips. Occasionally she extends them out in a gesture of welcome. Another time she moves towards the DJ with her arms raised and makes a chopping action in his direction. Later she remains on the spot, feet grounded and upper back hunched forward, with arms hanging down. As new tracks come on, she introduces even more variation: a sideways step in which one foot repeatedly crosses over; arms held softly forward as if dancing with a partner; and a gentle rolling of the shoulders. During a more upbeat number, she launches into a weighty jogging motion and then steps back and forward, pitching her torso to emphasize the

170

see-saw effect. She hops while turning on the spot, and then gently shuffles from side to side. Now she stamps back and forth, one hand on her hip, the other softly raised. She is immersed in the music and I am captivated too. A gentle hand on my shoulder breaks the spell. It is the elderly lady from the opposite table who welcomes me to the club and assures me that there is no trouble here.[2]

The subject of this chapter is Sunday Serenade, a British Caribbean dance club for the over-40s, located in Bridge Park Community Leisure Centre in Brentfield, North-West London.[3] Although Brent Council manages the venue, the club itself is set up each week by the event organizers in the centre's function suite. Situated just off the capital's North Circular ring road, the venue stands quietly down a drab-looking street. Inside, up the wide grey staircase, one of the regulars sits directly outside the function suite to collect the £5 entrance fee in a small metal tin. Yet through the double doors, the utilitarian space of a multipurpose leisure suite is transformed every Sunday night. A makeshift bar sits opposite the entrance offering a selection of beverages in plastic cups and to the right is the imposing sound system, where the DJs are based.[4] Huge speakers are spaced around the room and several tables line three of the walls, covered with white paper table cloths, tea lights in holders, small vases of flowers and a couple of packets of nuts. Such niceties, along with the flashing neon lights and a few strings of balloons, help disguise the everyday municipal facilities. What strikes me most, however, is the audible and physical impact of the sound. Its considerable volume and depth of tone positively envelop me in the dark enclosed space: my head rings, my chest pulses and my heart bangs. But it is the sight of Mirabelle, the single dancing woman, which visualizes this embodied affinity to the music and forms the starting point for my thinking.

As already detailed, I examine the matter of value in popular dance through a cultural studies approach. One of the criticisms directed at this field is its historic construction of Britishness and nation as rooted in 'whiteness'. Gilroy (1993) describes how the evolution of cultural studies marks an ethnocentric and nationalistic preoccupation with England and Englishness that fails to account for the presence of migrant communities within the British context. Baker et al. (1996) similarly trace how cultural studies produces a paradigm of homogeneity and belonging rooted in a binary of Britishness versus Others, in which 'black' is persistently placed in tension with 'English'. In response to this problematic dialectic, the intervention of a 'black British cultural studies' has come to contest the racist and essentialist view that black migrants and Britain respectively exist as 'fully formed and mutually exclusive cultural communities' (Gilroy, 1993, p. 7). Instead, its concerns lie with more complex enunciations of migrant communities through localized articulations of 'blackness' (Baker et al., 1996).

In a move against the elision or simplification of the black experience in Britain, in this chapter I seek to examine and identify the complexity represented in the popular dance practices of Sunday Serenade. Goldberg (2000) describes how the vernacular music and dance of the racialized Other are always devalued and marginalized as low culture. However, Hall (1992) argues that this marginalization offers a highly productive space through which articulations and negotiations of difference are enacted. It is here that I recall the dancing figure of Mirabelle, whose body appears to express a deep-felt commitment to the reggae music as it blasts out into the enclosed environment of Sunday Serenade. With this powerful image in mind, I recall Dent's (1992, p. 1) useful distinction between 'pleasure' and 'joy', in which the former is an internalized response to a commodified experience, while the latter is rooted in collective and 'non-market values' such as kindness, care and community.[5] Quickly dismissing the stereotypical reading of a 'natural joy' in the expressive practices of black people, Dent (1992) instead suggests that black popular culture offers a site through which identity can be interrogated. Thus, in the context of this chapter, I am less concerned with the internalized experience of pleasure, than with how the joy of dancing produces localized, and at times contradictory, expressions of value, identity and community at Sunday Serenade.

Longing for the homeland

9.30pm: People arrive

> Approximately one hour later, the club is still relatively empty, but Mirabelle continues to dance. Outside the leisure complex, a group of men stand smoking in the cool night air, including Desmond, with his shaved head and dapper pinstripe suit. Eventually, he extinguishes his cigarette and enters the club, greeting people with a shake of the hand or pat on the back. Delores, a big, smiling woman, bustles in straight from her bingo evening and heads towards the elderly seated couple, Evelyn and Clyde, all decked out in her Sunday best. After a quick catch-up, she goes to the bar for a can of Diet Coke. On the other side of the room, elegantly dressed in a white

satin top and a long black skirt, Martha, the wife of the bartender Winston, welcomes a string of couples as they steadily arrive. Stacey, a tall glamorous woman in heels and full 1950s-style skirt, crosses the dance floor, kissing Mirabelle hello on the way past. Almost half an hour later, people are still arriving. Many exchange a few words with Mirabelle as they enter, and all the while she dances to the heavy reggae beat.

The participants I describe above are those I have got to know through my fieldwork visits and several of whom I have interviewed. With the exception of Stacey, who is British-born but of Jamaican parentage, all of my interviewees were Jamaican-born and migrated to the United Kingdom, generally in child- or early adulthood; their ages ranged from 44 to 73.[6] I formally recorded field notes during visits on 21 January, 6 May, 13 May, 20 May and 10 June 2007, but attended the club (usually on a weekly basis) throughout the summer of 2007 and paid several occasional visits during the autumn of 2009. My presence as a white British researcher at a dance event primarily frequented by a British Caribbean community raises complex issues regarding the power relations in participant-based research.[7]

Ghandi (1998) identifies the difficulties inherent in researching marginalized groups in that, although their voices become heard, this exposes and perpetuates their subaltern status. She goes on to question whether a white scholar can ever hope to understand non-white communities (Ghandi, 1998). Gunaratnam (2003) offers some useful responses through her ontological study of research on race and ethnicity, which recognizes the constructed and relational dimensions of these categories. In a summary of 'race-of-interviewer effects' she argues that reflexivity within the interview context is a more fruitful approach than seeking racial matching of interviewer and respondent (Gunaratnam, 2003, p. 90).[8] This recognition of positionality conceives the interview as a dialogue space in which difference is acknowledged and reflected upon (Gunaratnam, 2003).

In remembering my first visit to Sunday Serenade, I recall feelings of anxiety, partly surrounding my racial difference, but also in relation to my position as a lone female attending a late-night club in an area of London with which I was unfamiliar. Yet I also recognize that, as a white, educated researcher investigating this dance event, I hold considerable power in my representation of this community. Although I was personally welcomed to the club by Evelyn, the elderly woman who greeted me on my first visit, my initial relations were awkward.

Figure 8.1   Stacey at Sunday Serenade. Photo copyright © Sherril Dodds.

To mask my insecurity at sitting alone, I attempted to take field notes while observing the dancing, although this only served to create a level of suspicion, which prompted Winston the bartender to question my intentions at the club (field notes, 13 May 2009).[9] This was a difficult confrontation, but when I explained my position as a dance academic and researcher, to some extent this eased my relationship with this dancing community as word seemed to get round regarding my personal and professional interest in the music and dance of Sunday Serenade. Consequently, several participants approached me to enquire about my research and I gained greater confidence in talking to people about their dance and music interests. Without exception, they were warm and willing respondents, keen to share their experiences. Indeed, after a period of absence, during my return to the club in autumn 2009 I was welcomed by several of the participants as a friend or companion rather than in the formal role of researcher. Yet, while I observe that I was able to overcome certain boundaries in terms of researcher–participant relations, this does not eliminate the issue of race as a positional and hierarchical structure. My presence and actions in the field are always circumscribed by my subjectivity as a white British researcher and I am conscious of this as I write about the dancing bodies at Sunday Serenade.

To return to the dancing figure of Mirabelle, I am tempted to read her as a quintessential Caribbean body. 'Dreamland', a well-known reggae anthem by Bunny Wailer, frequently plays at Sunday Serenade and I watch Mirabelle wave her outstretched arm in the air along to the lyrics, 'there's a land that I've heard about...' (field notes, 13 May 2007). Images of longing for a homeland resonate through Mirabelle's dance, her eyes closed, palm facing out, in a complex expression of solidarity, fantasy and remembering. Consequently, this evokes an idea that the participants in Sunday Serenade are united through a mythical heritage tracing back to a common African ancestry, which Gilroy (1987) describes as 'pan-Africanism', or to a Caribbean national identity, which Anderson (1991) conceives as an 'imagined community'. This notion of a unified past located in the memory of a homeland is seductive, given that the participants whom I interviewed spoke at length about how their dancing experiences at Sunday Serenade facilitated a remembering of their Caribbean heritage:

> I used to love the sound, 'cause I used to live in the countryside, you see. And they used to have a dance, say, once every two weeks in a special place, like. And I used to go there as a kid. I was only about

12. Going there and watching them dance. And I used to love the way they were dancing and I loved to hear the music. (Desmond, 10 July 2007)

Memories! Memories of, like, my growing-up days in Jamaica when my mum and my dad used to have this, we used to call it a record changer, they used to play on a Sunday afternoon. Memories most of it, just memories. (Francine, 2 June 2009)

Those memories, it never leave, it always there. Because it used to be good fun. We used to have very, very good fun. Because my mother, my father, my sister, brothers and aunts, everyone always dance together. And that is fond memory. And I could never, ever forget it. (Delores, 5 July 2007)

Because you're away from your homeland, how many years you are living in a different country, you still want to associate with the country, so no matter what happens: I was born in Jamaica and will always associate with Jamaica no matter what happens. (Claudia, 23 July 2009)

Each of the participants values a strong connection between the music and dance at Sunday Serenade and memories of Jamaica. Yet I would

Figure 8.2   Delores and her niece at Sunday Serenade. Photo copyright © Sherril Dodds.

argue that this direct corporeal relationship to a fixed Caribbean past is a problematic one.

Disrupting identity through music and dance

10.30pm: Everyone dances

> The club slowly fills up, although there continues to be a steady trickle of people through the door for at least another half-hour, and the mellow reggae sounds are gradually replaced by more upbeat tunes that comprise ska, rocksteady, soul, Motown and rhythm and blues music. Mirabelle remains one of the few dancing figures who occupy the centre of the dance floor, but the club is now littered with other moving bodies. Martha dances solo, using fast, energetic footwork and lively gesticulation; later I spot her with Winston performing a well executed jive. Stacey stands to the side of the room with a slightly younger crowd, stepping on the spot as she undulates her hips and rolls her shoulders in time to the music. She sings along to the track, enunciating it with expressive hand actions. Francine wears a brightly patterned top and short black skirt. Her hair is piled up in a head band and her eyes are painted with vivid purples and oranges. She dances flamboyantly, gyrating her hips, shoulders and torso. A ska track comes on and Desmond stands directly in front of the DJ decks and launches into a high-energy 'shuffling' motif. Watching Claudia, I see a flash of salsa. In addition to the regulars that I recognize, I observe a wide variety of dancing bodies and styles. A man in a stylish grey suit, with long dreadlocks tied at the back, is one of the rare few who briefly takes centre-stage. He performs nifty footwork, based on a rapid 'step-ball-change' action, which closely follows the rhythm of the music. Three women dance exuberantly to a Motown number, while two others stand side by side, dressed in elegant heels, skirts and hand-bags, swaying gently in unison to the track. I catch one man 'skank-ing' to a ska tune, arms crossing from side to side in front of his body with an accompanying rocking motion, and another woman executing a classic-looking twist. Many people 'slow dance' regard-less of the time of evening or genre of music. Some do this casu-ally, with a friend or acquaintance, chatting as they do so and then moving on. Others are locked intimately together, barely moving except for a slight tilting of the pelvis, a dance which Francine calls the 'cool and deadly'. Consequently, the single figure of Mirabelle

is replaced by a plethora of people displaying a range of highly individualized dance styles.

The above description contests an essentialist reading of Mirabelle as the representative Caribbean body at Sunday Serenade. The initial image of the solo reggae dancer typifying a lost Caribbean heritage gives way to a multiplicity of male and female bodies engaged in a diversity of dance and music practices.

The idea of the Caribbean as a stable and bounded nation is complicated by its histories of colonialism and migration. Murdoch (2007) identifies how the Spanish conquest of 1600 brought with it levels of labour and disease that almost eradicated the indigenous community, so now its contemporary population is primarily constituted by peoples who initially arrived through migration or slavery. Drawing on the work of Stuart Hall, Murdoch (2007) conceives the Caribbean as a creolized space and its identity as diasporic in character. This unfixing of a stable national heritage is further troubled through reflecting on the 'British Caribbean' experience of the participants at Sunday Serenade. Gilroy (1993) eloquently unsettles the category 'black British' through his assertion that it is neither unified nor fixed. He argues that black Europeans experience a 'double consciousness' in what appears to be an incompatible coupling of 'black' and 'white' that is rooted in national difference (Gilroy, 1993, p. 1).[10]

Within the British cultural imagination, this duality of racial and national inscription plays out in the symbolic imagery of the *Empire Windrush* as it came into dock in 1948 and marked the arrival of West Indian immigrants to Britain (Phillips and Phillips, 1999). In occupying an identity position as both black and British, the presence of this migrant community prompted an historical and material intervention in the absolutist paradigm of discrete cultural nationalisms (Gilroy, 1993). Consequently, the ontology of 'Black British' mobilizes a crisis of identity in which questions of heritage and authenticity are troubled, and a similar contestation or negotiation of national identity is staged through the participants in Sunday Serenade. While they all related their dancing experiences back to memories of their Caribbean heritage, it was equally apparent that their tastes and values concerning dance and music had also been informed by their British pasts.

Desmond formerly worked as a disc jockey in London from about 1971–85, playing at the Apollo Club in Willesden and the Candy Box in the West End. While the artists he played, 'Bob Marley, Gregory Isaacs, Freddie McGregor and Sugar Minott', are all Jamaican-born, their recording careers involve international performance, consumption and acclaim.

For instance, from the 1970s Bob Marley consciously internationalized his reggae compositions through speeding up the beat and adding blues rock guitar and gospel backing vocals (Davis, 2009); reggae artist Gregory Isaacs's material is performed in a 'romantic rock style' (Steffens, 2009); and Freddie McGregor's album *Anything For You* (2002) was nominated for a Grammy award by The Recording Academy of America (*http://www.freddiemcgregor.com*, accessed 16 October 2009). Tied to this interest in international recognition Desmond describes how he abandoned a recording career to disseminate reggae music to the audiences at his local music and dance venue: 'I love Bob Marley's music. Right. I love the message in his music. So I became a DJ from there at the Apollo Club.' The conscious internationalization of Marley's music offered Jamaican musicians access to European and American audiences familiar with these popular music styles and this cultural transmission was literally played out through Desmond's migrant passage from Jamaica to London.

The British Caribbean community of Sunday Serenade first encountered these transnational musical forms in such clubs. Indeed, Delores recounts attending the Apollo as a young woman, Evelyn (10 June 2007) frequently visited Hammersmith Palais and Desmond was a regular at

Figure 8.3   Desmond at Sunday Serenade. Photo copyright © Sherril Dodds.

The Flamingo in Wardour Street. Consequently the participants' formative dancing experiences took place as much in 1960s and 70s London
as they did in prelapsarian Jamaica and it is in these migrant contexts
that music and dance knowledges continue to be acquired.[11] Claudia
routes this learning experience back to her teenage years at Kilburn
Polytechnic in London:

> we used to go to parties and obviously you get to know the beats and
> new dances that came out. And at the party they'd be teaching you
> the latest dance and then you'd all do the same dance.

Thus I would argue that the participants in Sunday Serenade cannot be contained by an essentialist Caribbean identity. Gilroy (1993)
usefully problematizes the idea of a fixed nationalism through the
trope of the 'Black Atlantic' in which black British expressive practices
are constituted through Caribbean, American and African forms that
are recontextualized in a British frame. To explain this cultural transmission, Gilroy (1993) evokes the metaphor of the slave ship and its travels across the Middle Passage to illustrate how political and expressive
practices are carried across Europe, Africa, America and the Caribbean.
This model dismisses the idea of a national essentialism and replaces it
with the notion of transnational production.

Part of what seems to appeal to the participants in Sunday Serenade is
the diversity of music styles on offer, which largely reflect their remembered music experiences. I interpret this, however, not simply as a
passively situated reminiscing, but as an active reconnection to the imagined Jamaican homeland. Below is a sample of responses to my question
regarding the genres of music that drew participants to the event:

> Well everything actually, because I grew up with that music. I started
> from rock 'n' roll, Elvis Presley and Chubby Checker, well I come up
> to Chubby Checker and most of the black Americans and we had
> things like the merengue, which is South American-type, the salsa
> is taken from that part of the South as well, it come from the meren-
> gue, it's got a Spanish background to it, and calypso. (Raymond)

> The Alton Ellis, the John Holt, the Ken Boothe, that sort of
> music...Some of the modern stuff, R & B. Yes, the old Smokey
> Robinson, Patti LaBelle, Gladys Knight, that sort of era...I'm inter-
> ested in Motown as well. (Francine)

> I like, well my original music was reggae from the 1970s, and obvi-
> ously soul, soul music as well, but it's introduced me to a wider range

Figure 8.4 Francine from Sunday Serenade. Photo copyright © Sherril Dodds.

of music, my mother's age…so therefore I'm picking up on music that was my mother's tunes from her youth, when she was younger, and getting to learn about the sort of music. The ska and obviously rock 'n' roll. (Claudia)

What strikes me is the vast range of styles that emerge from a wide range of contexts within and beyond the Caribbean. At Sunday Serenade, I frequently hear popular African American music: for example, Sam Cooke's 'Twistin' The Night Away' (1962), Diana Ross and The Supremes's 'Where Did Our Love Go' (1964), Stevie Wonder's 'Signed, Sealed, Delivered' (1970) and The Jackson 5's 'Rockin' Robin' (1972). Although some of the music (in particular ska, rock steady and reggae) has strong associations with Jamaica, Heathcott (2003) describes them as transnational forms articulated in localized spaces of production and consumption. For example, first-wave ska, which emerged in the dancehalls of Jamaica in the early 1960s and is more typically played at Sunday Serenade than later styles, is indebted to traditional and contemporary musical sources that span British, American and Jamaican popular forms (Heathcott, 2003). Although I have already referenced the globalization of Bob Marley's music, there are further examples of how reggae is transnational in character. During one visit (6 May 2007), I heard the popular reggae version of 'Everything I Own' (1974) by Ken Boothe from Kingston, Jamaica, which was originally written by David Gates, from Tulsa, Oklahoma, as a soft-rock track for his American band Bread, but became a number one in the UK British popular music charts (Barrow and Dalton, 2001); at another (18 October 2009), the DJ played a reggae version of 'Blackbird', a song composed and performed by quintessential British pop band The Beatles. These few examples perfectly illustrate how musical styles and influences migrate and mutate across national borders.

Precisely the same diversity exists within the dancing bodies at Sunday Serenade. As Delores observes,

you never find everyone on the dance floor doing the same dance. Everyone do their thing a little bit different. So, it's absolutely gorgeous. I love it.

Of particular interest are the ways in which different styles are circulated as part of a migrational passage to Sunday Serenade. For instance, Raymond initially reflects upon his early dancing experiences in

Jamaica and identifies the impact of rock 'n' roll, as presented through white North American recording artists, on his dancing aspirations:

> it was mostly rock 'n' roll in them days, it was calypso then rock 'n' roll, course those days they'd have Bill Haley and his Comets just came in doing 'rock rock rock' and everyone want to dance like Billy Haley. And Elvis Presley, you know, 'Kissing Cousin', this sort of thing.

Yet he also recalls his early life in the United Kingdom in which he became friendly with a group of Irish men with whom he would socialize at an Irish working club and this too offered some formative dancing experiences:

> The Galtimore. Still going!...I used to go there and have a dance. In fact I was taught to do the steps, the Irish steps, by the Irish ladies.

Similar pedagogic encounters are recalled by other participants. As a British Caribbean woman, Martha's (27 May, 2007) acquisition of another dance style is not through her migrant passage, but through travel opportunities afforded by global tourism:

> Well, I went to Cuba last year and in Cuba they do a lot of salsa. And we went into the bushes and they had this restaurant and the guys who were playing the music and he was teaching me to do the salsa. So I caught on a little bit of it.

Likewise, Raymond recounts how he picked up linedancing during a holiday cruise, and as part of her leisure activities Evelyn attends ballroom dancing classes. Thus, in reflecting upon the lives of this British Caribbean community and their transnational music and dance practices, it is hardly surprising that I see examples of jiving, twisting, shuffling, skanking, salsa and the 'cool and deadly', along with all manner of highly individualized styles. This diversity of movement practices, performed by both men and women, could be conceived as an 'aesthetics of inclusion', which is further supported by the rhetoric of belonging that I explore later in the chapter. Yet I question whether I can unproblematically replace the essentialized Jamaican reggae body as typified by Mirabelle in my initial observations with a diverse community of dancers each engaged in coexistent, transnational, expressive practices.

The myth of multiculturalism

Gilroy (1993) comments on how the racial injustices of modernity have been replaced by a postmodernism which is characterized by an apolitical relativism. This critique, which lends itself to the inclusive philosophies of multiculturalism and cultural diversity, echoes elsewhere. Ghandi (1998) describes multiculturalism as a naïve utopia in its celebration of cultural diversity that neatly sidesteps difficult questions of social and economic inequity. Likewise, Bharucha (2000) positions it as an institutionalized concept that promotes an uncontested coexistence between different ethnic communities, but which results in a depoliticization of racial difference. Lo (2003) calls upon the terminology of 'hybridity' as a useful means to reflect upon the migrant experience. Her first understanding conceives hybridity as an unproblematic fusion of two discrete elements that salves notions of difference and is therefore populist and apolitical in style. She describes this in terms of a 'happy hybridity' typical of a postmodern relativism (Lo, 2003, p. 153). Thus a reading of Sunday Serenade as a uniform site of multicultural expression and its participants as the inhabitants of a coherent mix of British and Caribbean identities seriously neglects issues of difference and inequality.

Lo's second definition, however, employs a postcolonial lens as a politically reflexive means to understand hybridity, in that it has 'the potential to unsettle and dismantle hegemonic relations because it focuses on the process of negotiation and contestation between cultures' (2003, p. 153). Drawing on the linguistic work of Mikhail Bakhtin, she sees this as an 'intentional hybridity' which questions its position within a particular social and historical space (Lo, 2003, p. 154). Consequently, this state of 'in-betweenness' (Lo, 2003, p. 156) offers opportunity to critique hierarchies of race, nation and cultural identity. Bhabha (1990) also offers another useful lens for troubling essentialist categories of race and nation. He reflects upon nation as a totalizing discourse, but argues that 'the people' present a lived challenge to the coherency of this rhetorical hegemony. He describes how the people historically represent a 'national pedagogy' and in the living moment perform 'nation' through repeated quotidian acts. Yet a tension arises between the pedagogic and performative as individuals have the capacity to produce liminal performances that contest the coherence of nation. Bhabha (1990, p. 299) conceives this as a 'double-writing' or 'dissemi-*nation*', to describe how the people performatively expose its paradoxes. In relation to Sunday Serenade, the authority of the pedagogic construction of a unified British or Caribbean nation is destabilized through the embodied expressions of transnational dance and music productions that unsettle fixed notions of identity contained within the discrete borders of a cultural nationalism.

Values of belonging

While I dispute readings of Sunday Serenade either as an essentialist Caribbean community or as a harmonious site of multiculturalism, there are certainly clear indicators of belonging that bring me back to Dent's (1992) notion of a 'collective joy'. The participants whom I interviewed expressed a strong level of commitment to Sunday Serenade in that they had all been attending the club (usually on a weekly basis) for about three or four years. The organization of the space in which the club takes place creates an acute disjunction from the outside world. Set back from a bland concrete side street, in which a continuous hum of night-time traffic passes by, the club is hidden within an otherwise deserted leisure complex, behind the double doors of the function suite. Once inside, the dark space, fluorescent neon and thunderous bass-lines stake out a sensory enclosure that intensifies proximity with others through the stark contrast between inside and outside. Yet other values of belonging operate within the club beyond its function as a shared site of visual, sonic and kinetic pleasures.

First, the matter of age appears to produce an important point of connection between people as several participants reflected that the promotion of the club as an over-30s event was a clear attraction:

> One Sunday we were there feeling a bit bored and my friend said oh, if I could find somewhere to go, and I said, oh I heard this place advertising on the radio for the over-30s that I think it would suit us, so we decided to go. (Francine)

> When you see all those young people doing them thing, I mean there's no way I could get up and do as what them younger generation doing these last days. So I prefer to stick with the over-30s and over-50s, us go to Sunday Serenade. (Delores)

On one hand this identification of age might relate to participants' desire to hear music of the past that may not be of interest to a younger generation. On the other, this connection ties participants to values that they associate with a mature clientele:

> Well, there's no young kids screaming, shouting and running about, there's no guns, no knife culture, no hoodies. You name it! It's just pure, clean enjoyment. That's what it is. (Stacey)

I think it's nice, the fun is clean. You know it's clean, there's not a lot of smoking. You can go there, 'cause it's from 8 to 12 only and like Bank Holiday or special occasions, you'll get like an hour extra or so. You can go home and get up for work. You don't feel tired out when you're out. So it's nice, short and spicy. (Francine)

And the type of people that go to Sunday Serenade, I mean, you find if you go to a younger generation party these last days, majority of the time you seem to have some sort of trouble there…But when you go to Sunday Serenade everybody's so together. You've got none time to make trouble or argument with other people. You just get on with your own thing. (Delores)

The above quotations suggest a generational distancing from values associated with youth cultures and a privileging of moral virtues that produce a series of binary oppositions: good/bad, clean/dirty, safe/dangerous, old/young. While it may well be that the perception of youth as a source of social anxiety forms a common concern across a range of communities, Gilroy (1987) examines how British Caribbeans carry the 'representative burden' of black crime.[12] In a discursive analysis of official government reports on crime and policing, Gilroy (1987) carefully traces how representations of black criminality have been constructed to produce racial difference rooted in deviancy, unemployment and threat to the nation state. In the 1940s, 50s and 60s, social concerns directed at Caribbean migrants were rooted predominantly in fears of miscegenation and a housing crisis (Gilroy, 1987). The 1970s produced a turning point, however, in which black criminality was strategically employed to produce a moral panic concerning race, legality and nation (Gilroy, 1987). Irrespective of actual crime statistics, which Gilroy (1987) argues were relatively low and positioned within the context of white youth problems according to a 1973 Select Committee Report on Race Relations and Immigration, by 1976 a series of incidents between police and black youths centred around the cultural sites of British Caribbean discos, dancehalls and street festivals consequently tied black criminality to cultural expression. Given this legacy, it is perhaps not surprising that the participants in Sunday Serenade are keen to promote this event as a safe, clean space.

Building on these ideas of moral respectability, the second key value that produces a sense of community cohesion at Sunday Serenade is in relation to attire. While a small minority of participants attend in casual clothes, the majority clearly dress up for the occasion.

The women wear elegant skirts, dresses or evening trousers and the men come in smart trousers and shirts or two- or three-piece suits. Although the men are often dressed in darker tones, on occasions I have seen more flamboyant wear: one evening I saw a man in a white suit and shirt, with dreadlocks tied back under an enormous white fur hat; another wearing a white shirt, bow-tie and white baggy trousers; and Theobald, one of the regulars, in a matching red bow-tie and waistcoat. Not surprisingly, the participants are attentive to the importance of dress:

> Always wear a suit, most of the time I dress up. I like to look presentable. (Desmond)
>
> Well to me it's a special evening, so I dress up. Something that says I'm going out like to a party ... It's like you're going to a night club. I dress up. I dress up to go out on Sunday. (Claudia)

While I did not speak to participants about their religious beliefs as part of my interview schedule, there emerged a sense of occasion linked to a Sunday, which suggests a remembering of, or reconnecting to, the importance of this day in family life and an active re-creation of that formality at Sunday Serenade:

> Well, maybe as you notice, people do make an effort to look good and it looks better. It's not as if you're going to work. It's a Sunday. And originally, Sunday, you remember about the Sunday best? People go for the best on a Sunday! (Raymond)

For Stacey, her choice of attire signals a self-conscious identification with the past:

> I like to wear clothes that are kind of like back to that time, if you know what I mean. So I do wear a lot of '50s-style stuff because it actually goes with the style of the music, the style of the place and the style of the dance.

This indicates that the attention to dress allows participants to reimagine their Caribbean heritage within the context of Sunday Serenade. McMillan (2009) offers some useful ideas regarding the grooming and impression management of West Indian families. McMillan uses the trope of the 'front room' to examine how the Caribbean diaspora employs this living space as a public interface that produces questions

Figure 8.5 Theobald at Sunday Serenade. Photo copyright © Sherril Dodds.

of memory and identity in relation to experiences of migration, postcolonialism and globalization. He states:

> the dressing and maintenance of the front room reveals a form of 'impression management', as in the flexible presentation of self that brings up issues of 'good grooming' among people of African descent. (McMillan, 2009, p. 137)

He conceives these strategies of decorum and etiquette as a means to negotiate the diasporic experience. In doing so, he draws on Stuart Hall's notion of 'frontlines'/'backyard' whereby the former is the public intersection between black and white culture and the latter is a more private exploration of those differences. This raises some fascinating questions regarding the 'site/sight' of Sunday Serenade. With the exception of one individual, all of my interviews took place in the participants' 'front rooms'. These lived spaces did not always demonstrate the good grooming suggested by McMillan and instead displayed a wide spectrum of economic capital and social class: some participants had mortgaged properties in respectable postcode areas of central London, while others lived in rented accommodation that ranged from small houses on council estates to a single-room studio flat; some displayed great decorative finesse with plush furnishings and opulent ornamentation, while others were clearly of more limited means, including one which revealed extremely poor living conditions. This particular participant lived in a single room, littered with dirty ashtrays, bottles of alcohol and piles of old cassettes, with a mattress for a bed and a metal clothes rail for a wardrobe. Yet in spite of this debased home environment, he turned out to Sunday Serenade in absolutely immaculate dress.

Regardless of significant inequalities within participants' private lives, within the social space of Sunday Serenade sartorial etiquette is valued highly. Consequently, Sunday Serenade forms an important site in which social protocols are made visible. While the everyday realities of wealth and class are played out unevenly in the domestic setting (or 'backyard'), the public forum (or 'front line') of Sunday Serenade allows participants to stage their embodied affiliation with Caribbean music and dance practices through a model of community belonging that favours good personal grooming and high moral standards. At Sunday Serenade I therefore identify a reinscription of value that is less concerned with the capital worth and social status that circulate on 'the outside', than with the generational values and codes of dress enacted within.

While the participants I interviewed emphatically stated that the club is for anyone, the predominance of British Caribbeans (of Jamaican heritage in particular) cannot be ignored. Although I aim against readings that either unite participants through an essentialized Caribbean identity or lose them in an apolitical multiculturalism, the club fosters a strong sense of imagined community belonging:

> Well, a lot of them are people I know. It's a place where we meet up on a Sunday night. It's a special occasion for me all the time. I look forward to it every Sunday night. (Desmond)

> People just come and, as you probably will notice, that the people really come to enjoy, I keep telling the people come from all parts of London, even Luton and, you know, you go there for dancing. They enjoy three or four hours that you're there. And you just give it your best. Most people are non-stop dancers. You just keep dancing until the session finish. (Raymond)

> The majority of people there have been going since it opened, and we've all become like a little family. You know, if one doesn't turn up, somebody notices that you're not there and, you know, they're all friendly, they're all like my substitute mum and dad, if you know what I mean. So it's really nice. (Stacey)

Although the participants make no explicit reference to racial or national identifications, these are often played out at the event itself through acknowledgement of cultural affiliations and family belonging. For instance, participants are encouraged to share in each other's celebrations and one evening two people were called out by name so that everyone could wish them Happy Birthday; Winston and Martha were presented with a bouquet of flowers for their 34th wedding anniversary; and another moving back to St Lucia was blessed with good wishes (27 May 2007). The microphone at the DJ booth is frequently used as a tool to engender strong community relations, cultural interests and even political mobilization.[13] After playing the reggae anthem 'Soul Rebel' by Bob Marley, the DJ announces 'it's 26 years yesterday since Bob Marley passed away…the King!' (13 May 2007). Similarly, after 'We Are Family' by Sister Sledge, the event organizer states 'we are family and don't forget it' (20 May 2007). Later that evening, a woman spontaneously takes the microphone and tells people that they should not take notice of anyone else and they came here to have a good time so they should get on and party (20 May 2007). Thus notions of community, solidarity and unification resonate throughout the club event.

Paradoxically, Sunday Serenade does not value an 'aesthetics of inclusion' or belonging rooted in sameness as participants exercise a diversity of musical tastes and dance practices. Likewise, participants share radically different experiences of economic wealth, but enjoy common connections through age, etiquette and sartorial style. And the notion of 'family' does not refer literally to immediate blood relatives, but is imagined through a broad reconnection to a Jamaican heritage enacted within the circumscribed site of a London club, which speaks to a localized, extended and temporary sense of belonging. Although Sunday Serenade forms a transitory community, in that its membership is neither fixed nor permanent, its participants value and iterate performances of belonging.

The politics of diasporic identity

The field of diaspora studies offers a useful way to make sense of these articulations of community value and belonging. Diaspora refers to the displacement of people through migration or exile and constitutes an important challenge to fixed boundaries of nation and identity (Braziel and Mannur, 2003). Although the concept of diaspora often assumes dislocation from a homeland, as I stated at the beginning of this chapter I do not want to perpetuate the romantic myth that Sunday Serenade enacts a longing for a common point of origin in the form of an authentic Caribbean; instead, I am more concerned with how the 'lived experience' (Braziel and Mannur, 2003, p. 9) of diasporic identity is enacted and recontextualized within the host country. Lowe (2003) draws on the work of Antonio Gramsci to describe how subaltern communities are not recognized by the state. Although she argues that they are not a coherent and unified group, their marginal status suggests an allied position, which forms a political strength. She reflects on how essentialist categories, like black/white, majority/minority, are unsatisfactory means through which to delimit immigrant communities, which require more complex axes to describe their identities (Lowe, 2003). Indeed, identity is reframed as always in a process of becoming (Hall, 2003), thus perpetually mutating and reforming (Solomos and Back, 1996).

Yet questions of identity and political affiliation are complex. Hall (1996b) questions how to produce a solidarity of resistance while recognizing heterogeneity. In a critique of multicultural relativism, he calls for a new politics that 'engages' rather than 'suppresses difference' (Hall, 1996b, p. 169). Hall (2003) conceives diasporic identity as a 'play' of difference in that simple binaries of us/them, past/present do not suffice. As detailed earlier, these differences are quite literally played on the Sunday Serenade dance floor through the diversity of music and dance styles on display. In particular, Hall (2003, p. 240) rethinks British Caribbean identity through African, European and American 'presences' which acknowledges the heterogeneity and hybridity of the diasporic experience.[14] This again reflects the complex play of influences and traces that inform the embodied cultural practices at Sunday Serenade. Appadurai (2003, p. 39) suggests that part of the coping strategy for diasporas is to create 'invented traditions' that express kinship and identity through 'transnational spectacles' (2003, p. 42). Although Lowe also describes the diasporic experience as a loss of traditional culture she sees a more nuanced understanding of tradition that is 'partly inherited, partly modified, as well as partly invented' (Lowe, 2003, p. 136). Although Sunday Serenade could be read as a fabricated expression of a Caribbean identity, I argue that it plays out 'difference' in a far more complicated staging of people's diasporic histories, which includes Jamaican and British pasts that have facilitated multiple embodied engagements with transnational music and dance forms. In Hall's (2003) terms, these multifarious 'presences' set into play the contested identities of British Caribbeans within the site/sight of the dance floor. Situated in a complex position of 'in-betweenness' (Lo, 2003) or 'dissemi-*nation*' (Bhabha, 1990), the participants in Sunday Serenade are never singularly British or Jamaican. In response they seek to reconnect with an imagined Jamaica, but all the while bearing traces of their transnational migration. Sunday Serenade therefore offers a spatialized gathering through which the instabilities of their dislocated identities are temporarily fixed through performative acts of 'family belonging' articulated through values of dance, etiquette and grooming.

Although the concept of diaspora forms a helpful strategy through which to conceptualize the traces of past and present expressive practices emerging from passages of music and dance that cross Africa, America, Britain and the Caribbean and intersect within the embodied experience of Sunday Serenade, I seek not to lose sight of other material realities that this community faces. Lowe (2003) references Frantz Fanon in a warning of how the bourgeoisie can replace the colonial order in diasporic contexts so that social and economic relations continue to ensure separatism. Consequently, Sunday Serenade must not be read as a diasporic community in isolation, but the relations between diaspora and host nation need also to be addressed.

During the interviews, several of the participants reflected on how matters of race had impacted upon their lived experiences of Britain. Although at various times Desmond, Raymond and Claudia mentioned social events that were racially mixed, the participants also commented on how British Caribbeans were initially marginalized within the context of British social life and, as a consequence, had to produce their own music and dance events:

> Well, in early days, you have to break into these things, you know. In those days there were the first Race Relations Act, I think in about 1962 or something. Prior to that they could easily say, sorry you can't come in...And then we organized our own functions at small organizations that we belonged to. We used places like the Porchester Hall and Lyceum Ballroom, that sort of thing, and organized dances. (Raymond)

> At those times, no, there weren't any. Unless you make a little party, if it's your birthday, you'd have your friends round and you offer them a drink or they might bring a little drink with them. And then you might have a little dance, we used to put on the records and play it in the house. (Evelyn)

> In those days the Lyceum Ballroom, I think those were the ones organized by my mum, well 'cause she was an entertainments manager for a club, a West Indian club that was in this side of London, so we used to go out a lot. In those days, as Afro-Caribbeans, they didn't have our entertainment so we had to put it on ourselves. (Claudia)

Participants employ precisely the same strategy with Sunday Serenade. The club is organized by British Caribbeans who draw on their own resources to provide entertainment that arguably services their diasporic needs. Notably, while the £5 entrance fee primarily covers venue and sound system hire, the relatively low admission price reflects the inclusive ethos of the club. This micro-economy therefore facilitates opportunities for British Caribbeans to participate in expressive practices perceived as important to their sense of cultural identity. Furthermore, this economic capital circulates within the control of British Caribbean producers and consumers and is therefore safeguarded from commercial exploitation by the economic mainstream. Consequently, historical practices of exclusion are contested through strategies of inclusion, which produces a further reinscription of value.

Goldberg (2000) conceives racial knowledge and difference as an articulation of power and Solomos and Back (1996, p. xiv) describe race as a 'discursive category' that demarcates social difference, but which also produces material realities. Thus, while racial identity can be understood as a construction or representation, the social inequities it produces impact upon the historical realities of people's lives. Hall (1996b) therefore argues that race needs to be read in relation to other social formations and economic practices and the interview data evidences how members of Sunday Serenade were faced with the materialities of racial injustice. As Evelyn recalls,

> It wasn't very easy for black people. It was very very tough ... We didn't even know that we could get loans from the banks to get somewhere to live. We didn't know we could get a council flat, we didn't know nothing. No-one guide us along. (Evelyn)

Indeed, Raymond explains how the Bridge Park Community Leisure Centre, where Sunday Serenade takes place, was created to accommodate the needs of black British people in the local area.

> Well you must have heard in the media black-on-black killing and all that sort of thing in them areas, so when they thought of this centre, can't remember how much it cost to build, opened by Prince Charles and that sort of thing, so it meant to be a good place, but bad boys used to infiltrate the place and give it a bad name. But it is a good place really.

The issues that Raymond raises here articulate the complex reality of black British life. The idea that black British people need a site for community activity attests to the sentiments outlined above in which participants experienced a disenfranchisement from the cultural practices, social networks and economic opportunities awarded to white British subjects. Sunday Serenade takes place within the London Borough of Brent, which 'is one of only two Boroughs in England and Wales where, for the first time, "BME" [Black and Minority Ethnic] groups now represent a greater proportion than white groups' (Brent Council, 2004, p. 5).[15] Within the borough, 'close to a quarter of Brent's resident population is deemed to be living in overcrowded conditions' (Brent Council, 2004, p. 5) and 'unemployment rates are highest amongst Black or Black British' (Brent Council, 2004, p. 15). It is then ironic that Prince Charles, one of the most representative figures of the British establishment and its imperialist heritage, was invited to open the centre. Raymond's comment 'so it meant to be a good place' recognizes that Prince Charles as the white British heir of the monarchy validates the centre through his privileged relationship to race, nation and power. As discussed earlier, underpinning this is an historical and racially bound power relationship situated around moral and social value and, although Raymond does not describe the 'bad boys' who challenge the values and aspirations for the centre in racial terms, his earlier reference to 'black-on-black killings' clearly positions the problem within the black community. This speaks to an uncomfortable awareness of the way that British Caribbeans are read through the racial lens of black criminality (Gilroy, 1987) and Raymond's insistence that it is a 'good place' echoes Evelyn's reassurance during my first visit to Sunday Serenade that there is 'no trouble here'.

Although Skeggs (2004) focuses on class identity, she argues that class constitutes an inscription that can only be understood through other subject positions like race, gender, nation and so on, and while some people have the power to use these inscriptions as a resource, others are fixed by them. For Skeggs (2004, p. 6), class is a 'knowledge position' that reflects the interests of a particular group and views others through limited representations. She describes how nation forms one of the value systems that produces symbolic belonging and how whiteness is inscribed at the centre of that power and therefore represents national belonging (Skeggs, 2004). The importance of addressing class in relation to race and how that intersection produces particular values and knowledge emerges in other areas of scholarship. Goldberg (2000, p. 166) references Gunnar Myrdal's concept of the 'underclass' to describe those peoples underemployed and disenfranchised in postindustrial society. He goes on to argue that the popular media read the underclass racially as an 'undeserving poor' on the basis of black stereotypes linked to drug use, welfare reliance, laziness and criminality. From this, Goldberg (2000, p. 170) employs the term 'racially marginalized' to include both economic and racial poverty. Similarly, Gilroy (1987) recognizes how class and race intersect within the history of British immigration and therefore black British communities are unified and essentialized as working class.

These ideas resonate strongly in relation to the interview data and the 'racial marginalization' experienced by participants, which includes restricted access to social, cultural and economic opportunities, also extends to profession. Although some of the participants are retired, areas of employment, both past and present, covered the following professions and sectors: DJ, bus driver, carer, machine operator, Post Office worker, British Rail administrator, cashier, launderette assistant, customer services and insurance. From the participants' descriptions, this work primarily falls into the categories of unskilled or semi-skilled labour in that it requires little specialist training. Only one of the participants whom I interviewed was a 'management professional' and none had entered into full-time Higher Education.[16] While I recognize fully that my interview sample includes only a small cross-section of people attending a venue in a London borough low in socioeconomic wealth, these findings significantly complicate the relativist and apolitical ideal of the multicultural or postnational community and instead call attention to the 'intentional hybridity' or 'dissemi-*nation*' that Lo (2003) and Bhabha (1990) respectively discuss as a troubling exposure of the social, cultural and economic paradoxes encountered by migrant communities.

While I do not set out to simplify and homogenize the lived experiences of this British Caribbean community, several of the participants commented on how the event serves as a form of escape from their quotidian existence:

> Like I said before, it's my way of expressing all those pent-up feelings during that week. It's just a way of releasing, you know? Yeah, just releasing the pressure for those couple of hours that you're there. And that's it, it's all gone. It's like going on holiday, you know, and you forget about everything and it all clicks back into place as soon as you go back. (Stacey)

> It's lovely. It's nice. You forget all your cares, you forget all your troubles. You know, you're free, you're just with it. You forget about everything else. Your cares, your trouble and your woe, you know? You know, dancing is a great part of one's life. (Evelyn)

> I work hard and that's the only time you really get to unwind with your friends and feel good within yourself. I might in the day say, I'm feeling really tired, I'm not going there and even if I go I'm not gonna dance, but as soon as I hear the music start playing, oh you forget about tiredness. (Francine)

> It take away all your problem...but, you know, when you're dancing you forget all about it. I mean, go to Sunday Serenade on Sundays and maybe the problem is there Sunday, you go and you dancing, you dance that problem away. And then maybe Monday it might come back [laughs] and then Sunday, you can go dance it off again. So I think dancing play a good part in my life really. I just love it. (Delores)

Although ideas of escapism are commonly referenced in relation to vernacular dance practice, I equally wish to acknowledge the challenging realities of the participants' racialized class position which emerges through the interview data. [17]

Visible dancing values at Sunday Serenade

As an end to this chapter, I want to make claim for the capacity of the dancing body at Sunday Serenade to negotiate, contradict and resist a hegemonic British nationalism. These black British dancing bodies refuse to be contained by an essentialist Caribbean identity that longs for a mythical homeland, nor do they coexist as an apolitical, postnational utopia. Instead these bodies participate in a complex performance of transnational music and dance practices that call upon traces of African, American, British and Caribbean expressive cultures and which can be conceived as an 'aesthetics of inclusion'. As several scholars suggest, black popular expression frequently operates outside the logocentric limitations of Western culture, thus offering opportunities to articulate difference and resistance (Bhabha, 1994; Gilroy, 1987; Hall, 1992). Consequently, through their diasporic heterogeneity, the dancing bodies of Sunday Serenade trouble fixed categories of race, nation and cultural absolutism and their associated binaries of black/white, English/Other, good/bad and so on. Yet in spite of this diversity, Sunday Serenade engenders a strong sense of community belonging through social etiquette, sartorial expression, shared moral values and a commitment to dancing as an embodied reenactment of the participants' British Caribbean pasts. This reinscription of value marks an expression of difference; yet one that is rooted in the inclusive discourse of 'family belonging'. Tied also to this diasporic experience are the social, cultural and economic inequities that have shaped the participants' class identities within their contemporary British lives. In response, these practices of exclusion are opposed through strategies of inclusion.

A series of visual metaphors are also contained within the chapter: the way in which participants envision an uncorrupted and idealized Jamaican heritage, although their music and dance practices constitute examples of 'transnational spectacle'; how the rhetoric of multiculturalism is blind to the social and economic difference that British migrants face; how generational values are embodied through etiquette and dress; and how the enclosed site of Sunday Serenade is hidden from outside view, although inside it displays performances of belonging. In order to make sense of these lived contradictions, Graeber's (2001) 'theory of action' offers a useful lens through which to understand the 'performances of value' that underpin the dancing and material identities of the participants in Sunday Serenade. As identified in Chapter 5, Graeber (2001) argues for a theory of value that resides in actions, which provides a useful strategy for considering the embodied values articulated through the dancing body. Thus in Graeber's terms, whether it is the production of commodities or creative expression, human action produces particular relations of social value. Indeed, Graeber (2001) uses the examples of 'chanting' and 'money' to argue that both share common characteristics of value: they can provide 'measures of value' in that they signal greater or lesser degrees of worth; they are 'media of value' in that they are the material means through which value is expressed; and they are an 'end in themselves' as they are seen to embody value itself.[18] In view of this, the dancing bodies at Sunday Serenade may be viewed as measures, media and embodiments of value.

For Graeber (2001) value ultimately requires public recognition and comparison. Hence any kind of commodity exchange or public performance constitutes a creative action that produces value. Furthermore, Graeber (2001) suggests that visibility and invisibility of 'currency' are central to understanding value. While money is generally invisible (in that one cannot adorn oneself with it), it is associated with an unseen capacity for action; visible wealth on the other hand is conceived as a means to persuade others how to act towards the self (Graeber, 2001, p. 104). These metaphors of sight provide a useful apparatus for envisioning the paradoxical articulations of value at Sunday Serenade. On one hand, the participants' economic wealth and its relationship to class position are not rendered visible at Sunday Serenade. As suggested earlier, the variety of living conditions and the professional status of the participants are made invisible at Sunday Serenade and carry little value within its social context. This lack of material wealth and social power reflects the marginalized position of the British Caribbean diaspora within the lived reality of British life. Yet the visible values of decorative niceties, sartorial taste, high moral standards, generational expectations and a shared commitment to a range of music and dance expressions produce a set of social relations amongst the members of Sunday Serenade that articulate high levels of cultural capital within this diasporic community.

Yet, in developing Graeber's thinking, I identify how the participants of Sunday Serenade are not passively shaped by value, but through their actions set about a reenvisioning of value: their experiences of social and economic exclusion are contested through inclusive practices of belonging; irrespective of social and economic wealth, the cultural capital of etiquette, morality and good grooming is privileged; and belonging is not collapsed into sameness, but articulated through diverse dancing bodies. I also identify a reclaiming of popular entertainment from commercially situated pleasures of the capitalist economy. Through the strategic intervention of a micro-economy, the participants create their own site of popular expression through this self-sustaining practice: the small £5 fee covers basic costs, while offering access to the participants' situated consumption of black popular music and dance. In Dent's (1992) terms, Sunday Serenade neatly sidesteps the capitalist pleasures of the commercial popular and instead privileges the joy of community values. Yet these measures of sight expose a striking gap between socioeconomic power and cultural worth. Beyond the temporary site of Sunday Serenade, participants lack visible value in their racial and class inscription. In view of this, I see why they envision, or in the words of Bunny Wailer, conceive an alternative 'dreamland'. These paradoxical embodiments of value undoubtedly display the contested power relations of black British worth.

Conclusion: The Value of Popular Dance

Since the explosion of social dance forms at the beginning of the twentieth century, popular dance has traditionally been awarded low measures of social and intellectual merit. In Chapter 1 I argued that we exist in a world shaped by value, which includes systems of economic, aesthetic, political and social capital and investment. Consequently, we perpetually negotiate and produce scales of significance and frameworks of worth. While academia has sought to repress or ignore the value structures that inform its work, its interests and methods are rooted in value judgements. These scholarly expressions of worth have significantly impacted on the artistic sphere through their legitimization of the Western art canon, which in dance terms privileges the elite domain of theatre art dance. Yet, in the last few decades of the twentieth century a relativist privileging of all cultural forms replaced the absolutist belief in inherent cultural worth. In response, the popular idiom has come back with a force, dancing on the canon in its Doc Marten boots, stiletto heels, old skool trainers and all other kinds of vernacular footwear that depart from the traditional ballet slippers or barefoot performances of modern stage dance. In light of this, popular dance now supplies a subject of keen interest within the discipline of dance studies.

In response I argued that popular dance is not passively subject to existing modes of dance research, but that it has stimulated significant changes to the way that dance is conceived and theorized. In Chapter 2 I traced how cultural studies values the popular and conceives culture as an arena of dynamic power relations. In particular, I drew on its attention to participant experience as a means to interrogate how dancing communities construct meaningful value systems. Yet I also took note of the way that cultural studies research focuses on the conditions of production. From this I observed that the measures of significance and worth produced by popular dancing communities are not autonomously created, but are responsive to networks of social, economic, political and aesthetic value already in circulation. While cultural studies offers useful theoretical and methodological tools for the study of popular dance that attend to its production, transmission and consumption, it neglects to consider how the moving body can articulate, negotiate and re-imagine social identities and cultural formations. As I demonstrated in Chapter 4, which I come to shortly, dance studies affords the dancing body a much greater sense of agency.

In Chapter 3 I sought to make sense of what the term 'popular dance' encompasses. The concept of the 'popular' emerges as an unstable and historically contested category and, for this reason, I argued that it is more usefully understood as an intellectual approach to dance that takes place under a range of conditions. This slipperiness demonstrates how the popular undergoes complex processes of distribution and reinvention and its capacity for mutation offers important directions for how it might be addressed. Given that popular dance developed rapidly in response to processes of industrialization and urbanization, it needs to be examined through its historical conditions of production. Questions of context also come to the fore in that the popular occurs across 'street', stage and screen locations and ranges from amateur participation to professional entertainment. In view of this, the politics of site and issues of purpose enter the field of interrogation. As I noted, popular dance shifts and evolves through a complex system of cultural exchange between commercial leisure and media industries and the participants engaged in its practice. Consequently, questions regarding the political economy and consumption are key to understanding the workings of the popular. Indeed, the way in which popular dance circulates across different communities, through the global systems of mass communication or through face-to-face interaction, prompts bodily practices to engage in processes of appropriation, hybridization and reinvention. Therefore the relationship between transnational forms and localized reception produces questions of identity, authenticity and ownership.

In Chapter 4 I examined the treatment of popular dance within dance studies scholarship, particularly in relation to the cultural studies approaches outlined above. Given the dynamic and mutable character of popular dance as it migrates across different sites, I suggested that popular dance research demands a broader frame of analysis that attends to its contexts of production and consumption. Yet I also noted that dance studies awards the dancing body far greater significance as a *locus* of agency and power. Consequently, I sought to explore how the dancing body is dialectically shaped by and responsive to frameworks of social, political and economic value. In Chapter 5 I aimed to develop a method for reading value as articulated through the dancing body. In this chapter I excavated paradigms of value that conceptualize it as an economic system of exchange; as an expression of taste cultures inscribed, although not determined, by class-based knowledge; and as an articulation of aesthetic discrimination that is largely unexplored in relation to the popular idiom. In dance terms, I am interested in how these factors shape value formations and how dancing participants can potentially negotiate and resist their regulatory frameworks. I therefore set out in Part II of the book to interrogate how these structures and responses are discursively and performatively signalled through the dancing body. I conceive this as an embodied value, which exists not as a universal measure of worth but as a locally situated enunciation of significance.

In Part II, I employed qualitative methods, in particular participant observation and interviews, through which to explore the meanings and belief systems that inform popular dance activity. This close attention to the individuals who engage in these embodied practices offers a robust apparatus to interrogate constructions of value within the field of popular dance. From the three case study examples under investigation, I observed how these dancing communities demonstrate a passionate commitment to and investment in the dance events that form a significant part of their lives. Furthermore, I explored how each dancing community exists within a set of economic relations; how they express taste cultures that mobilize concepts of class, race, gender and nation; and how each produces an aesthetic value rooted in movement expression.

In Chapter 6, I examined how neo-burlesque striptease artists produce a regime of value that closely aligns the genre with late nineteenth- and early twentieth-century burlesque, but which reflects the meanings and values of its contemporary performance context. The economic exchange that takes place between performers and audiences inevitably sets up expectations regarding the codification of the striptease act; however, as the small-scale venues under investigation offer little opportunity for high financial return, this allows for a greater performance radicality, which is evident from the creative diversity on display. Within the neo-burlesque community, concepts of autonomy, inclusivity and empowerment are valued. Although diversity is fostered in relation to representations of the female body, evidence of racial and class inclusion is less apparent. The notion of tease forms a key aesthetic in neo-burlesque performance and serves as a critical performance strategy that allows performers to inhabit and take pleasure in normative representations of femininity, while offering a performative critique of those gendered embodiments through a choreography of facial commentary.

In Chapter 7, I showed how subcultural communities use pogoing, headbanging and skanking to convey aesthetic appreciation, individual technical skill, community interactions, dance floor politics and an 'aesthetics of excess', which relates both to the extreme physicality of the movement and to the high level of investment in participants' musical tastes. For punk, metal and ska fans, this embodied commitment produces feelings of pleasure, agency and transformation. While notions of community are emphasized and evidenced through gender inclusion, class diversity and a leftist politics which is played out through the etiquette of the dance floor, the predominance of white dancing bodies signals the issue of racial exclusion. In relation to economic matters, these performances of fandom occur within a framework of capitalist exchange, although this is placed in tension as musicians seek to solicit the interest of dancing participants as a means to secure their continued financial gain. To make sense of the competing relations between the music industry, the band members and the embodied actions of music fans, I employed the concept of play to demonstrate how subcultural members produce, regulate, negotiate and destabilize the complex, and at times paradoxical, network of values that constitute the live gig event.

In Chapter 8, I examined how the participants at a British Caribbean dance hall value an 'aesthetics of inclusion', both through a rhetoric of belonging and through the diversity of transnational music and dance forms staged at the event. I argued that the commitment to inclusion is a performative response to experiences of exclusion. The men and women of Sunday Serenade refuse to be contained by hegemonic frameworks of race, class and nation and instead reconfigure their own systems of value rooted in sartorial taste, generational etiquette and moral standards. Through a basic micro-economy, this dancing community distances itself from the commercial mainstream in order to service its diasporic interests. I draw on the metaphor of visibility to argue that, although the discourse of multiculturalism erases the social and economic realities of black British life, the participants in Sunday Serenade contest this exclusion through a reinstatement of value that articulates the joy of belonging.

When I embarked on this research, I did not intend to produce a model of value that could be consistently applied across popular dance practice. Rather, I sought to examine the localized structures of value embodied by the dancing participants in relation to their particular movement practice. Yet my findings indicate some cumulative conclusions regarding the value of popular dance. In observing and reflecting upon their dancing experiences, the participants articulate a sophisticated, although sometimes contradictory, set of corporeal enunciations around issues of value that speak to concepts of gender, sexuality, class, age, race and nation. These embodied expressions of value do not exist in isolation from the social, political, aesthetic and economic frameworks that underpin popular dance events. Rather, these dancing values both respond to and reconstitute the conditions in which they are created and consumed. Consequently, the embodied values that are produced within and receptive to the localized contexts of popular dance production have the capacity to maintain, negotiate, destabilize and reinvent the wider network of social values that circulate around movement practice.

In reflecting upon their dancing experiences, some common themes emerge across the participants' interview data. The first is a clear sense of 'imagined community' engendered through these dance events that speak to issues of inclusion and belonging, particularly in relation to bodies that are situated on the margins of society. In the case of neo-burlesque striptease, this is articulated through its affirmation of female bodies that sit outside the idealized representations of contemporary media culture; with the punk, metal and ska fans, this is through the collective embrace offered to those perceived as outsiders; and with Sunday Serenade, this is through the rhetoric of family belonging for British Caribbeans who have been historically subject to social and economic exclusion. The second key theme is the importance of 'play' within each dancing community. In neo-burlesque striptease, tease is employed both as a seductive play on the audience and as a means to critique and re-imagine representations of female display; at punk, metal and ska gigs, there is a play between observing, policing and transgressing subcultural codes of behaviour; and at Sunday Serenade, there is a play of difference as absolute categories of race and nation are contested through the British Caribbean experience.

The third area of commonality lies in the profound sense of pleasure (or joy) that emanates from the dancing experience. Without fail, all of the participants not only described the intense pleasures derived from the physicality of movement, but also voiced pleasure in the transformational capacities of dance. On the neo-burlesque stage, artists experience a sense of agency and power through the thrill of disrobing before an affirmative public audience; punk, metal and ska fans speak of a compulsive embodied response to the music which produces emotional, physiological and personal benefits; and for the participants of Sunday Serenade, the dancing expresses a joy of collective belonging. The final theme that emerges is rooted in the way that participants conceive the dance as offering an escape or release from everyday life. Yet I am cautious of reproducing the safety valve paradigm in which dance is presented within a functionalist argument that positions it as a temporary departure from social norms, but which offers no opportunities for transgression or transformation.

In acknowledgment of participant responses, I argue instead that these dancing experiences constitute an existence 'alternative' to quotidian life in which participants do not escape from their subject positions, but rather confront these complicated matters of identity in the act of dancing. Through neo-burlesque striptease, performers deal with troubled questions of female spectacle and normative femininities; at music gigs, punk, metal and ska fans negotiate positions of insider and outsider, consumerism and agency, and responsibility and rebellion; and at Sunday Serenade, participants work through their affinity to the Caribbean within the context of their contemporary British lives. It is therefore not surprising that participants award their dancing experiences such high levels of value. In spite of the elitist view that has sought to repress the cultural worth of popular dance, the three dancing communities firmly reject this position. They capitalize on their dancing bodies to create a sense of belonging, enter into opportunities for play, participate in the production of pleasure and address important matters of identity. These precious embodiments of value surely signal the worth of popular dance.

Notes

Acknowledgements

1. Every effort has been made to secure permission from the participants to include excerpts from their interviews in this book.

Introduction: Let's Dance!

1. I was registered for a BA (Hons) Creative Arts in dance and drama from 1987–90 and for an MA Dance Studies from 1992–3.
2. This was a cover version of the 1962 original by Chris Montez.
3. See *http://en.wikipedia.org/wiki/Special:Search/Let's_Dance!* (accessed 28 February 2011).
4. In Chapter 3 I interrogate the label 'popular dance' as a defining concept and develop a working definition for the purposes of this book.
5. I explore this new area of work in detail in Chapter 4.
6. When I commenced work on this book, I knew that I wanted to prepare a monograph on popular dance and that I was keen to employ a methodology that combined cultural studies approaches and fieldwork methods, but the concept of value as the principal research focus had not yet developed. I therefore began research on the punk, metal and ska fans, shortly followed by the neo-burlesque fieldwork. It was only as I began to analyse the interview data from the punk, metal and ska fans that the concept of value really emerged in relation to how they reflected on their dancing practices. This then prompted me to consider how popular dance as a subject has been valued within the academy.

1   Dancing on the Canon

1. Malnig makes reference to McNamara's observation that theatre studies traditionally focuses on the 'great moments' of its performance history, thus ignoring its 'minor forms' of popular entertainment (McNamara cited in Malnig, 2009, p. 1), and argues that the same applies to the neglect of popular dance within the dance studies legacy.
2. While several scholars note the neglect of value as a subject within the arts and humanities, they acknowledge that questions of value have played a far more significant role within the disciplines of economics and philosophy (Connor, 1992; Fekete, 1987; Graeber, 2001).
3. From the 1970s the influence of literary critical theory, in particular semiotics, structuralism and post-structuralism, clearly impacted on the arts and humanities disciplines through its method of textual interpretation (Adshead-Lansdale, 1999; Barker, 2000). A more detailed interrogation of textual analysis takes place in Chapter 2.

4. The development of women's and gender studies, queer theory, critical race theory and postcolonial studies are testament to the presence of a humanist, and therefore 'value-laden', position within contemporary cultural and critical theory (Connor, 1992).
5. Although there is a tradition of dance anthropology and ethnochoreology that examines traditional or indigenous dance practices, these studies have typically focused on non-Western dance or European folk dance rather than dance within popular formations (see Buckland, 1999b and Thomas, 2003).
6. Buckland makes reference here to Matthew Arnold and his followers in the 'culture and civilization' tradition, which was vehemently opposed to the emerging popular cultures of the early twentieth century. As a cultural critic and educational reformer, Arnold expressed moral and intellectual concerns over the decline of traditional folk cultures in response to the 'culture of the masses' that emerged through industrialization (see Turner, 1990). This cultural movement is also addressed in Chapter 2 in reference to the literary criticism of F. R. Leavis.
7. See Browning, 1995; Buckland, 2002; Daniel, 1995; Delgado and Muñoz, 1997; Dixon Gottschild, 2002; George-Graves, 2000; Malnig, 1992 and 2009; Malone, 1996; McMains, 2006; Osumare, 2007; Pini, 2001; Savigliano, 1995; Stearns and Stearns, 1994; Valis Hill, 2000.
8. In Chapter 4 I provide a detailed analysis of how contemporary writing within dance studies utilizes a cultural theory approach.
9. Included within the literature that Ward discusses are key cultural studies texts (Chambers, 1986; Hebdige, 1979; McRobbie, 1984).
10. Frith's work on value is further developed in his monograph *Performing Rites: On the Value of Popular Music* (1996).
11. Further discussion of the contemptuous attitude to popular culture evident through mass culture theory and the work of the Frankfurt School takes place in Chapters 2 and 3.
12. The subject of cultural populism is explored in Chapter 2.
13. See Moore (2010) for a synopsis of U2's critical and commercial achievements (*http://www.oxfordmusiconline.com/subscriber/article/grove/music/46259*, accessed 15 February 2010).

2   The Value(s) of Cultural Studies

1. Although the CCCS is widely regarded as the institutional foundation of cultural studies, Turner (1990) credits the work of other centres in the intellectual development of cultural studies: Centre for Television Research (Leeds, 1966), Centre for Mass Communication Research (Leicester, 1966), Glasgow Media Group (1974) and the Open University's Mass Communications and Society course (1977) and Popular Culture degree (1982).
2. It is of note that two other scholars are also credited for their early influence on the field of cultural studies. Edward Thompson's *Making of the English Working Class* (Harmondsworth: Penguin, 1963) is a British social history that demonstrates an interest in 'lived culture' and subjective experience (Hall, 1996a; Turner, 1990). Although his understanding of agency is said to be romantic and humanist, the importance of this text lies in its focus on

working class life (Turner, 1990). The other scholar is Stuart Hall who took up the directorship of the CCCS from 1969–79. Hall's major contribution to cultural studies has been the development of its structuralist strand and for an insight into this area of his work see Turner (1990), Grossberg (1993) and Morley and Chen (1997).

3. See Bennett (1993), Hall (1996a) and Turner (1990) for further debates on the limitations of Williams's understanding of culture as a 'way of life'.

4. Although considerable research has been devoted to the study of popular practices in cultural studies, high art or scientific discourse are equally valid subjects of examination (Agger, 1992; Nelson et al., 1992).

5. See Grossberg (1993) and Strinati (1995) for a detailed explanation of how Althusser's and Gramsci's work has been appropriated by, and influenced, the field of cultural studies.

6. For an extended debate on why cultural studies has both committed itself and failed to achieve political aims through social policy and action see Agger (1992), Ang (1996), Bennett (1993 and 1996), Garnham (1997), Gitlin (1997), McRobbie (1997), Murdock (1997) and Thomas (1997).

7. Ethnographic fieldwork practices are often linked with the culturalist strand (Barker, 2000).

8. For an exposition and critique of culturalism and structuralism, see Grossberg (1993) and Hall (1996a).

9. This is particularly evident in the area of 'screen theory', for example, which is concerned with the textual construction of spectatorship rather than the social character of the audience (McGuigan, 1992).

10. Garnham (1997, p58) acknowledges that the mode of production does have an element of historical stability because of the 'social investment' in its construction and the 'social dangers' of its collapse.

11. The scholar who has become notably associated with 'uncritical populism' and is repeatedly attacked for his position on this is John Fiske (Frow, 1995; McGuigan, 1992; Morris, 1996; Kellner, 1997). McGuigan (1992) argues that Fiske inverts the mass culture critique, in that he dismisses any ideological work in operation within popular culture and places complete emphasis on 'semiotic democracy' by focusing solely on the pleasures and meanings that the consumer invests in popular forms.

12. So pervasive is this line of thinking that Morris (1996) cynically imagines a master disk that perpetually recycles the hackneyed notions of pleasure and resistance in an endless series of cultural studies texts.

13. This is not a call for a return to the 'mass culture critique' in which the consumer is positioned as a passive 'cultural dupe' manipulated by the ideological workings of the culture industry, but an urge for caution against an unquestioning celebration of popular idioms.

14. I focus here on the early youth cultures/subcultures research that emerged from the CCCS rather than the more recent developments in post-subcultural theory, which I examine in Chapter 7. While some of the scholars under investigation specifically employ the label 'subcultures' (Brake, 1985; Hebdige, 1979), others are concerned with the idea of 'youth cultures' more broadly (Chambers, 1985; McRobbie, 1984; Willis, 1990).

15. Helen Thomas also offers an excellent critique of some of the work that I address in *The Body, Dance and Cultural Theory* (2003).

16. See Bennett (2001) and Berger (1999).
17. Female vocalists Siouxsie Sioux, Toyah Wilcox and Poly Styrene, and all-female bands the Slits and the Raincoats were closely associated with the punk movement. (See *http://www.oxfordmusiconline.com/subscriber/article/grove/music/46845*, Richard Middleton, accessed 15 February, 2010).
18. See Desmond (1997) for a detailed examination of how popular dance is frequently read through an essentialized understanding of race, class and gender.
19. Exceptions here are Chambers's analysis of mods and Northern soul, both of which involved males dancing (1985).
20. See also 'Fame, Flashdance and Fantasies of Achievement' (McRobbie, 1990), which develops key themes addressed in 'Dance and Social Fantasy' (McRobbie, 1984).
21. The work of Bourdieu is addressed further in Chapter 5.

3   What Is Popular Dance?

1. Reay (1998) also suggests that the cultural practices of early modern England cannot be simplistically bifurcated between the gentry and the poor. He references other groups (such as lower-level merchant families, tradesmen and craftsmen) who were prominent socially, economically, politically and culturally.
2. I will return to aspects of Buckland's (1983) definition later in the chapter as these tie in with key arguments developed in popular music studies and cultural studies.
3. I will come back to some of these definitions, which variously see the popular in relation to 'many' or 'not art', later in the chapter.
4. The model for Buckland's (1983) structural comparison is Green's (1978) critique of Lloyd (1970). Lloyd's research is devoted to music definitions and in the framework he provides classical and folk are polarized on a spectrum with popular located in between. Green updates this structural paradigm which Buckland (1983) has employed in relation to dance.
5. In Buckland's defence it is important to note that she does offer some definitions of popular dance, which I examine later in this chapter. She also duly recognizes that the oppositional categories that distinguish classical and folk are far from absolute in that dance practices often cross boundaries of classification, and exceptions and contradictions are easily revealed.
6. As stated earlier, the romantic image of a traditional rural community has been critiqued for its primitivist perspectives (Burke, 1981).
7. For interesting accounts of how cultural practice shifts across the high/low boundary see Carter's (2005) study of ballet within the popular Victorian and Edwardian musical hall and Storey's (2003) mapping of how opera has been reinvented as both high art and popular entertainment.
8. Art schools, along with the pub rock scene, were a common place to showcase new punk bands, particularly as these small-scale venues were situated outside the stadium rock context of which punk musicians were so critical (Wicke, 1993).
9. Some figures do exist for popular dance in vernacular settings, such as statistics regarding attendance, which are cited on websites for 'dance

associations' or in the context of 'social surveys'. Yet the reliability of this data can not be guaranteed.

10. The 'Frankfurt School' refers to the work of a group of German Jewish intellectuals associated with the Institute of Social Research (established in 1923) that included Theodor Adorno, Max Horkheimer, Herbert Marcuse and Walter Benjamin (Strinati, 1995).

11. Although the pogo had little to offer in the way of commercial exploitation, in the *Guardian Unlimited*, Jones (2003) reports a fitness regime in America called 'Punk Rock Aerobics', which employs pogoing as part of the movement routine.

12. Notably, punk allowed young people, and women in particular, to enter the music business (Laing, 1985; Shaar Murrray, 1991; Wicke, 1993).

13. For instance, see Daniel's (1995) study of rumba in which she discusses it in the context of postrevolutionary Cuba, and its popularization and commercialization through Hollywood film and the ballroom context; and Osumare's (2000) research on hip hop in Hawai'i in which she argues that the globalization of the form creates an intertext in which its original meanings and values interface with local indigenous interpretations of the dance to create new performative identities.

14. See Thomas (1997) for a critique of the 'dominant ideology' model: in that this assumes a historical universalism, it is debatable whether a dominant group has a unified set of ideas that can serve the interests of a minority, and it is inconceivable that a monolithic framework such as this can exist within a complex society.

4   Writing Popular Dance

1. The inclusion of popular dance within the undergraduate curriculum can be seen at the following British universities: HE3 *Popular Dance* module at the University of Surrey; HE2 *From Street to Stage* and HE3 *Social Dance* modules at Kingston University; HE2 *Dance as Popular Practice* module at De Montfort University; and a BA *Dance: Urban Practice* at the University of East London.

2. Palatine is a British higher-education subject centre in dance, drama and music (http://www.palatine.ac.uk/, accessed 13 January 2010).

3. I primarily focus on academic journal articles within the field of dance studies, in particular *Dance Research Journal*, *Dance Research* and *Discourses in Dance*, although I am aware that dance scholars frequently publish in journals associated with other research disciplines. Given the paucity of published work within dance scholarship of the 1980s and 1990s that focuses on popular dance, I also draw on conference proceedings of the Society of Dance History Scholars published up to and including the year 2000 as part of this survey.

4. See De Frantz (2002b), Jackson (2001), LaBoskey (2001), Malone (1996), Monaghan (2001), Stearns and Stearns (1994) and Valis Hill (1992).

5. See Cook (2000), Malnig (1998), Martin (2009), Ponzio (1996), Robinson (2009), Skinner (2008), Sommer (2001), Stern (2000), Szwed and Marks (1988) and Thomas and Cooper (2002).

6. For studies of ragtime see Cook (2000), George-Graves (2009) and Robinson (2009); for tap see De Frantz (2002b), Stearns and Stearns (1994) and Valis Hill (1992); for salsa see Bosse (2008), McMains (2009) and Skinner (2008); for hip hop see Jackson (2001), Osumare (2000, 2002, 2007) and Zanfagna (2009); for dancehall see Cooper (2000), Hope (2004), Ryman (2004) and Stanley Niaah (2004); for club dance see Buckland (2002), Gore (1997), Hall (2008); Lawrence (2009), Pini (1997) and Sommer (2001); for lindyhop see Jackson (2001), Monaghan (2001), Monaghan and Dodson (2000) and Usner (2001); and for ballroom see Malnig (1998), McMains (2001, 2006) and Penny (1999).

7. This is mirrored in cultural studies which has almost exclusively focused on the dance activities of the young (Thomas and Cooper, 2002).

8. See Jackson (2001) for a well argued proposition that in African American vernacular dance improvisation is a form of choreography. This perspective challenges ethnocentric discourses that try to separate improvisation from choreographic design.

9. The one exception to this is McMains's (2001) study of Latin DanceSport, which constitutes a live competition event. Notably, DanceSport is a particularly bounded event in the sense that there is a strictly codified vocabulary and presentation of the dancers, which allows the author to approach the 'dance event' as a text. McMains also uses photographs as another textual reference to support her discussion of 'racial/ethnic referents' (2001, p. 54) within DanceSport competition.

10. For ethnographic studies see Bosse (2008), Daniel (1991), Gonzalez (2003/04), Jackson (2001), Osumare (2000, 2002 and 2007), Penny (1999), Skinner (2008), Sommer (2001), Stanley Niaah (2004), Stern (2000), Thomas and Cooper (2002) and Usner (2001). For historiographic approaches see Banes and Szwed (2002), Cook (2000), Doolittle (2001), Lawrence (2009), Malnig (1998), Malone (1996), Monaghan and Dodson (2000), Robinson (2009), Szwed and Marks (1988), Valis Hill (1992 and 2009), Wagner (1986) and Wall (2009).

11. Penny (1999) is a notable exception in that much of her data is statistical.

12. I acknowledge that, whereas cultural studies tends to be commodity-centred in its research, popular dance studies frequently focuses on live practice. Therefore, in reference to commodities, the producers and consumers of commodity culture tend to be different groups of people; in relation to popular dance practice, however, the producers (i.e. creators) and participants can be one and the same.

5 Embodiments of Value

1. For a useful exposition of the impact of Marxism on popular culture theory see Strinati (1995).

2. In answer to Bourdieu's structuralist correlation between class and cultural taste, Frow (1995) attempts to reframe the relationship between class and value through his concept of the 'knowledge class'.

Part II: Dancing Values

1. I detail the precise number of interviews and field visits in each case study chapter.

6 'Naughty but Nice': Re-Articulations of Value in Neo-Burlesque Striptease

1. A 'rogering' is a colloquialism for the sexual act in British slang.
2. Although there exists an emerging tradition of male and transgender neo-burlesque striptease, this study focuses specifically on female artists. Traditionally, female neo-burlesque performers strip down to g-strings and pasties (small discs, decorated with sequins and tassels, that shield the nipples).
3. In London I attended *Hip Hip* and *Burly Q* at Bethnal Green Working Men's Club, *Blues and Buns Burlesque* at Volupté, *Ska Burlesque* at the Amersham Arms, the *Wam Bam Club* at the Soho Revue Bar and performances at the Brickhouse, the Volstead Club, Koko and the *Feminist Neo-Burlesque Symposium* at the Central School of Speech and Drama; and in New York, I visited *Hot Box Burlesque* and *Mr Choade's Upstairs/Downstairs* at the Slipper Room, *Starshine Burlesque* at Rififi's, *This is Burlesque* at Corio's and *Le Scandal* at The Cutting Room.
4. See Allen (1991), Buszek (2006), Pullen (2005), Roach (2007), Schaefer (1997), Shteir (2004) and Willson (2008).
5. See Dentith (2000), Hutcheon (2003), Mulkay (1988), Palmer (1993), Ross (1998) and Simpson (2003).
6. See Athorne (2005), Blanchard (2003), Gumbel (2003), Harris (2004) and Shepard (2005).
7. Although Thompson and the British Blondes had arrived in New York with a well established career on the London stage behind them, there is a scarcity of material that documents this period of their work (Pullen, 2005).
8. *Cartes de visites*, or 'calling cards', which were popularized from the 1850s, depicted a photograph of the 'card carrier' and were distributed as a means of showing her or his social and cultural standing (Buszek, 2006, p. 32).
9. *Tableaux vivants* were theatre spectacles in which nude or scantily clad women replicated still-life images from classical art (Shteir, 2004); concert saloons were insalubrious bars that offered cheap dining with 'theatrical entertainment' by provocatively dressed waitresses (Shteir, 2004, p. 16); and dime museums 'displayed the human body – particularly the female body – as a scientific curiosity' (Shteir, 2004, p. 17).
10. These particular clubs are British, although Liepe-Levinson (2002) identifies a similar boom in upmarket strip clubs in North America and Canada.
11. There are well established burlesque scenes in Birmingham and Edinburgh in the United Kingdom and in Seattle and San Francisco in the United States, for example.
12. Although I have traced the lineage of neo-burlesque through histories of burlesque and striptease performance, I acknowledge that this theatrical

practice is situated in a wider history of female performance. Within the field of arts practice, there have been radical interrogations and critiques of the female body in the work of performance artists such as Annie Sprinkle, Bobby Baker and Rose English. While none of the neo-burlesque artists whom I interviewed referenced this body of work as influential on their own practice, I suggest that feminist performance practice has undoubtedly offered female artists alternative paradigms for the staging of the body. For further discussion of this work see Harris (1999) and Schneider (1997).

13. The writing on her vest referred to former US President George W. Bush.
14. Although the majority of neo-burlesque acts are performed using recorded or live music accompaniment, Amber Topaz generally sings as part of her performance.
15. Dita von Teese, from the United States, and Immodesty Blaize, from the United Kingdom, are perhaps the most high-profile neo-burlesque artists within the cultural mainstream. Von Teese has published a richly illustrated book about herself, *Burlesque and the Art of Teese* (2006), and regularly headlines spectacular Las Vegas shows, and Blaize has produced a burlesque documentary *Burlesque Undressed* (2010) and has performed at prestigious events such as the Cartier International party and the Dior Rouge launch (see *http://www.immodestyblaize.com/*, accessed 3 February 2010).
16. 'Pee Wee Herman' (Paul Reubens) was an American children's television presenter who was arrested in 1991 for masturbating in an adult film theatre, which caused a serious public scandal (*http://en.wikipedia.org/wiki/Pee-wee_Herman*, accessed 14 December 2008).
17. I am conscious that the act of teasing can range from a gentle mockery to an uncomfortable provocation. While the neo-burlesque performers that I observed for this research work at the playful end of the spectrum, there are artists, such as Empress Stah (*http://www.empressstah.com/*, accessed 3 February 2010) and Luci Fire (*http://www.lucifire.com/*, accessed 3 February 2010), who employ sexually explicit and confrontational imagery that has the capacity to disturb or offend.
18. The 'big reveal' is the term used by burlesque artists to refer to the ultimate display of the disrobed breasts.
19. Although Liepe-Levinson (2002, p. 117) identifies the use of 'facial choreography' in modern striptease, she does not read it as a strategy of critique.
20. See Harris (1999) and Doane (1992) for a full discussion of 'masquerade' and its application to female performance.
21. One of the critiques of Butler is that she does not sufficiently explain the distinction between 'performativity' and 'performance'; for further discussion see Gere (2001) and Harris (1999).

7 Pogoing, Headbanging and Skanking: Economies of Value in Dancing Subcultures

1. I have changed the names of my informants to protect their privacy and when I first introduce each one I reference the full interview date.
2. There exists a well developed body of literature that attends to club cultures and Thornton's (1997) work in particular conceives the multiples genres

of dance music through subcultural affiliations (see Chapter 2). For the purposes of this chapter, however, I choose not to address clubbing subcultures as I am particularly interested in subcultural dance practices that occur within the context of a live music gig rather than a 'DJ set' in which recorded music is played. I am also conscious that nascent work exists in dance studies that examines clubbing subcultures (see Buckland, 2002 and Hall, 2008), whereas research into pogoing, headbanging and skanking is virtually absent.

3. See Gelder and Thornton (1997) for a useful exposition and critique of this work.

4. Angela McRobbie's work (1991 and 1994), which attends to the cultural practices of young teenage women, forms an important counterbalance to the predominantly masculine bias of the CCCS research.

5. There are two main strands of research that characterize 'post-subcultural studies': the first attempts to develop new theoretical models through which to analyse subcultures, such as Butler's concept of 'performativity' and Bourdieu's work on 'cultural capital'; and the second seeks to find ways of conceiving youth activity beyond the notion of a discrete 'subculture' (Weinzierl and Muggleton, 2003).

6. In a useful discussion of the relations between fandom and subcultures, Sandvoss (2005) suggests that there is an overlap between fans and subcultures in that both have a sustained emotional investment in a form, although subcultural groups may not define themselves as fans and not all fans are part of a subculture. He suggests that subcultures tend to be theorized as collectives rather than individuals and are concerned with style, communality and interaction (Sandvoss, 2005). It is important to note, however, that while the concept of 'fan' exists in common parlance, the way that fans perceive their interests and behaviours may not align with theoretical framings of fandom.

7. While I acknowledge that this self-selected group of informants does not entirely fit with the CCCS subcultural model of 'young, white, male and working class', I align my work with other scholarship on subcultures that recognizes subcultural affiliations across broader ranges of gender, age and class (see Bennett, 2006 and Muggleton, 2000).

8. Although I have listed their official employment status, several of the informants were heavily involved in other kinds of 'work' tied to their punk interests: Mikey was part of a local collective that produced and promoted punk gigs; Pete produced and managed a well developed punk website (*http://www.punk4life.co.uk*); and Melanie also produced a heavily utilized punk website from which she ran her own mail order business for punk clothes and accessories (*http://www.punkoiuk.co.uk*).

9. In addition to their 'day jobs', Sonny worked as a radio and club DJ and Chris ran a ska club (*http://www.clubska.com*).

10. For research on slam dancing see Tsitsos (1999).

11. For further discussion of 'moshing' see Fonorow (1997) and Tsitsos (1999).

12. Heathcott (2003) provides a useful explanation of first-, second- and third-wave ska: 1960s first-wave ska emerged within the context of urban Jamaica and is characterized by 'horn-dominated instrumentation, syncopated

rhythms, up-tempo timing, and down-beat emphasis' (Heathcott, 2003, p. 184); 1970s 'two-tone ska' developed within the London and Coventry club scene and was typified by bands such as 'the Beat, Madness and the Specials' (Heathcott, 2003, p. 184); third-wave 'ska punk' came from the USA and combines 'punk rock sound with ska rhythm and instrumentation' (Heathcott, 2003, p. 185). For a detailed discussion of first-wave ska music see Barrow and Dalton (2001).

13. The link between ska music and 'shuffling' is supported by my field data from Sunday Serenade, in which several informants from the club described shuffling as one of the key dances associated with ska music (see Chapter 8).

14. This type of 'skanking' or 'ska dancing' is also in evident at Sunday Serenade (see Chapter 8).

15. This generic style of rigid movement and clenched fists was typified in the 'nutty dance', a dance performed by the members and fans of 1980s second-wave ska band Madness, which would involve people walking in a line. The walk however demanded an emphatic step using flexed knees and flexed arms, with clenched fists, moving in opposition. The movement was staccato and the rigid torso would lurch alternately forwards and backwards with each step.

16. In an attempt to create a more diverse sample, I tried hard to secure an interview with a black British woman who regularly attended ska gigs, but unfortunately she was unavailable due to family commitments.

17. At the time of interviewing the informants, Tony Blair was the British prime minister and had adopted a political position that was broadly described as New Labour.

18. In the interview data, all of the respondents made reference to changes in personal style that responded to their subcultural interests, such as tattoos, piercing, dyeing hair or alternative modes of dress and make-up.

8 'There's a Land That I've Heard About': Envisioning Value at Sunday Serenade

1. As with Chapter 7, I have changed names to respect informant privacy and I note the interview date on the first occasion that I draw on an informant's interview data.

2. This indented description and the subsequent two passages are a composite of field notes, as each evening follows the same pattern. It commences with Mirabelle, one of the regulars, dancing alone for up to an hour before other people slowly start to arrive. Unlike the majority of participants, who prefer to dance around the edges of the room, Mirabelle takes great pleasure in dancing in the centre.

3. The event is advertised through RJR 94FM radio, which describes itself as 'the outlet of choice for homesick Jamaicans' (*http://www.rjr94fm.com/*, accessed 28 September 2009). Sunday Serenade is promoted as a dancehall for the over-30s and, although there are occasionally participants who are in their 20s, the majority are over 40 and includes those in their 70s and beyond. Out of eight regular participants that I interviewed, the two youngest were 44.

4. Gilroy describes sound systems as a type of mobile disco, although they are 'many thousands of times more powerful than a domestic record player' (1987, p. 216) and the 'sound that they generate has its own characteristics, particularly an emphasis on the reproduction of bass frequencies' (1987, p. 217).

5. Dent (1992) attributes this theorization of 'pleasure' and 'joy' to the work of Cornel West.

6. I formally interviewed eight participants outside the club environment, but spoke to a range of people informally at Sunday Serenade evenings. I approached people to interview because they had taken an interest in my research and/or because they appeared particularly committed to dancing at the club. The following details the names of interviewees and their ages when they migrated to the United Kingdom: Desmond arrived at 14; Raymond arrived at 21; Stacey is British-born; Martha arrived at 18; Evelyn arrived at 21; Francine arrived at 33; Claudia arrived at the age of 3; and Delores arrived at 19. Although all of the participants I interviewed were Jamaican, I spoke to one man, Theobald, who originates from Dominica.

7. Although the majority of participants are black British, there is an elderly white British male who is a regular attendee, I have seen a white British woman on one occasion and my contact who recommended the club, Sonny (my ska informant from Chapter 7), is a white British male who sometimes visits Sunday Serenade.

8. Gunaratnam's (2003) critique of racial matching in interviews is that it is predicated on essentialist beliefs and overlooks other interests, such as age or gender for instance.

9. My note-taking activity had caused such suspicion that Winston initially asked me to which press agency I belonged. I have heard informally that there have been some moves to close down the club, so people are understandably wary of any individuals whose behaviour does not sit within the usual practices of the club space.

10. The notion of a 'double consciousness' is indebted to the work of W. E. B. DuBois (Gilroy, 1993).

11. I use the idea of a 'prelapsarian Jamaica' to convey how the participants conceive their Caribbean existence as a pure and idealistic distillation of their cultural heritage.

12. Hall (1996b, pp. 164–5) employs the 'burden of representation' to describe the way that black people are subject to stereotypical representations over which they have no control. He argues that these representations are formative rather than reflective and produce real effects beyond their discursive realm. In response, black people have sought to resist such representations through their expressive practices.

13. In a discussion of sound systems, Gilroy comments on how the DJ, MC and/or 'toaster' who play the music 'emerge as the principal agents in dialogic rituals of active and celebratory consumption. It is above all in these performances that black Britain has expressed the improvisation, spontaneity and intimacy which are key characteristics of all new world black musics, providing a living tradition between them and African traditions of music-making' (1987, p. 217). The same kind of spontaneous commentary takes place at Sunday Serenade before, after and during tracks,

sometimes in relation to the music and sometimes in relation to the gathered community.

14. Hall's (2003) notion of presences or traces is rooted in Jacques Derrida's linguistic concept of *'différance'*, which means both 'to differ' and 'to defer'. Consequently meaning is never finished in that it is always shifting to allow additional or supplementary meanings, although traces of the original remain. Hall suggests that this concept is useful for conceiving a non-essentialized Otherness as it challenges fixed binaries, although there is a danger of an endless linguistic play that fails to recognize the political. Hall (2003) counters this in his own understanding of *'présences Africaine/Européene/Américaine'* which he respectively considers through the troubled politics of African slavery, European colonialism and 'New World' creolization.

15. These statistics are taken from a report published by Brent Council (2004) (see *http://www.brent.gov.uk/directorate.nsf/Files/LBBA-2/$FILE/census_ammend.pdf*, accessed 11 December 2009) based on the 2001 Census.

16. The 'management professional' whom I interviewed currently works in the area of human resources and had completed a professional qualification through evening classes accredited by the Institute of Personnel Management.

17. See Chapter 2 for a critique of social dance and the 'safety valve' argument and Chapter 7 as an example of how subcultural dancing communities imagine popular dance as a 'temporary release'.

18. Graeber's analysis of 'chanting' is based on communal ceremonies enacted by the Kayapo society of Brazil (2001).

Bibliography

Abbing, H. (1996) 'The Artistic Conscience and the Production of Value' in Klamer, A. (ed.) *The Value of Culture: On the Relationship Between Economics and Arts*. Amsterdam: Amsterdam University Press.

Abercrombie, N. and Longhurst, B. (1998) *Audiences: A Sociological Theory of Performance and Imagination*. London: Sage.

Adshead-Lansdale, J. (ed.) (1999) *Dancing Texts* London: Dance Books.

Agger, B. (1992) *Cultural Studies as Critical Theory*. London and Philadelphia: Falmer.

Aharonian, C. (1983) 'A Latin-American Approach in a Pioneering Essay' in Horn, D. (ed.) *Popular Music Perspectives 2*, Papers from the Second International Conference on Popular Music Studies, Reggio Emilia, 19–24 September, 52–65.

Allen, R. (1991) *Horrible Prettiness: Burlesque and American Culture*. Chapel Hill, NC and London: University of North Carolina Press.

Anderson, B. (1991) *Imagined Communities: Reflections on the Origin and Spread of Nationalism*, 2nd edn. London: Verso.

Ang, I. (1996) 'Culture and Communication: Towards an Ethnographic Critique of Media Consumption in the Transnational Media System' in Storey, J. (ed.) *What is Cultural Studies?* London: Arnold.

Appadurai, A. (2003) 'Disjuncture and Difference in the Global Cultural Economy' in Braziel, J. E. and Mannur, A. (eds) *Theorizing Diaspora*. Oxford: Blackwell.

Atkinson, P. (1990) *The Ethnographic Imagination: Textual Constructions of Reality*. London and New York: Routledge.

Athorne, S. (2005) 'Watch the Bawdy; Burlesques', *The Sunday Times*, 17 April, 25.

Baker, H. et al. (1996) 'Introduction: Representing Blackness/Representing Britain: Cultural Studies and the Politics of Knowledge' in Baker, H. et al. (eds) *Black British Cultural Studies: A Reader*. Chicago IL and London: University of Chicago Press.

Banes, S. and Szwed, J. F. (2002) 'From "Messin' Around" to "Funky Western Civilization": The Rise and Fall of Dance Instruction Song' in DeFrantz, T. (ed.) *Dancing Many Drums: Excavations in African American Dance*. Madison, WI: University of Wisconsin Press.

Barker, C. (2000) *Cultural Studies: Theory and Practice*. London: Sage.

Barker, K. (1987) 'Dance and the Emerging Music Hall in the Provinces', *Dance Research*, V: 2, 33–42.

Barker, M. and Beezer, A. (1992) *Reading into Cultural Studies*. London: Routledge.

Baroni, M. and Callegari, L. (1983) 'The History and Origins of Popular Music' in Horn, D. (ed.) *Popular Music Perspectives 2*, Papers from the Second International Conference on Popular Music Studies, Reggio Emilia, 19–24 September, 317–33.

Barrow, S. and Dalton, P. (2001) *The Rough Guide to Reggae: The Definitive Guide to Jamaican Music, From Ska Through Roots to Ragga*, 2nd edn. London: Rough Guides.

Bharucha, R. (2000) *The Politics of Cultural Practice: Thinking Through Theatre in an Age of Globalization*. Hanover, CT: Wesleyan University Press.

Becker, S. (1987) 'A *Femme Fatale* Communicates Through Dance', Proceedings of the Society for Dance History Scholars 10th Annual Conference, University of California, Irvine, 13–15 February, 45–52.

—— (1989) 'Jack Cole in Hollywood', Proceedings of the Society for Dance History Scholars 12th Annual Conference, Arizona State University, 17–19 February, 8–14.

Bennett, A. (2001) *Cultures of Popular Music*. Berkshire and Philadelphia, PA: Open University Press.

—— (2006) 'Punk's Not Dead: The Continuing Significance of Punk Rock for an Older Generation of Fans', *Sociology*, 40: 2, 219–35.

Bennett, A. and Kahn-Harris, K. (2004) 'Introduction' in Bennett, A. and Kahn-Harris, K. (eds) *After Subculture: Critical Studies in Contemporary Youth Culture*. Basingstoke: Palgrave.

Bennett, T. (1986) 'The Politics of the "Popular" and Popular Culture' in Bennett, T. Mercer, C. and Woollacott, J. (eds) *Popular Culture and Social Relations*. Milton Keynes and Philadelphia, PA: Open University Press.

—— (1993) 'Useful Culture' in Blundell, V. et al. (eds) *Relocating Cultural Studies: Developments in Theory and Practice*. London: Routledge.

—— (1996) 'Putting Policy into Cultural Studies' in Storey, J. (ed.) *What is Cultural Studies?* London: Arnold.

Berger, H. M. (1999) *Metal, Rock and Jazz: Perception and the Phenomenology of Musical Experience*. Hanover, CT and London: Wesleyan University Press.

Bernstein, J. M. (1987) 'Aesthetic Alienation: Heidegger, Adorno, and Truth at the End of Art' in Fekete, J. (ed.) *Life After Postmodernism: Essays on Value and Culture*. New York: St Martin's Press.

Bhabha, H. (1990) 'Dissemination: Time, Narrative, and the Margins of Modern Nation' in Bhabha, H. (ed.) *Nation and Narration*. London: Routledge.

—— (1994) *The Location of Culture*. London: Routledge.

Billig, M. (1997) 'From Codes to Utterances: Cultural Studies, Discourse and Psychology' in Ferguson, M. and Golding, P. (eds) *Cultural Studies in Question*. London: Sage.

Birrer, F. (1983) 'Definitions and Research Orientation: Do We Need a Definition of Popular Music?' in Horn, D. (ed.) *Popular Music Perspectives 2,* Papers from the Second International Conference on Popular Music Studies, Reggio Emilia, 19–24 September, 99–105.

Blanchard, J. (2003) 'Va Va Va... Voom; New-Age Burlesque Strips Away X-rated Sleaziness, Resurrects Old-Time Tease, Humor and Skits', *The Washington Times*, 13 June, B01.

Blundell, V. et al. (eds) (1993) *Relocating Cultural Studies: Developments in Theory and Practice*. London: Routledge.

Bollen, J. (2001) 'Queer Kinesthesia: Performativity on the Dance Floor' in Desmond, J. (ed.) *Dancing Desires: Choreographing Sexualities On and Off Stage*. Madison, WI: Wisconsin University Press.

Bosse, J. (2008) 'Salsa Dance and the Transformation of Style: An Ethnographic Study of Movement and Meaning in a Cross-Cultural Context', *Dance Research Journal*, 40: 1, 45–64.

Bourdieu, P. (1984) *Distinction: A Social Critique of the Judgement of Taste*. London: Routledge.

Brake, M. (1985) *Comparative Youth Culture: The Sociology of Youth Subcultures in America, Britain and Canada*. London: Routledge.

Braziel, J. E. and Mannur, A. (2003) 'Nation, Migration, Globalization: Points of Contention in Diaspora Studies' in Braziel, J. E. and Mannur, A. (eds) *Theorizing Diaspora*. Oxford: Blackwell.

Brown, G. (1996) 'Where Angels Fear to Tread', *The Independent* Arts, 30 March, 7.

Browning, B. (1991) 'The Body Articulate: Racial Identification in the Samba in Dance in Hispanic Cultures', Proceedings of the Society of Dance History Scholars 14th Annual Conference, New World School of the Arts, Miami, Florida, 8–10 February, 1–29.

—— (1995) *Samba: Resistance in Motion*. Bloomington, IN: Indiana University Press.

Buckland, F. (2002) *Impossible Dance: Club Culture and Queer World-Making*. Hanover, CT: Wesleyan University Press.

Buckland, T. (1983) 'Definitions of Folk Dance: Some Explorations', *Folk Music Journal*, 4: 4, 315–32.

—— (1999a) 'All Dances are Ethnic, but Some are More Ethnic Than Others: Some Observations on Dance Studies and Anthropology', *Dance Research*, XVII: 1, 3–21.

—— (ed.) (1999b) *Dance in the Field: Theories, Methods and Issues in Dance Ethnography*. Basingstoke: Macmillan.

Burke, P. (1981) 'The "Discovery" of Popular Culture' in Samuel, R. (ed.) *People's History and Socialist Theory*. London and Boston, MA: Routledge and Kegan Paul.

—— (1999) *Popular Culture in Early Modern Europe*. Aldershot: Ashgate.

Burnett, R. (1999) *The Global Jukebox: The International Music Industry*. London: Routledge.

Butler, J. (1999) *Gender Trouble: Feminism and the Subversion of Identity*. London and New York: Routledge.

Buzsek, M. E. (2006) *Pin-Up Grrrls: Feminism, Sexuality, Popular Culture*. Durham, NC: Duke University Press.

Carter, A. (2005) *Dance and Dancers in the Victorian and Edwardian Music Hall Ballet*. Aldershot: Ashgate.

Chambers, I. (1985) *Urban Rhythms: Pop Music and Popular Culture*. London: Macmillan.

—— (1986) *Popular Culture: The Metropolitan Experience*. London and New York: Methuen.

Christiansen, R. (2001) 'Dancing Dogs' Macho Magic has had its Day', *The Mail on Sunday* Review, 18 February, 72.

Clifford, J. (1986) 'Introduction' in Clifford, J. and Marcus, G. (eds) *Writing Culture: The Poetics and Politics of Postmodernism*. Berkeley, CA and Los Angeles: University of California Press.

Cohen-Stratyner, B. (2001) 'Issues in Social and Vernacular Dance', *Dance Research Journal*, 33: 2, 121–3.

Collins, J. (ed) (2002) *High-Pop: Making Culture into Popular Entertainment*. Oxford: Blackwell.

Connor, S. (1992) *Theory and Cultural Value*. Oxford: Blackwell.

—— (1993) 'The Necessity of Value' in Squires, J. (ed.) *Principled Positions: Postmodernism and the Rediscovery of Value*. London: Lawrence and Wishart.

Conrad, P. (2001) 'Who Let the Dogs Out?' *The Observer* Review, 11 February, 6.

Cook, J. W. (2006) 'Master Juba, the King of all Dancers! A Story of Stardom and Struggle from the Dawn of the Transatlantic Culture Industry', *Discourses in Dance*, 3: 2, 7–20.

Cook, S. (2000) 'Talking Machines and Moving Bodies: Marketing Dance Music before World War I', in *Dancing in the Millennium* Conference Proceedings, Washington, 19–23 July, 75–83.

Cooper, C. (2000) 'Lady Saw Cuts Loose: Female Fertility Rituals in Jamaican Dancehall Culture', in *Dancing in the Millennium* Conference Proceedings, Washington, 19–23 July, 79–87.

Copeland, R. and Cohen, R. (eds) (1982) *What is Dance? Readings in Theory and Criticism.* Oxford: Oxford University Press.

Crease, R. (2000) 'Divine Frivolity: Movement and Vernacular Dance', in *Dancing in the Millennium* Conference Proceedings, Washington, 19–23 July.

Crisp, C. (2003) '*Tap Dogs* Rebooted', *The Financial Times* Arts, 8 August, 15.

Cutler, C. (1983) 'What is Popular Music?' in Horn, D. (ed.) *Popular Music Perspectives 2,* Papers from the Second International Conference on Popular Music Studies, Reggio Emilia, September 19–24, 3–12.

Daniel, Y. (1991) 'Changing values in Cuban Rumba, a Lower Class Black Dance Appropriated by the Cuban Revolution', *Dance Research Journal,* 23: 2, 1–10.

—— (1995) *Rumba: Dance and Social Change in Contemporary Cuba.* Bloomington, IN and Indianapolis, IN: Indiana University Press.

Davis, S. (2009) Reggae. *http://www.oxfordmusiconline.com/subscriber/article/grove/music/23065* (accessed 16 October 2009).

De Frantz, T. (2002a) *Dancing Many Drums: Excavations in African American Dance* Madison, WI: University of Wisconsin Press.

—— (2002b) ' "Being Savion Glover": Black Masculinity, Translocation, and Tap Dance', *Discourses in Dance,* 1: 1, 17–28.

Delgado, C. F. and Muñoz, J. E. (eds) (1997) *Every-Night Life: Culture and Dance in Latin/o America.* Durham, NC: Duke University Press.

Dent, G. (1992) 'Black Pleasure, Black Joy: An Introduction' in Dent, G. (ed.) *Black Popular Culture.* Seattle: Bay Press.

Dentith, S. (2000) *Parody.* London: Routledge.

Desmond, J. (ed.) (1997) *Meaning in Motion.* Durham, NC & London: Duke University Press.

—— (2000) '*Terra Incognita*: Mapping New Territory in Dance and Cultural Studies', *Dance Research Journal,* 32: 1, 43–53.

Dixon Gottschild, B. (2002) *Waltzing in the Dark: African American Vaudeville and Race Politics in the Swing Era.* New York: St. Martin's Press.

Doane, M. A. (1992) 'Film and the Masquerade: Theorizing the Female Spectator' in Caughie, J. and Kuhn, A. (eds) *The Sexual Subject: A Screen Reader in Sexuality.* London: Routledge.

Dodds, S. (1997) 'Dance and Erotica: The Construction of the Female Stripper' in Thomas, H. (ed.) *Dance in the City.* Basingstoke: Macmillan.

—— (2001) *Dance on Screen: Genres and Media from Hollywood to Experimental Art.* Basingstoke: Palgrave.

—— (2008) '*Mad Hot Ballroom* and the Politics of Transformation' in Lansdale, J. (ed.) *Decentring Texts.* Basingstoke: Palgrave.

—— (2009) 'From Busby Berkeley to Madonna: Music Video and Popular Dance' in Malnig, J. (ed.) *Ballroom, Boogie, Shimmy Sham, Shake: A Social and Popular Dance Reader.* Urbana and Chicago, IL: University of Illinois Press.

Doolittle, L. (2001) 'The Trianon and On: Reading Mass Social Dancing in the 1930s and 1940s in Alberta, Canada', *Dance Research Journal,* 33: 2, 11–28.

Duerden, R. (1999) 'Michael Clark' in Bremser, M. (ed.) *Fifty Contemporary Choreographers*. London: Routledge.

Dunagan, C. (2007) 'Performing the Commodity-Sign: Dancing in the Gap', *Dance Research Journal*, 39: 2, 3–22.

During, S. (ed.) (1993) *The Cultural Studies Reader*. London: Routledge.

Elster, J. (1986) *An Introduction to Karl Marx*. Cambridge: Cambridge University Press.

Featherstone, M. (1991) 'The Body in Consumer Culture' in Featherstone, M., Hepworth, M. and Turner, B. (eds) *The Body: Social Process and Cultural Theory*. London: Sage.

Fekete, J. (1987) 'Introductory Notes for a Postmodern Value Agenda and Vampire Value, Infinitive Art, and Literary Theory: A Topographic Mediation' in Fekete, J. (ed.) *Life After Postmodernism: Essays on Value and Culture*. New York: St Martin's Press.

Ferguson, M. and Golding, P. (eds) (1997) *Cultural Studies in Question*. London: Sage.

Fiori, U. (1983) 'Popular Music: Theory, Practice, Value', in Horn, D. (ed.) *Popular Music Perspectives 2*, Papers from the Second International Conference on Popular Music Studies, Reggio Emilia, 19–24 September, 13–23.

Fiske, J. (1992) 'The Cultural Economy of Fandom' in Lewis, L. A. (ed.) *The Adoring Audience: Fan Culture and Popular Media*. London: Routledge.

Foley, B. (2005) *Undressed for Success: Beauty Contestants and Exotic Dancers as Merchants of Morality*. Basingstoke: Macmillan.

Foley, C. (2001) 'Perceptions of Irish Step Dance: National, Global and Local', *Dance Research Journal*, 33: 1, 34–45.

Fonarow, W. (1997) 'The Spatial Organization of the Indie Music Gig' in Gelder, K. and Thornton, S. (eds) *The Subcultures Reader*. London and New York: Routledge.

Franks, A. H. (1963) *Social Dance: A Short History*. London: Routledge and Kegan Paul.

Frith, S. (1991) 'The Good, the Bad, and the Indifferent: Defending Popular Culture from the Populists', *Diacritics*, 21: 4, 101–115.

—— (1996) *Performing Rites: On the Value of Popular Music*. Cambridge, MA: Harvard University Press.

—— (1997) 'Popular Culture' in Payne, M. (ed.) *A Dictionary of Cultural and Critical Theory*. Oxford: Blackwell.

—— (2001) 'Pop Music' in Frith, S. et al. (eds) *The Cambridge Companion to Rock and Pop*. Cambridge: Cambridge University Press.

Frith, S. and Horne, H. (1987) *Art into Pop*. London: Methuen.

Frow, J. (1995) *Cultural Studies and Cultural Value*. Oxford: Oxford University Press.

Gammond, P. (ed.) (1991) *The Oxford Companion to Popular Music*. Oxford: Oxford University Press.

García, D. (2009) 'Embodying Music/Disciplining Dance: The Mambo Body in Havana and New York City' in Malnig, J. (ed.) *Ballroom, Boogie, Shimmy Sham, Shake: A Social and Popular Dance Reader*. Urbana and Chicago, IL: University of Illinois Press.

Garnham, N. (1997) 'Political Economy and the Price of Cultural Practice' in Ferguson, M. and Golding, P. (eds) *Cultural Studies in Question*. London: Sage.

Gelder, K. and Thornton, S. (eds) (1997) *The Subcultures Reader.* London and New York: Routledge.

George, N. (2002) 'Dance and Identity Politics in American Negro Vaudeville: The Whitman Sisters, 1900–1935' in DeFrantz, T. (ed.) *Dancing Many Drums: Excavations in African American Dance.* Madison, WI: University of Wisconsin Press.

George-Graves, N. (2000) *The Royalty of Negro Vaudeville: The Whitman Sisters and the Negotiation of Race, Gender and Class in African American Theater, 1900–1940.* New York: St Martin's Press.

—— (2009) '"Just Like Being at the Zoo": Primitivity and Ragtime Dance' in Malnig, J. (ed.) *Ballroom, Boogie, Shimmy Sham, Shake: A Social and Popular Dance Reader.* Urbana and Chicago, IL: University of Illinois Press.

Gere, D. (2001) '29 *Effeminate Gestures*: Choreographer Joe Goode and the Heroism of Effeminacy' in Desmond, J. (ed.) *Dancing Desires.* Madison, WI: University of Wisconsin Press.

Ghandi, L. (1998) *Postcolonial Theory: A Critical Introduction.* New South Wales: Allen and Unwin.

Gilroy, P. (1987) *There Ain't No Black in the Union Jack.* London: Routledge.

—— (1993) *The Black Atlantic: Modernity and Double Consciousness.* London and New York: Verso.

Gitlin, T. (1997) 'The Anti-Political Populism of Cultural Studies' in Ferguson, M. and Golding, P. (eds) *Cultural Studies in Question.* London: Sage.

Goldberg, T. (2000) 'Racial Knowledge' in Back, L. and Solomon, J. (eds) *Theories of Race and Racism: A Reader.* London: Routledge.

Gonzalez, A. (2003/04) 'Mambo and the Maya', *Dance Research Journal,* 35: 2/36: 1, 131–45.

Gore, G. (1997) 'The Beat Goes On: Trance, Dance and Tribalism in Rave Culture' in Thomas, H. (ed.) *Dance in the City.* London: Macmillan.

Graeber, D. (2001) *Toward an Anthropological Theory of Value.* New York: Palgrave Macmillan.

Gray, A. (2003) *Research Practice for Cultural Studies.* London: Sage.

Green, M. (1996) 'The Centre for Contemporary Cultural Studies' in Storey, J. (ed.) *What is Cultural Studies?* London: Arnold.

Greskovic, R. (1999) 'Karole Armitage' in Bremser, M. (ed.) *Fifty Contemporary Choreographers.* London: Routledge.

Grossberg, L. (1992) 'Is There a fan in the House? The Affective Sensibility of Fandom' in Lewis, L. A. (ed.) *The Adoring Audience: Fan Culture and Popular Media.* London: Routledge.

—— (1993) 'The Formations of Cultural Studies: An American in Birmingham' in Blundell, V. et al. (eds) *Relocating Cultural Studies: Developments in Theory and Practice.* London: Routledge.

Gumbel, A. (2003) 'Give 'Em the Old Razzle Dazzle', *The Independent on Sunday,* 9 March, 18.

Gunaratnam, Y. (2003) *Researching 'Race' and Ethnicity: Methods and Knowledge and Power.* London: Sage.

Hall, J. (2008) 'Mapping the Multifarious: The Genrification of Dance Music Club Cultures' in Lansdale, J. (ed.) *Decentring Texts.* Basingstoke: Palgrave.

Hall, S. (1992) 'What is this "Black" in Black Popular Culture?' in Dent, G. (ed.) *Black Popular Culture.* Seattle: Bay Press.

224   *Bibliography*

Hall, S. (1996a) 'Cultural Studies: Two Paradigms' in Storey, J. (ed.) *What is Cultural Studies?* London: Arnold.

—— (1996b) 'New Ethnicities' in Baker, H. et al. (eds) *Black British Cultural Studies: A Reader.* Chicago, IL and London: University of Chicago Press.

—— (2003) 'Cultural Identity and Diaspora' in Braziel, J. E. and Mannur, A. (eds) *Theorizing Diaspora.* Oxford: Blackwell.

Hall, S. and Jefferson, T. (1976) *Resistance Through Rituals: Youth Subcultures in Post-War Britain.* London: Routledge.

Hanna, J. L. (1979) *To Dance is Human: A Theory of Nonverbal Communication.* Austin, TX: University of Texas.

—— (1998) 'Undressing the First Amendment and Corseting the Striptease Dancer', *The Drama Review,* 42: 2, 38–69.

—— (2000) 'Ballet to Exotic Dance – Under the Censorship Watch' in *Dancing in the Millennium* Conference Proceedings, Washington, 19–23 July, 230–4.

Harris, C. (1998) 'Introduction Theorizing Fandom: Fans, Subculture and Identity' in Harris, C. and Alexander, A. (eds) *Theorizing Fandom: Fans, Subculture and Identity.* New York: Hampton Press.

Harris, G. (1999) *Staging Femininities: Performance and Performativity.* Manchester: Manchester University Press.

Harris, P. (2004) 'Who Said Burlesque Was Dead?' *The Observer,* 9 March, 23.

Harris, T. (ed.) (1995) *Popular Culture in England, c1500–1850.* Basingstoke: Palgrave.

Heathcott, J. (2003) 'Urban Spaces and Working-Class Expressions Across the Black Atlantic: Tracing the Routes of Ska', *Radical History Review,* 87: 183–206.

Hebdige, D. (1979) *Subculture: The Meaning of Style.* London: Methuen.

Herrnstein Smith, B. (1983) 'Contingencies of Value', *Critical Inquiry,* 10: 1, 1–35.

—— (1987) 'Value Without Truth-Value' in Fekete, J. (ed.) *Life After Postmodernism: Essays on Value and Culture.* New York: St Martin's Press.

Hills, M. (2002) *Fan Cultures.* London and New York: Routledge.

Hirst, P. (1993) 'An Answer to Relativism' in Squires, J. (ed.) *Principled Positions: Postmodernism and the Rediscovery of Value.* London: Lawrence and Wishart.

Hoggart, R. (1957) *The Uses of Literacy.* London: Chatto and Windus.

Hope, D. (2004) 'Ninja Man, the Lyrical Don: Embodying Violent Masculinity in Jamaican Dancehall Culture', *Discourses in Dance,* 2: 2, 27–43.

Hubbard, K. and Monaghan, T. (2009) 'Negotiating Compromise on a Burnished Wood Floor: Social Dancing at the Savoy' in Malnig, J. (ed.) *Ballroom, Boogie, Shimmy Sham, Shake: A Social and Popular Dance Reader.* Urbana and Chicago, IL: University of Illinois Press.

Hutcheon, L. (2003) *The Politics of Postmodernism,* 2nd edn. London: Routledge.

Hutera, D. (2001) *'Tap Dogs' The Times* Arts, 16 February, 15.

Hutter, M. (1996) 'The Value of Play' in Klamer, A. (ed.) *The Value of Culture: On the Relationship Between Economics and Arts.* Amsterdam: Amsterdam University Press.

Inglis, F. (1993) *Cultural Studies.* Oxford: Blackwell.

Jackson, J. (2001) 'Improvisation in African-American Vernacular Dancing', *Dance Research Journal,* 33: 2, 40–53.

Jays, D. (1996) 'Of Myths and Men', *Dance Now,* 5: 2, 72–5.

Jenson, J. (1992) 'Fandom as Pathology: The Consequences of Characterization' in Lewis, L. A. (ed.) *The Adoring Audience: Fan Culture and Popular Media*. London: Routledge.

Jensen, J. and Pauly, J. (1997) 'Imagining the Audience: Losses and Gains in Cultural Studies' in Ferguson, M. and Golding, P. (eds) *Cultural Studies in Question*. London: Sage.

Johnson, R. (1996) 'What is Cultural Studies Anyway?' in Storey, J. (ed.) *What is Cultural Studies?* London: Arnold.

Kahn-Harris, K. (2004) 'Unspectacular Subculture?: Transgression and Mundanity in the Global Extreme Metal Scene' in Bennett, A. and Kahn-Harris, K. (eds) *After Subculture: Critical Studies in Contemporary Youth Culture*. Basingstoke: Palgrave.

Kassabian, A. (1999) 'Popular' in Horner, B. and Swiss, T. (eds) *Key Terms in Popular Music and Culture*. Oxford: Blackwell.

Kellner, D. (1997) 'Overcoming the Divide: Cultural Studies and Political Economy' in Ferguson, M. and Golding, P. (eds) *Cultural Studies in Question*. London: Sage.

Klamer, A. (ed.) (1996) *The Value of Culture: On the Relationship Between Economics and Arts*. Amsterdam: Amsterdam University Press.

LaBoskey, S. (2001) 'Getting Off: Portrayals of Masculinity in Hip Hop Dance in Film', *Dance Research Journal*, 33: 2, 112–20.

Laing, D. (1985) *One Chord Wonders: Power and Meaning in Punk Rock*. Milton Keynes: Open University Press.

LaPointe-Crump, J. (2000) 'Conversations in Celluloid: An Almanac of Dance Theory and the Dance Film' in *Dancing in the Millennium* Conference Proceedings, Washington, 19–23 July, 293–7.

Lawrence, T. (2009) 'Beyond the Hustle: 1970s Social Dancing, Discotheque Culture and the Emergence of the Contemporary Club Dancer' in Malnig, J. (ed.) *Ballroom, Boogie, Shimmy Sham, Shake: A Social and Popular Dance Reader*. Urbana and Chicago, IL: University of Illinois Press.

Levene, L. (1997a) 'Bound but Not Gagged', *The Independent*, 20 March, 10.

—— (1997b) 'Tobias Tak', *The Independent* Reviews, 6 May, 11.

—— (2001) 'Repetition is Such a Strain', *Sunday Telegraph* Review, 25 February, NA.

Lewis, L. A. (ed.) (1992) *The Adoring Audience: Fan Culture and Popular Media*. London: Routledge.

Liepe-Levinson, K. (2002) *Strip-Show: Performances of Gender and Desire*. London and New York: Routledge.

Lo, J. (2003) 'Beyond Happy Hybridity: Performing Asian-Australian Identities' in Ang, I. et al. (eds) *Alter/Asians*. Sydney: Pluto Press.

Lowe, L. (2003) 'Heterogeneity, Hybridity, Multiplicity: Marking Asian-American Differences' in Braziel, J. E. and Mannur, A. (eds) *Theorizing Diaspora*. Oxford: Blackwell.

Malbon, B. (1999) *Clubbing: Dancing, Ecstasy, Vitality*. London: Routledge.

Malnig, J. (1992) *Dancing Till Dawn: A Century of Exhibition Ballroom*. New York: Greenwood.

—— (1998) 'Athena Meets Venus: Visions of Women in Social Dance in the Teens and Early 1920s', *Dance Research Journal*, 30: 2, 34–62.

—— (2001) 'Introduction', *Dance Research Journal*, 33: 2, 7–10.

Malnig, J. (2009) 'Introduction' in Malnig, J. (ed.) *Ballroom, Boogie, Shimmy Sham, Shake: A Social and Popular Dance Reader*. Urbana and Chicago, IL: University of Illinois Press.

Malone, J. (1988) ' "Let the Punishment Fit the Crime": The Vocal Choreography of Cholly Atkins', *Dance Research Journal*, 20: 1, 11–18.

—— (1996) *Steppin' on the Blues: The Visible Rhythms of African American Dance*. Urbana and Chicago, IL: University of Illinois Press.

Martin, C. (2009) 'Reality Dance: American Dance Marathons' in Malnig, J. (ed.) *Ballroom, Boogie, Shimmy Sham, Shake: A Social and Popular Dance Reader*. Urbana and Chicago, IL: University of Illinois Press.

Matluck Brooks, L. (1989) 'The Philadelphia Dancing Assembly in the Eighteenth Century', *Dance Research Journal*, 21: 1, 1–6.

Marx, K. (1867; ed. 1957) *Capital: Volume One*. London: Dent.

McDonagh, D. (1979) *Dance Fever*. New York: Random House.

McGuigan, J. (1992) *Cultural Populism*. London: Routledge.

—— (1997) 'Cultural Populism Revisited' in Ferguson, M. and Golding, P. (eds) *Cultural Studies in Question*. London: Sage.

McLellan, D. (1975) *Marx*. London: Fontana.

McMains, J. (2001) 'Brownface: Representations of Latin-ness in Dancesport', *Dance Research Journal*, 33: 2, 54–71.

—— (2006) *Glamour Addiction: Inside the American Ballroom Industry*. Middletown, CT: Wesleyan University Press.

—— (2009) 'Dancing Latin/Latin Dancing: Salsa and Dancesport' in Malnig, J. (ed.) *Ballroom, Boogie, Shimmy Sham, Shake: A Social and Popular Dance Reader*. Urbana and Chicago, IL: University of Illinois Press.

McMillan, M. (2009) 'The West Indian Front Room: Reflections on a Diasporic Phenomenon', *Small Axe*, 135–56.

McRobbie, A. (1984) 'Dance and Social Fantasy' in McRobbie, A. and Nava, M. (eds) *Gender and Generation*. Basingstoke: Macmillan.

—— (1990) *'Fame, Flashdance* and Fantasies of Achievement' in Gaines, J. and Herzog, C. (eds) *Fabrications: Costume and the Female Body*. London: Routledge, 1990.

—— (1991) *Feminism and Youth Culture*. London: Macmillan.

—— (1994) *Postmodernism and Popular Culture*. London: Routledge.

—— (1997) 'The Es and the Anti-Es: New Questions for Feminism in Cultural Studies' in Ferguson, M. and Golding, P. (eds) *Cultural Studies in Question*. London: Sage.

Middleton, R. (1983) 'Popular Music, Class Conflict and the Music-Historical Field' in Horn, D. (ed.) *Popular Music Perspectives 2*, Papers from the Second International Conference on Popular Music Studies, Reggio Emilia, 19–24 September, 24–45.

—— (1997) *Studying Popular Music*. Milton Keynes: Open University Press.

Miller, T. and McHoul, A. (1998) *Popular Culture and Everyday Life*. London: Sage.

Monaghan, T. (2001) 'Why Study the Lindy Hop?' *Dance Research Journal*, 33: 2, 124–7.

Monaghan, T. and Dodson, M. (2000) 'Has Swing Dance Been Revived?' in *Dancing in the Millennium* Conference Proceedings, Washington, 19–23 July, 317–20.

Morley, D. (1997) 'Theoretical Orthodoxies: Textualism, Constructivism and the "New Ethnography" in Cultural Studies' in Ferguson, M. and Golding, P. (eds) *Cultural Studies in Question.* London: Sage.

Morley, D. and Chen, K. (eds) (1997) *Stuart Hall: Critical Dialogues in Cultural Studies.* London: Routledge.

Morris, M. (1996) 'Banality in Cultural Studies' in Storey, J. (ed.) *What is Cultural Studies?* London: Arnold.

Muggleton, D. (2000) *Inside Subculture: The Postmodern Meaning of Style.* Oxford: Berg.

Mukerji, C. and Schudson, M. (eds) (1991) *Rethinking Popular Culture: Contemporary Perspectives in Cultural Studies.* Berkeley, CA and Los Angeles: University of California Press.

Mulkay, M. (1988) *On Humour: Its Nature and its Place in Modern Society.* Cambridge, Polity.

Mungham, G. and Pearson, G. (eds) (1976) *Working Class Youth Cultures.* London: Routledge and Kegan Paul.

Murdock, G. (1997) 'Base Notes: The Conditions of Cultural Practice' in Ferguson, M. and Golding, P. (eds) *Cultural Studies in Question.* London: Sage.

Murdoch, H.A. (2007) ' "All Skin" Teeth is Not Grin': Performing Caribbean Diasporic Identity in a Postcolonial Metropolitan Frame', *Callaloo,* 30: 2, 575–93.

Nahachewsky, A. (1995) 'Participatory and Presentational Dance', *Dance Research Journal,* 21: 1, 1–15.

Nelson, C. et al. (1992) 'Cultural Studies: An Introduction' in Grossberg, L. et al. (eds) *Cultural Studies.* London: Routledge.

Norris, C. (1993) 'Old Themes for New Times: Postmodernism, Theory and Cultural Politics' in Squires, J. (ed.) *Principled Positions: Postmodernism and the Rediscovery of Value.* London: Lawrence and Wishart.

Ostlere, H. (2003) 'Improvography/Savion Glover', *The Financial Times,* 19 December, 10.

Osumare, H. (2000) 'Performance and Performativity in Global Hip Hop: Hawai'i as Case Study' in *Dancing in the Millennium* Conference Proceedings, Washington, 19–23 July, 334–8.

—— (2002) 'Global Breakdancing and the Intercultural Body', *Dance Research Journal,* 34: 2, 30–45.

—— (2007) *The Africanist Aesthetic in Global Hip-Hop.* New York and Basingstoke: Palgrave.

Palmer, J. (1993) *Taking Humour Seriously.* New York: Routledge.

Penny, P. (1999) 'Dance at the Interface of the Social and the Theatrical: Focus on the Participatory Patterns of Contemporary Competition Ballroom Dancers in Britain', *Dance Research,* XVII: 1, 47–74.

Phillips, T. and Phillips, M. (1999) *Windrush: The Irresistible Rise of Multi-Racial Britain.* London: Harper Collins.

Pini, M. (1997) 'Cyborgs, Nomads and the Raving Feminine' in Thomas, H. (ed.) *Dance in the City.* London: Macmillan.

—— (2001) *Club Cultures and Female Subjectivity.* Basingstoke: Palgrave.

Plotnitsky, A. (1987) 'Interpretation, Interminability, Evaluation: From Nietzsche Toward a General Economy' in Fekete, J. (ed.) *Life After Postmodernism: Essays on Value and Culture.* New York: St Martin's Press.

Ponzio, B. (1996) 'Mythic Images of the American West and the Renewed Popularity of Country Western Dance', *Speaking of History: Dance Scholarship in the 90s* Proceedings of the SDHS 19th Annual Conference, University of Minnesota, Minneapolis, Minn, 13–16 June.

Prato, P. (1983) 'Musical Kitsch: Close Encounters Between Pops and Classics' in Horn, D. (ed.) *Popular Music Perspectives 2*, Papers from the Second International Conference on Popular Music Studies, Reggio Emilia, 19–24 September, 375–86.

Prentice, C. (1998) '*Tap Dogs' The Scotsman*, 30 June, 17.

Pullen, K. (2005) *Actresses and Whores: On Stage and in Society*. Cambridge: Cambridge University Press.

Reay, B. (1998) *Popular Cultures in England 1550–1750*. London and New York: Longman.

Roach, C. (2007) *Stripping, Sex and Popular Culture*. Oxford: Berg.

Robinson, D. (2009) 'Performing American: Ragtime Dancing as Participatory Minstrelsy', *Dance Chronicle*, 32, 89–126.

Ross, A. (1998) *The Language of Humour*. London and New York: Routledge.

Ross, C. (1995/96) '*Stomp* and *Tap Dogs'*, *Dance Theatre Journal*, 12: 3, 47–8.

Ruccio, D., Graham, J. and Amariglio, J. (1996) ' "The Good, the Bad and the Different": Reflections on Economic and Aesthetic Value' in Klamer, A. (ed.) *The Value of Culture: On the Relationship Between Economics and Arts*. Amsterdam: Amsterdam University Press.

Rust, F. (1969) *Dance in Society*. London: Routledge and Kegan Paul.

Ryman, C. (2004) 'Bouyaka (Boo-ya'h-kah): A Salute to Dancehall', *Discourses in Dance* 2: 2, 5–7.

Sabin, R. (ed.) (1999) *Punk Rock: So What?* London: Routledge.

Sandvoss, C. (2005) *Fans: The Mirror of Consumption*. Cambridge: Polity Press.

Savigliano, M. (1995) *Tango and the Political Economy of Passion*. Boulder, CO: Westview.

—— (1996) 'Fragments for a Story of Tango Bodies (on Choreocritics and the Memory of Power)' in Foster, S. (ed.) *Corporealities: Dancing Knowledge, Culture and Power*. London and New York: Routledge.

Schaefer, E. (1997) 'The Obscene Seen: Spectacle and Transgression in Postwar Burlesque Films', *Cinema Journal*, 36: 2, 41–66.

Schneider, R. (1997) *The Explicit Body in Performance*. London and New York: Routledge.

Sedgwick, P. and Edgar, A. (eds) (1999) *Key Concepts in Cultural Theory*. London and New York: Routledge.

Shaar Murray, C. (1991) *Shots From the Hip*. London: Penguin.

Shepard, A. (2005) 'High Jinks; New Burlesque', *The Times*, 5 February, 26.

Shepherd, J. (1983) 'Definition as Mystification: A Consideration of Labels as a Hindrance to Understanding Significance in Music' in Horn, D. (ed.) *Popular Music Perspectives 2*, Papers from the Second International Conference on Popular Music Studies, Reggio Emilia, 19–24 September, 84–98.

Shilling, C. (1993) *The Body and Social Theory*. London: Sage.

Shresthova, S. (2004) 'Swaying to an Indian Beat...Dola Goes my Diasporic Heart: Exploring Hindi Film Dance', *Dance Research Journal*, 36: 2, 91–101.

Shteir, R. (2004) *Striptease: The Untold History of the Girlie Show*. Oxford: Oxford University Press.

Shuker, R. (1997) *Understanding Popular Music*. London: Routledge.

Shuker, R. (1998) *Key Concepts in Popular Music*. London: Routledge.

Simpson, P. (2003) *On the Discourse of Satire: Towards a Stylistic Model of Satirical Humour*. Philadelphia, PA: John Benjamins.

Skeggs, B. (2004) *Class, Self, Culture*. London and New York: Routledge.

Skinner, J. (2008) 'Women Dancing Back-and-Forth: Resistance and Self-Regulation in Belfast Salsa', *Dance Research Journal*, 40: 1, 65–77.

Sklar, D. (2000) 'Reprise in Dance Ethnography', *Dance Research Journal*, 32: 1, 70–7.

Solomos, J. and Back, L. (1996) *Racism and Society*. Basingstoke: Macmillan.

Sommer, S. (1998) 'Tap Dance' in Cohen, S. J. (ed.) *International Encyclopedia of Dance*, Vol. 6, New York and Oxford: Oxford University Press.

—— (2001) '*C'mon to my House*: Underground-House Dancing', *Dance Research Journal* 33: 2, 72–86.

Soper, K. (1993) 'Postmodernism, Subjectivity and the Question of Value' in Squires, J. (ed.) *Principled Positions: Postmodernism and the Rediscovery of Value*. London: Lawrence and Wishart.

Squires, J. (1993) 'Introduction' in Squires, J. (ed.) *Principled Positions: Postmodernism and the Rediscovery of Value*. London: Lawrence and Wishart.

Stahl, G. (2003) 'Tastefully Renovating Subcultural Theory: Making Space for a New Model' in Muggleton, D. and Weinzierl, R. (eds) *The Post-Subcultures Reader*. Oxford: Berg.

Stanley Niaah, S. (2004) 'A Common Genealogy: Dance-Hall, Limbo and the Sacred Performance of Space', *Discourses in Dance*, 2: 2, 9–26.

Stearns, M. and Stearns, J. (1994) *Jazz Dance: The Story of American Vernacular Dance*. New York: Da Capo.

Steffens, R. (2009) Isaacs, Gregory. *http://www.oxfordmusiconline.com/subscriber/article/grove/music/49965* (accessed 16 October 2009).

Stern, C. (2000) 'The Implications of Ballroom Dancing for Studies of "Whiteness"' in *Dancing in the Millennium* Conference Proceedings, Washington, 19–23 July, 394–9.

Storey, J. (ed.) (1996) *What is Cultural Studies?* London: Arnold.

—— (1997) *An Introduction to Cultural Theory and Popular Culture*, 2nd edn. Hemel Hempstead: Prentice Hall/Harvester Wheatsheaf.

—— (ed.) (1998) *Cultural Theory and Popular Culture*, 2nd edn. London: Prentice Hall.

—— (2003) *Inventing Popular Culture*. Oxford: Blackwell.

Stratton, J. (1983) 'What is Popular Music?' *Sociological Review*, 31: 2, 293–309.

Strinati, D. (1995) *An Introduction to Theories of Popular Culture*. London: Routledge.

Studlar, G. (1995) 'Douglas Fairbanks: Thief of the Ballets Russes' in Goellner, E. and Shea Murphy, J. (eds) *Bodies of the Text: Dance as Theory, Literature as Dance*. New Brunswick, NJ: Rutgers University Press.

Suchting, W.A. (1983) *Marx: An Introduction*. Sussex: Wheatsheaf.

Szwed, J. and Marks, M. (1988) 'The Afro-American Transformation of European Set Dances and Dance Suites', *Dance Research Journal*, 20: 1, 29–36.

Taylor, V. (2000) 'The Historic Present: Ballet as a Utopian Myth in Popular Culture' in *Dancing in the Millennium* Conference Proceedings, Washington, 19–23 July, 415–20.

Thomas, S. (1997) 'Dominance and Ideology in Culture and Cultural Studies' in Ferguson, M. and Golding, P. (eds) *Cultural Studies in Question*. London: Sage.

Thomas, H. (2003) *The Body, Dance and Cultural Theory*. Basingstoke: Palgrave Macmillan.

Thomas, H. and Cooper, L. (2002) 'Dancing Into the Third Age: Social Dance as Cultural Text – Research in Progress', *Dance Research*, 20: 1, 54–80.

Thornton, S. (1997) *Club Cultures: Music, Media and Subcultural Capital*. Cambridge: Polity, 1997.

Tsitsos, W. (1999) 'Rules of Rebellion: Slamdancing, Moshing, and the American Alternative Scene', *Popular Music*, 18: 3, 397–414.

Turner, G. (1990) *British Cultural Studies*. London: Unwin Hyman.

Usner, E. (2001) 'Dancing in the Past, Living in the Present: Nostalgia and Race in Southern California Neo-Swing Dance Culture', *Dance Research Journal*, 33: 2, 87–101.

Valis Hill, C. (1992) 'Buddy Bradley: The "Invisible" Man of Broadway Brings Jazz Tap to London in American Dance Abroad – Influence of the United States Experience', Proceedings of the SDHS 15th Annual Conference, University of California, California, 14–15 February, 77–84.

—— (2000) *Brotherhood in Rhythm: The Jazz Tap Dancing of the Nicholas Brothers*. Oxford: Oxford University Press.

—— (2009) 'From Bharata Natyam to Bop: Jack Cole's 'Modern' Jazz Dance' in Malnig, J. (ed.) *Ballroom, Boogie, Shimmy Sham, Shake: A Social and Popular Dance Reader*. Urbana and Chicago, IL: University of Illinois Press.

Van den Braembussche, A. (1996) 'The Value of Art: A Philosophical Perspective' in Klamer, A. (ed.) *The Value of Culture: On the Relationship Between Economics and Arts*. Amsterdam: Amsterdam University Press.

Van Heusden, B. and Klamer, A. (1996) 'The Value of Culture: A Dialogue Between Barend van Heusden and Arjo Klamer' in Klamer, A. (ed.) *The Value of Culture: On the Relationship Between Economics and Arts*. Amsterdam: Amsterdam University Press.

Van Ulzen, K. (1997/98) 'Cast of Steel', *Dance Australia 93*, December/January, 24–5.

Wagner, A. (1986) Terpsichore and Taxi-Dancers: American Anti-Dance Attitudes Proceedings of the Society for Dance History Scholars 9th Annual Conference, City University of New York, 14–17 February, 217–26.

Wall, T. (2009) 'Rocking Around the Clock: Teenage Dance fads from 1955 to 1965' in Malnig, J. (ed.) *Ballroom, Boogie, Shimmy Sham, Shake: A Social and Popular Dance Reader*. Urbana and Chicago, IL: University of Illinois Press.

Ward, A. (1993) 'Dancing in the Dark: Rationalism and the Neglect of Social Dance' in Thomas, H. (ed.) *Dance, Gender and Culture*. London: Macmillan.

Webster, D. (1996) 'Pessimism, Optimism, Pleasure: the Future of Cultural Studies' in Storey, J. (ed.) *What is Cultural Studies?* London: Arnold.

Weeks, J. (1993) 'Rediscovering Values' in Squires, J. (ed.) *Principled Positions: Postmodernism and the Rediscovery of Value*. London: Lawrence and Wishart.

Weinzierl, R. and Muggleton, D. (2003) 'What is "Post-Subcultural Studies" Anyway?' in Muggleton, D. and Weinzierl, R. (eds) *The Post-Subcultures Reader*. Oxford: Berg.

Wicke, P. (1983) 'Popularity in Music: Some Aspects of a Historical Materialist Theory for Popular Music', in Horn, D. (ed.) *Popular Music Perspectives 2*, Papers from the Second International Conference on Popular Music Studies, Reggio Emilia, 19–24 September, 47–51.

—— (1993) *Rock Music: Culture, Aesthetics and Sociology.* Cambridge: Cambridge University Press.

Williams, D. and Farnell, D. (1995) 'Editorial Foreword', *Journal for the Anthropological Study of Human Movement,* 8: 3, 73–9.

Williams, R. (1958) *Culture and Society.* London: Chatto and Windus.

Williams, R. (1961) *The Long Revolution.* London: Chatto and Windus.

Willis, P. (1978) *Profane Culture.* London: Routledge Falmer.

—— (1990) *Common Culture.* Milton Keynes: Open University Press.

Willson, J. (2008) *The Happy Stripper: Pleasure and Politics in New Burlesque.* London: I B Tauris.

Winter, M. (2001) 'Juba and American Minstrelsy' in Dils, A. and Cooper Albright, A. (eds) *Moving History/Dancing Cultures.* Middletown, CT: Wesleyan University Press.

Wright, B. (2004) 'Speaking the Unspeakable: Politics of the Vagina in Dance-Hall Docu-Videos', *Discourses in Dance,* 2: 2, 45–59.

Young, T. (1999) 'Dancing on Bela Lugosi's Grave: the Politics and Aesthetics of Gothic Club Dancing', *Dance Research,* XVII: 1, 75–97.

Zanfagna, C. (2009) 'The Multiringed Cosmos of Krumping: Hip-Hop Dance at the Intersections of Battle, Media, and Spirit' in Malnig, J. (ed.) *Ballroom, Boogie, Shimmy Sham, Shake: A Social and Popular Dance Reader.* Urbana and Chicago, IL: University of Illinois Press.

Index